Accounting For Success:

Guide To Short Case Resolution

Competency is tied in to respect for teaching,
within the bounds of professional ethics.

My deep thanks to the translators
at Whitehall Richmond Communications, Inc.

AB + Publications

Accounting For Success:

Guide To Short Case Resolution

by

Sylvie Deslauriers, PhD, MSc

FCPA, FCA, FCMA, CPA (FL), CMA (US)

Professor of Accounting Cases

at the University of Québec at Trois-Rivières, Canada

AB + Publications

Accounting For Success: Guide To Short Case Resolution

by Sylvie Deslauriers, PhD

Cover design: Sabina Kopica, Audrey Morasse

P.O. Box 38
St-Alban
Canada
G0A 3B0
info@ABplusPublications.com
www.ABplusPublications.com

ISBN 978-0-928067-05-4 (paperback)

ISBN 978-1-928067-06-1 (eBook-pdf)

Legal deposit: 2015
Library and Archives Canada
Bibliothèque et Archives nationales du Québec

Other books by Dr. Sylvie Deslauriers:

EASY $UCCESS, 2013.

CGA = COMPETENCY, 2013.

TEACHING TIPS FOR ACCOUNTING CASES, 2012.

Guide To Short Case Resolution

FOREWORD

My book is intended for students and candidates called upon to resolve multi-subjects integrated cases during their accounting studies.

The ideas set out in this book result from over thirty years of experience in case resolution, which experience derives from university teaching, consulting work performed for public accounting firms and the marking of professional exams. Incidentally, over the years, I have taken part in more than 75 national marking centers.

The resolution of a multi-subjects case, within the confines of a particular context, represents one of the greatest challenges encountered throughout accounting studies. My objective is to promote learning on your part by developing a practical and structured approach. To this end, I have illustrated my comments by using examples taken, among others, from the detailed analysis of a short case appended hereto.

Case resolution and analysis enable you to apply your knowledge and to exercise your judgment under various circumstances, with a view to undeniably enhancing any studies in accounting you may undertake. In this vein, I simply wish for you to appreciate the drafting of your cases.

It is with great pleasure that I share with you the sum of all my work, in the hope of fostering your own Success.

Dr. Sylvie Deslauriers

CONTENTS

CONTENTS (continued)

Part 1
Reading And Annotating A Case

Identify The Case Parameters
Flesh Out Useful Information
Annotating A Case Efficiently

"As soon as you notice something peculiar, repeated, that occurs simultaneously, or that is sequenced in some manner or a connection, take the time to jot it down."

© Deslauriers Sylvie, *Easy $uccess*, AB + Publications, 2013, page 17.

Part 1
Reading And Annotating A Case

An active and structured reading of a case is a crucial step in any simulation process or examination. An adequate understanding of the information and case facts supplied will help you successfully plan, and then resolve, problems or issues. Generally speaking, reading should take up at least one quarter, and sometimes even up to one third, of the time allotted for resolution of a case. For instance, reading should take between 17 and 23 minutes for a 70 minute-long case.[1]

Identify The Case Parameters

A case is a situational exercise or a scenario that calls for the resolution of problems or issues, within a specific environment. Each case is made up of components which, when combined, make it unique. A topic to be analyzed or a computation to be made may form part of more than one case, however the approach and the contents will be different from one case to the next.

It appears to me to be critical to identify as soon as possible, to understand, and then to take into account, the particulars of a case in order to properly focus one's efforts. These particulars **act as a guide and reference framework throughout your reading of the case**. I consider that the context, the role and the requirement(s) make up the case parameters.

- **CONTEXT.** What is the basic information that needs to be highlighted in order to better understand the environment of the subject entity?

  E.g.: The entity has no management information for decision-making.

  A6: The estimated life of the product is generally three years or less.

- **ROLE.** From which angle should the problems or issues be tackled? What personality are you being asked to take on in the case?

  A3: You work for Hi & Lo, an accounting firm that was newly appointed as DFT's auditor. This means, among others, that problems or issues must be analyzed from an external point of view. Anne, for instance, would not approach the questions in the same manner since she holds the in-house position of Chief Financial Officer.

- **REQUIRED/REQUIREMENT.** What is the work required? What are the problems or issues?

  One must first identify the principal requirements and then determine the various topics to discuss or analyze.

  ISSUE: Accounting issues of significance (A3)

  Topics: Revenue Recognition (A5), Research and Development (A6), etc.

---

1 This volume contains a great many examples illustrating advanced concepts. When these examples are taken from the Digital Future Technologies (DFT) case, which appears in Appendix A, the reference appears in round brackets (A…).
The case information is highlighted in yellow whereas what is being asked appears in green highlighting. Theoretical concepts are highlighted in orange.
I suggest that you start by reading the DFT case (A3 to A8). Do not hesitate to refer to it throughout your reading process.

Understanding the requirements, within the framework of the role to be played, helps to determine the topics to analyze.

Flesh Out Useful Information

The resolution of a case takes place in a restricted – if not tight – time frame, and this is especially true of short cases. It is crucial to develop one's ability to **quickly** and **properly** understand the information supplied. To this end, I suggest you conduct your reading of a case in two phases: 1- Overview of the information provided and 2- Detailed reading of the case.

1- *Overview Of The Information Provided*

This first step doesn't take very long, at most 2 or 3 minutes for a 70-minute case. The objective is to take cognizance of all the information provided by fleshing out as soon as possible the components of one of the case parameters. A proper determination of your duties and responsibilities is crucial to the drafting of a relevant answer.

To this end, I suggest you look for the paragraph(s) describing the requirements by examining, first of all, the end of the descriptive portion of the "text" of the case, immediately prior to the exhibits. Read **these sentences and paragraphs describing and specifying what is required** twice rather than just once. Make sure, as soon as possible, that you grasp fully what role you are to play, because it will influence the manner in which you read and interpret the case information. Where the case has a "Required" section, start by reading this section.

DFT CASE

The final paragraph of the descriptive portion of text of the DFT case clearly states what is expected of the candidate. It is very useful to read it from the outset and to take the time to absorb the significance of the work to do. In this type of paragraph, EACH WORD COUNTS.

For instance, take the following sentence: (A3)

"He is particularly concerned about issues that affect earnings because management is anticipating a more profitable year than previous years."

On the one hand, a close reading enables one to realize that the **impact on earnings** will have to be mentioned following the analysis of each of the accounting issues. It would be futile, for instance, to devote time to the impact on the balance sheet, since this is quite simply not the perspective requested. On the other hand, this sentence sets out **management's** expectations with respect to **earnings**. In this role as external auditor, you will have to be diligent, in light of the potential bias which management may exhibit.

One must next peruse each of the paragraphs of the case to flesh out a requirement, question or topic to tackle. Any information that specifies what you must do must be flagged. To this end, I suggest that you pay particular attention:

– to sentences ending with a question mark, since you will likely be required to answer the question asked;	E.g.: "Do you suggest that I take steps to list these shares on the stock exchange? If so, what documents must I prepare?"
– to sentences appearing in quotation marks, as they may contain an opinion that requires you to comment or an express requirement on the part of the employer or client;	E.g.: When you met with Alice, she confessed to you "that she had no idea what price she should offer her sisters for the redemption of their unit".
– to sentences alluding to your role. N.B.: The letters "CPA", for instance, ought to draw your attention.	E.g.: "You have been chief accountant for a short while and you are required ..." A3: One can search for the name "Kin" throughout the text, since he is your immediate supervisor.

POINT OF VIEW

It is important to identify the key parameters or reference points of a case since they color the reading and interpretation of any information you read thereafter.

Being able to grasp the particulars of the case within the first few minutes is an undeniable asset.

When you know, for instance, that "Management is now part of a new bonus program that is based on earnings before interest, income taxes, depreciation, and amortization (EBITDA)." (A3), you will pay greater attention to anything that may impact this number, from the very first line of the case.

I suggest that you then leaf through the contents of the exhibits in order to take stock of the materials placed at your disposal to resolve the case. For instance, an exhibit setting out a financing offer means that you need to consider this offer as part of the duties entrusted to you. Similarly, the existence of a statement of "**Projected** net income" (A7) is a hint in and of itself. Not to mention that there is a **new** bonus program (A3) and you are being asked to analyze the **accounting issues of significance** (A3). Therefore, you must, as soon as possible, "HUNT FOR ANY MISTAKES"!

Note also the headings and sub-headings throughout the case, in particular those appearing in the exhibits. For instance, by honing in on the heading "Inventory Delivery Problem" or "Bank Concerns", you already have gained an overview of the problems or issues to be resolved. When you read, elsewhere in the wording of the case, that speed of delivery is a key factor to achieving success in the industry or that there is a delay in the production of the monthly financial statements, this will grab your attention to a much greater extent.

2- *Detailed Reading Of The Case*

From the outset, I would like to state that reading a case is not a passive or strictly linear activity. Merely reading the words or glancing at the financial reporting will not suffice. One must flesh out the features of the subject entity, understand what is going on, and classify the information in order to be able to adequately resolve the various problems or issues.

POINT OF VIEW

It is not as easy as one would think to determine the ideal amount of time to devote to the reading of a case. One must fully understand the information provided while leaving sufficient time to resolve the problems or issues. Some candidates read too quickly or start to write their answer before having read the whole case. One then notices "reading mistakes" which invalidate part of their answer. A problem that requires resolution may not have been picked up or the entity's manner of proceeding may not have been properly understood. Since the deal with Indo-Tech was signed (A5), for instance, it would be useless, as an audit procedure, to suggest asking if a contract exists. On the other hand, some candidates spend so much time reading the case that they are unable to resolve it adequately.

One must, starting with the first case simulations,

learn to allocate time between the reading and resolution of a case.

I, personally, write under the heading "CONTEXT" (or BACKGROUND) the specific particulars of the case. What is different or unusual? What is likely to influence the answer? What is not there in all cases? Although one can gather this information as one reads through the case, it is noteworthy that it is usually placed at the outset of the case, in the presentation of the subject entity. One can note, among others, the size of the entity (e.g.: family business), the industry (technology company (A3)), the significant dates (e.g.: period end), the key success factors (e.g.: product quality), the strengths, weaknesses, threats and opportunities (e.g.: fixed costs maintained at a low level), the objectives, needs, biases and behavior of the stakeholders (e.g.: strong risk aversion), the practices and policies of the entity (e.g.: requiring a minimum return of 9% for any new project), as well as any constraints (e.g.: limited sources of financing).

DFT CASE

The particulars of the DFT case are listed on page A8. For instance, the fact that DFT is a technology company (A3) implies a rapid obsolescence of its products, in a potentially competitive environment. Similarly, noting that DFT targets an average margin of 40% for products and 60% for services (A4) will prove to be useful in the event it becomes necessary to compute gross profit.

These remarks raise an important point, namely that the specifics of the context which one thus picks up on are "sometimes" useful, but not always. One must use them wisely, where circumstances warrant, and perhaps even in more than one location throughout the answer.

Furthermore, a reading of the case ought to enable you to identify specifically what the topics to analyze are, in light of the role you are called upon to play and of what is required. One must, consequently, be alert to any sentence or case facts that may contribute to specifying what is to be done. Where the employer or client is wondering about certain questions, expresses a request or issues an opinion on this or that, one must take note of it. Your objective is to finish reading the last sentence of the case with a list in hand of what may be analyzed in the answer to the case.

DFT CASE

In the discharge of your duties as auditor, the DFT case requests the preparation of a memo basically dealing with any accounting issues and their impact on the audit (planning and procedures). You are given this information as of the first minute of the simulation. As you read the case, you must thereafter search for the topics – and sub-topics – to resolve within each of these issues. Where, for instance, the case explains the terms of the non-recurring engineering (NRE) contract (A5), one must, first of all, ensure that one understands the nature of this unusual agreement. One must then ask oneself questions while not losing sight of what is required in the case.

What are the accounting aspects that require analysis?

As such, one should consider that there may be more than one aspect at play in order not to restrict one's thinking. In the case at hand, the accounting for the discount of $225,000 is the topic to latch on to. More specifically, one must determine WHEN to record this price reduction (discount): in the current period or in the following period.

What is the impact on the audit?

One may consider the effect of this new event on audit planning (risk), and then develop procedures that take into account the specific risks arising therefrom.

First and foremost, one must uncover the new topics, whether current or future. In point of fact, one must be alive to anything that is different or unusual, especially for the current period. "What is pending or ongoing?" One must answer this question, within the case parameters. While you are reading, you must constantly ask yourself the following: "What are the problems or issues to be resolved?", "What questions are unresolved?", "What is wrong within this entity?" and "What is in flux?".

POINT OF VIEW

Reading a case is a process that requires discipline and concentration, since one can never lose sight of any of the reference parameters (context, role, requirement).
For instance, a candidate might wonder why DFT agreed to give a client a $225,000 discount. While the question may be interesting, it is simply not relevant in the discharge of duties as an auditor who has been called upon to discuss matters of accounting and audit.

Within the specific context of a case,

one must limit oneself to the role one has been asked to play,

in light of the work to be done.

Some problems or issues are easier to spot than others. Their presentation or description leaves no doubt as to the nature of what needs to be discussed; these are "explicit" (or "direct") topics. Such is not always the case: indeed, a case **may** contain problems or issues that are "less explicit or non-explicit" (or "indirect"). These types of issues are characterized by the following:

- *Problems or issues that are "less explicit or non-explicit" fall within the case parameters.* They are perhaps not as obvious to identify as those that are explicit, however they are undeniably part of what is required. Let us suppose, for instance, that the work to be performed is the assessment of the purchase price of a business based on its future cash flows. Under these circumstances, one must also estimate future profit since the entity is required to pay over 10% of such profit to the inventor of a patent. Although this step is **non-explicit**, the computation of the net future income is critical, as part of an **explicit** requirement to estimate future cash flows so as to assess the purchase price. Unless it is requested somewhere, it would not be appropriate, for instance, to give business advice to the purchaser based on the fact that he "has no experience in the field". In and of itself, this information does not warrant the occurrence of such a less explicit issue.

CONTEXT ROLE REQUIRED

↘ ↓ ↙

CASE FACTS

↓

ISSUE/TOPICS

DFT CASE

In the DFT case, several case facts lead us to realize that management has intentionally manipulated the information in order to show net income in excess of $14 million (M). First, one must consider, from the outset, the existence of a "potential" bias on the part of management in maximizing the amount of the bonus. In his explanation of the work to be done, Kin, your immediate supervisor, specifically draws your attention to this possibility (A3). Secondly, it is apparent that most of the adjustments made to net income – in particular those close to the fiscal year-end – increase the EBITDA (A7).

This repetition of the direction of the impact must attract your attention.

One can also observe that the new bonus program has garnered the interest of management in particular. This is raised on more than one occasion in the case: "...management is anticipating a more profitable year than previous years" (A3) and "Anne believes that everyone in the program will receive a bonus." (A6).

It is important to realize that the identification and interpretation of this non-explicit issue takes place within the case parameters. It is in his or her capacity as **external auditor** that the candidate must ask himself or herself questions as to the implications of what he or she is observing.

A less explicit or non-explicit problem or issue falls within the parameters of one of the explicit requirements of the case, as part of the role to be played.

- *The case always provides case facts enabling the identification of a less explicit or non-explicit problem or issue.* And, most of the time, in light of their nature, there are more than one, spread out in various locations throughout the case. For instance, when there is significant doubt about the entity's ability to continue as a going concern, there will most certainly be several items of information pointing in this direction. Hence, there will be a cash deficit, the income statement will show losses for the past two years or suppliers will demand payment of goods upon delivery. In reality, at some point, one must acknowledge the existence of a common feature among the various case facts. When this occurs, one must usually backtrack and re-read certain parts of the case in order to get a broader picture, and then complete the assessment of the situation.

  This will enable you to issue a clear and substantiated finding with respect to the existence of the less explicit issue.

POINT OF VIEW

It is not easy, especially in the first simulated case, to identify a less explicit or non-explicit problem or issue. A candidate that focuses only on what appears at first blush risks not being aware of their occurrence.

Of course, there is not a less explicit or non-explicit problem or issue in every case, since the possibilities are, all in all, rather limited. Aside from that which is mentioned above, the production at full capacity, a cash flow deficit, the existence of "shady" dealings or related-party transactions as well as a lack of independence of the external auditor are factors to consider.

Where financial data – very often financial statements – is provided in the exhibit, I suggest that you start by examining this exhibit prior to any other. Besides being able to take cognizance of the entity's financial state, this enables you to flesh out what is unusual or problematic at an earlier stage during your reading. One must learn how to quickly flesh out key aspects. Try to identify that which seems different from a "standard" business by focusing a little longer on the items specific to the industry. The current year must be the initial focus of your perusal, although the comparison to the previous year is also often revealing.

WHAT ARE THE PATTERNS, RELATIONSHIPS, AND TRENDS?

Having already considered the financial reporting, your reading of the other parts of the case will be more exhaustive. For instance, noticing that the item Accounts receivable has doubled since the previous fiscal year, although sales have remained constant, will heighten your awareness and make you spot any case facts with respect to the existence de doubtful accounts. Always conduct your reading by taking into account the case parameters. If you know, for instance, that the business is in need of liquidity to carry out a capital project, you will pay attention to the investments, the assets and the existing structure of the non-current (long-term) financing. Finally, to ensure that observations are diversified, one can take a brief glance at each of the following categories: profitability, liquidity, coverage and activity.

FINANCIAL REPORTING ITEMS TO IDENTIFY

Items to identify	Examples (DFT CASE, Exhibit III (A7))
Basic Information	– "Projections" (FUTURE therefore unaudited) – Year-end: September 30
Most Significant Items (in terms of variations or percentage)	– Revenue as well as the Cost of sales, by extension, are the items, which were subjected to significant adjustments.
Riskiest Items (those in respect of which future benefits are more uncertain or which require an estimation of the situation)	– A significant amount of Research and development (R&D) is expensed. – Since projections are involved, several items include estimations that need to be validated.
Unusual Items	– The amortization expense has been included in several items: Cost of sales, R&D costs, General & administrative expenses. N.B.: This observation is especially important regarding the method of computation of the bonus based on the EBITDA.
Inconsistencies, biases and contradictions	– The majority of the adjustments made result in an increase in net income. – The adjusted EBITDA of $15,860,000 exceeds the target of $14,000,000.
Derogations from standards, rules, laws, policies, etc.	– Grants were recognized as revenue, which is not in compliance with accounting standards.
Key Ratios (specifically those that are of interest to creditors or management)	– Since management bonuses are based on EBITDA, this is the focus. – A quick glance at the main ratios – without computing them – does not allow for detection of any particular problems.

POINT OF VIEW

I insist on advising you as follows: try to adapt to each of the cases you are writing. The uniqueness of each of them requires its own reaction.

Some candidates try to "force" the issue by systematically looking for a non-explicit problem or issue in all cases. Others automatically calculate 4 to 6 ratios as soon as they see financial statements.

One must limit oneself to what is useful for the case under study.

Ask oneself questions? DEFINITELY YES
Systematically adopt the same behavior in all cases? DEFINITELY NOT

In light of the restricted time frame in which to complete a case, it often happens – despite one's good intentions – that the reading speeds up as time flies. Hence, the first pages are read with greater scrutiny whereas the latter pages are read a little too fast. From experience, I can tell you that important information is frequently found in the last paragraphs of a case. For instance, let us examine the last page of the DFT case (A7). In the rush to start writing his or her answer, a candidate could gloss over this page too quickly, although it contains very important information. Worse yet, he or she could decide to return to it, if necessary, during the drafting per se. This is rarely a good idea, since, in particular in this example, one must understand the nature of the adjustments carried out in order to properly analyze the various topics. We will revisit this issue a little later but know this:

It is important to link the various items of information in order to conduct a complete analysis of the situation.

Finally, I wish to suggest to you that you pay particular attention to the layout of the information. Is the information provided to you by type of product, by division or by country? Are the figures expressed in kilograms, hours or square meters? Is reference made on more than one occasion to the date or year? These are case facts in and of themselves. As well, be alert to repetitions, similarities, contradictions and synchronisms. For instance, a desire to stimulate management into contributing to profitability – *by way of an indicator of earnings for the current period* – by being innovative and developing new products – *which is generally an activity over the medium term* – is incoherent. (A4)

UNDERSTANDING THE REQUIREMENT

↓

RELEVANCE OF THE ANSWER

Annotating A Case Efficiently

I would now like to make you aware of the usefulness of annotating a case. Although I devote an entire section to them, one must say that annotations are written directly on the case – or on a separate piece of paper – as you read the case. To the extent that time constraints prevent you from reading the entire text twice or from thinking of summarizing it, annotating a case efficiently greatly assists in the planning and drafting of your answer. Since relevant information appears throughout the case, a methodical reading is in order to be able to properly grasp what is going on.

In other words, annotations serve to **classify the information** and **enable you to quickly locate it**. The longer the case, the more useful annotations can be. And, finally, there is the not insignificant benefit derived from reading and then annotating a case, namely that they help you remain focused on the task at hand.

POINT OF VIEW

There are many ways of annotating a case. Some highlight the text, sometimes with different colors, whereas others underline and circle important words. The number and scope of annotations also vary from one person to the next; some candidates need to write more than others. I urge you to experiment with various methods in order to discover what suits your personality best.

Pages A3 to A7 illustrate the manner in which I annotate a case. This is what one must consider:

- *Highlight the specifics of the context.* One must, of course, identify and understand them, but also remember to refer to them or use them while drafting. It is also possible to rewrite this information in the form of Reading Notes (A8) in order to be in a position to quickly glance at them. It is a useful reminder of their existence. I also know that several candidates highlight them by simply using a different color.

- *Flesh out explanations or clarifications of the role and the requirement.* Personally, in light of the significance of these parameters, I flag them separately, always using a green highlighter (A3). Incidentally, since I re-read this information more than once, I also sometimes circle key words outlining the work to be done, or yet again, I recopy the essence of what is required on a separate page. This is especially useful where the requirement is unusual, where the problems or issues are difficult to identify or the topics to be discussed are complex.

POINT OF VIEW

While reading, it is possible that ideas that are useful to the resolution of the case will come to mind. It is then tempting to start writing the answer. As mentioned above, I suggest you read the case in its entirety in order to be in a position to assess and consider all the available information in one fell swoop. An analysis which is embarked on too quickly is in danger of being incomplete or even of becoming useless when one takes into consideration the last of the case information.
If you fear forgetting these ideas, scribble them quickly on a working copy or on a separate sheet, and wait for the right time to expatiate on them.

- *Identify the problems and issues to discuss.* I use the left-hand margin exclusively for this purpose. I write down both the problem or issue involved and the topic to be discussed. If necessary, I add a reference such as *(a)*, *(b)*, *(c)*, ... or ①, ②, ③, ... For instance, I write "ACCT" as well as the topic involved next to each of the accounting issues identified. I also jot down each of the parts of a topic as follows: "REV 1.5M" and "REV 1.85M" (A5). Where a paragraph contains information useful to more than one aspect of the requirement, I write it down to make sure I do not forget anything (e.g.: "R&D – ZEUS / ACCT AUDIT" (A6)). The abbreviation "R" which stands for "risk" can easily be written down. And, finally, the word "BONUS" can appear in strategic locations throughout the case.

One must acknowledge that some cases structure information in such a way that it is easy to find one's bearings. A simple bracket may be sufficient to signal the presence of information on a capital project, for instance. In other circumstances, an exhibit, or two in the DFT case (A4, A5), may contain information relating to more than one topic. One must then order this information and take the time to identify, in each of the paragraphs, the topic(s) to be discussed.

POINT OF VIEW

I am frequently able – and I urge you to do the same – to determine the significance of a topic as I am reading.

I generally use the following signs or abbreviations:

IMPORTANT TOPICS: "IMP" OR "+++ "
TOPICS OF LESSER IMPORTANCE: "+/–"
NOT VERY IMPORTANT / INSIGNIFICANT TOPICS: "SEC"

N.B.: It happens frequently that a case will contain no unimportant or insignificant topics.

As needed, I occasionally add, in the right-hand margin, a brief comment, an opinion, a calculation or a key word. For instance, the term "cash" could refer to the items to consider under the cash basis of accounting. As for the symbol "$", it denotes, for instance, the information to consider in the adjustment of the net income amount (A5, A6). Or yet, writing the abbreviations "W" for "weakness", "PROS" for "advantage" or "CONS" for "disadvantage" allows one to identify upon reading the contents of certain parts of the work to be done. In addition, a "wow", a "?", "!", an arrow or any other sign you like can be quite revealing. Remember, the usefulness of annotations is to enable you to quickly locate the information you are looking for.

➢ *Highlighting (or underlining) important words.* I urge you to read a paragraph in its entirety – or sometimes to split it up into parts – before proceeding to do this. This will allow you to step back a bit and ask yourself what is truly important in the information provided. Otherwise, everything may end up in yellow! The words or expressions to focus on are those that help define the problems or issues or which provide case facts or arguments enabling their resolution.

  For instance, the fact that DFT "abandoned the development" of the Ares product may be used to justify expensing deferred development costs. On the other hand, the fact that the development "can be leveraged for a new product" will support the current position, which involved capitalizing costs. (A6) Therefore, one must, upon reading the case, try to anticipate the use of the information or case facts identified. I will revisit this issue in Part 3.

  The more you practice, the easier you will recognize these words or expressions that must attract your attention upon reading.

  Here are a few examples:

  "**new**" (A3), "never", "all", "recently", "**constantly** reinvest…" (A4), "**DFT is confident** it will do…" (A5), "**unexplained** variations", "**three** financing alternatives", "the system was developed by the **bookkeeper**", "accrue an **estimate** of..." (A6), "**key** information", etc.

READ

+

UNDERSTAND

↓

ORGANIZE

POINT OF VIEW

Remember one important thing, namely that what you have written on the case itself does not form part of the answer. Incidentally, it frequently happens that the candidate will leave in the text of the case a simulation or investigation he or she conducted. This means that one must restrict the use of annotations to what is strictly essential. Also, since these annotations are for the exclusive use of the candidate, they may, and must, be very succinct. It is therefore possible for you, for instance, to write "P" for "Product" and "S" for "Service" (A5), or to develop your own referencing system.

Give your annotations a personal touch so that they are significant **for you** and so that **you** are easily able to find **your** bearings.

Occasionally, candidates jot down a few notes on a separate page (e.g.: A8). Although these Reading Notes usually appear at the very end of the answer, they are not always read or evaluated by the person grading the case. Once again, one must focus on what is essential and proceed in that manner only if it is useful to you. Personally, I sometimes write down a few notes, on a working copy. For instance, I summarize on this scrap piece of paper the information regarding a situation, which is difficult to grasp, or I draw a diagram, which is hard to create on-screen.

➢ *Ensure that you understand the information properly.* In point of fact, you must develop tricks, under the circumstances, that enable you to understand what is going on. For instance,

- Make journal entries in order to visualize the accounting of a complex transaction.
- Draw a timeline where the sequence of events is under consideration (A3).
- Reconcile adjustments in projected net income where there are many of them (A7).
- Draw an audit diagram illustrating the flow of accounting documents throughout the entity.
- Place the information with respect to the two leases in a comparative chart.

POINT OF VIEW

The reading of a case requires one essential quality, namely: objectivity. This means that one must read and understand the information but refrain from ascribing to it a meaning it does not have. Resist the urge to add words to the text.

One must pay close attention to the written facts, BLACK ON WHITE.

One must not "read between the lines" or "speculate".

For instance, a client tells you "that the employees at the Burlington plant are threatening to strike". One should definitely not assume, unless information is provided to that effect, that the same will hold true for all the business' other plants.

That which is not written in a case is not there or does not exist.

- *Tie the various items information together.* It frequently happens that a given topic will be addressed in more than one location throughout the case. One will note, for instance, that the Zeus product is introduced on page A4 (July meeting), and that it is referred to again on page A6 (September meeting). One must find a way to link these two items of information in order to acknowledge, for instance, that the expectations regarding this new product did not materialize. Personally, I write a reference to each of them at all locations where they appear in order to be able to access all the available information when the time comes to resolve this topic. The reference to A4-2 is to page A4, 2nd paragraph. I also sometimes quickly rewrite the relevant information.

POINT OF VIEW

To me, it appears especially important to establish a link between qualitative and quantitative information. Too often, financial data is considered separately even though it can contribute to a better understanding of what is going on. One must, therefore, develop a reflex of making such data, whatever form it may take or contents it may contain, interact with the rest of the text.

Personally, upon reading the DFT case, I frequently consulted the projected net income in Exhibit III (A7) in order to complete or validate any of the items of information I had read. For instance, where I read that "The bonus begins to accumulate once EBITDA exceeds $14 million" (A3), I will immediately estimate or calculate the projected EBITDA in my mind (A7).

N.B.: In order to be able to easily revert to an exhibit containing financial data, I stick a "Post-it ".

Part 2
Planning One's Answer

Validate What Is Required/The Requirements
Determining The Importance Of Topics To Be Analyzed
Crafting One's Answer

"It is not always possible to find the time to do everything, but one must find the time to do everything that is important."

Part 2
Planning One's Answer

Between the end of the reading of a case and the beginning of the drafting of the answer, I strongly suggest that you take a moment to reflect. Whether by making a mental note or by writing it down, you must ensure that you adequately plan the time you have left. Especially in a short case scenario, time flies by quickly and each minute is precious. It appears to me to be all the more necessary to confirm the direction your answer will take towards that which is important, or relevant.

Validate What Is Required/The Requirements

One must correctly grasp the case parameters, since they inform the drafting of the answer. It is a good idea to re-read the paragraph(s) explaining what is required/the requirements so as to ensure that all the problems and issues have been identified. For instance, in the DFT case, one is required to analyze the impact of the accounting issues both on "audit planning" AND on "the procedures to be performed" (A3). The two aspects must necessarily form part of the answer. One must also keep in mind the requirement that the problems and issues must be approached from the point of view of an external auditor. Therefore, it would not be appropriate, for instance, to provide business advice.

One way or another, one must set out the list of the topics to discuss in the answer. I previously explained that I write the topics I have identified during my reading in the left-hand column of the case. I sometimes write this list of topics, and sub-topics, on a separate page in order to gain an overall picture of what needs to be done. This is especially useful where there are many topics or they are spread out in different locations throughout the case. Besides determining the topics that must be included in the answer, one must make sure **to identify as precisely as possible** that which must be discussed or resolved. Where the starting point is erroneous or imprecise, it is difficult for the analysis that follows to be appropriate.

DFT CASE

Let us take the example in the "Indo-Tech" section (A5). As soon as one starts reading the three paragraphs in question, one must look for the topic(s) to be discussed, within the case parameters.

Let us start with the accounting issue. The text refers to the unusual terms of the deal signed with Indo-Tech, focusing in particular on the variation of inventory. A candidate reading too quickly might think that the accounting topic to be discussed relates to inventory. He or she might then embark on a discussion of the accounting for this asset at the lesser of cost and net realizable value, for instance. That would not be very useful, quite simply because the critical aspect to discuss does not involve inventory. Incidentally, I know that some candidates who simulated the DFT case wrongly believed that goods on consignment were involved.

In point of fact, "Revenue Recognition" is the topic to discuss. The text, incidentally, refers on more than one occasion to the notion of "transfer of ownership", a notion that is inherent in the recognition of revenue from the sale of goods. That is a hint in and of itself. In reality, the question to be resolved is the following: "WHEN one must recognize revenue?". Therefore, one must take a step back in order to specifically identify the pending issue, in light of the information provided. Nothing here leads one to believe that the inventory has been improperly accounted for.

It is crucial to properly identify the case parameters.

POINT OF VIEW

From experience, I can tell you that not adequately identifying the topic or aspect to be analyzed is one of the greatest obstacles to success in a case. A discussion of the accounting of inventory, no matter how good its quality, cannot replace a required discussion of revenue recognition.

In light of how far you have progressed in your studies, you are in a position to discuss a great number of topics. The challenge involves knowing how to choose from among the broad array of knowledge you have acquired what to say for the answer to be appropriate.

In light of the restricted time frame in which to resolve a case,
it is absolutely crucial to get on the right track from the outset.

In a mass of information, it is sometimes difficult to distinguish what needs to be done. What is the problem to be solved? What is not as it should be? It is not always obvious to distinguish a problem from the case facts that enable one to flesh it out. In other words, one must not confuse a given problem with the cause(s) of its occurrence, or with the consequences of its existence.

Let us assume, for instance, that a business gives away an all-expenses-paid trip to its two best salespersons. Let us also assume that the external auditor realizes that sales were recorded in the books towards the end of the current period for goods to be delivered at the beginning of the next period. The early recording of these sales results in an overvaluation of net income.

Too hasty a reaction would be to state that the problem involves granting a bonus to salespersons based on sales during the fiscal year, while, in fact, this is not true. Fundamentally, this is an issue of deficiency in internal control, since the cutoff for transactions between periods has not been properly established. Giving the best sellers a free trip probably very squarely meets the stated goal, which is to motivate them. To be sure one has properly identified the problem, one should ask oneself the following question: "If the business stops giving away a free trip to its best sellers, is everything settled?" NO!, because other errors relating to the allocation of transactions between periods can subsist.

cause(s)	**PROBLEM**	consequence(s)
↓	↓	↓
early recording of sales	deficiency in internal control	overvaluation of net income
	↑ ↑ ↑	

In the DFT case, the problem does not lie in wanting to pay bonuses to management, but rather in knowing on what basis to compute them. (A3, A37)

The above example raises, once again, the need for properly identifying the problem at issue. A candidate who erroneously believes that the problem to be solved is the manner of rewarding or incentivizing salespersons (or management) will naturally develop his or her answer in that direction. He or she might, among others, analyze other means of promoting sales growth, and ultimately suggest the one that appears most apposite to him or her under the circumstances. On the one hand, such a reply does not resolve the fundamental problem of the deficiency in internal control. On the other hand, in the capacity of external auditor, this discussion would not really be appropriate.

In the determination of topics to discuss, also consider the following:

- *One must take into account the source of the information placed at your disposal.* Notes taken by you or your immediate supervisor carry greater credibility than information found on the Web, for instance.

DFT CASE

There is a difference between the two exhibits of the DFT case, which provide a summary of the meeting with Anne, the Chief Executive Officer (CEO). Exhibit I (A4), which details the meeting held in July, introduces the DFT corporation in a general and factual manner. There are no topics to speak of that need resolving upon a reading of this exhibit. A good deal of information will, however, be useful to the resolution of topics appearing elsewhere in the case.

As for Exhibit II (A5), it summarizes a more recent meeting. It describes "events [that] have occurred since July", which is a hint in and of itself of their greater significance. You should, therefore, not be surprised to see that most of the topics to be analyzed are contained in this exhibit.

- *The same item of information can be used more than once, for different aspects.* Some candidates read a paragraph, identify a topic for discussion, and move on to the next without any further inquiry. The risk inherent in proceeding in this manner is that they may not glean an exhaustive list of what needs to be done. Let us return to the example in the "Indo-Tech" section of the DFT case (A5). An analysis of the information previously enabled us to identify the accounting issue as relating to Revenue recognition. One must understand that this same basic information will also be used in the analysis of the impact on audit planning and the procedures to be performed.

- *The identification of a topic may require consideration of several case facts,* which are sometimes spread out in various locations. Once you have completed your reading of the case, I suggest you take a step back and look at the information in its entirety.

  Are there repetitive comments?

  Did one notice similar situations?

  What is essentially flowing in the same direction?

  This brief moment of reflection may enable you to flesh out the occurrence of an issue that is less explicit or non-explicit or of an important consideration. Examples include a risk of fraud, an especially high financial risk, a series of poor management decisions or the professional negligence of a colleague. In the DFT case, you might become more acutely aware of the inherent influence of the bonus program on the accounting treatment of fiscal year-end events (A7).

PROBLEM IDENTIFIED

↓

RELEVANT ANSWER

Determining The Importance Of Topics To Be Analyzed

To me, it seems crucial to assess the importance of each of the topics to be dealt with, as against each other. Where certain topics are more important than others, one must make sure to analyze them appropriately. Since the time to complete a case is always limited, this is a skill that one must absolutely develop. Generally speaking, a more important topic requires a greater depth of analysis. As mentioned in Part 1, I rank topics in three categories: important topics, topics of lesser importance and not very important (insignificant) topics. From experience, I can tell you that, in order to successfully complete a case:

One must **attempt to analyze all** – or nearly all – the **important topics** and,

if possible, part of the topics of lesser importance.

Thus, one must take into account the information available and DETERMINE WHAT IS IMPORTANT, IN LIGHT OF THE CASE PARAMETERS. In this respect, I suggest that you consider simultaneously one or more of the criteria below.

CRITERIA TO CONSIDER IN THE DETERMINATION OF THE IMPORTANCE OF A TOPIC

Criteria to consider	Examples
Significance of the amounts involved Tip: An item become important if it represents anywhere from 5% to 15% of a baseline – net income, revenue, total assets. Observation: The impact on the stakeholders must be considered.	– The impairment loss of $100,000 on production equipment (A6), when compared to the projected net income of $7,351,000 (A7), is minor. One can therefore drop this topic of little significance (not very important). – The preparation of a budget requires a determination of future revenue. This business markets three different products. One can make a more detailed calculation for the two main products and use a mere hypothesis for the third, which represents 6% of the revenues from ordinary activities.
Role to be played Tip: One must determine the chief reason why you are being hired. What skills are being called upon? From which perspective is one to approach the work to be performed?	– Although several tax ideas may come to mind while you are reading the DFT case, dealing with them is irrelevant to the answer. On the one hand, this simply forms no part of what is required. On the other hand, since the bonus program is aiming for a pre-tax amount, namely EBITDA, this reduces the importance of the item Income taxes. (DFT CASE)

CRITERIA TO CONSIDER IN THE DETERMINATION OF THE IMPORTANCE OF A TOPIC

Criteria to consider	Examples
Risks and uncertainties Tip: One must consider the nature or impact of the topic of discussion. Does it involve significant cash inflows or cash outflows? Does it have the potential of changing the findings or recommendations? Does it require estimations to be made?	– Inventory, having a current value of $1.85M is presently located in India. Aside from the significance of the amount, one must say that the unusual deal entered into with Indo-Tech, as well as the physical remoteness of the inventory, make this an important topic to be dealt with by the auditor. (A5) – Revenue recognition is a more important problem when no amount has been received. Hence, it is more important to determine when to account for an amount of $500,000 receivable in one year than to know when to recognize an amount already received.
Distinctive features of the industry Tip: One must ask oneself what is characteristic of the industry in which the entity operates. What is peculiar and not found in other industries?	– The business is in retail sales. Inventory management is more likely to be an important topic than management of receivables. – When a not-for-profit entity is involved, one must think about including additional information in the financial statements, such as a description of the operations, performance indicators and budgetary data.
Timeline Tip: One must look at the deadline or expiry, closing or due date; the closer this date is in time, the more likely the topic is to be important.	– A company is contemplating building a new plant in the next three years. Since the time horizon is far off, this topic will likely be of little importance, even if the facts mention that the President is adamant about this project.
Available information Tip: The nature and quantity of information available for analytical purposes may be a hint in and of themselves. What is the opinion of any of the stakeholders? How long is the text devoted to this topic?	– An entire exhibit is devoted to the reporting of the adjustments to the computation of projected net income. (A7) It is therefore necessary to examine the impact of each of the accounting issues on this income. This is also warranted by the frequent reference to the existence of the new bonus program based on the EBITDA in the qualitative segment of the case.

SPECIFIC REQUIREMENT

↓

SPECIFIC ANSWER

↓

SUCCESS

- Each topic or aspect of a topic must be assessed separately. In the DFT case, for instance, one needs to inquire about the deferred development costs for two different products: Zeus and Ares. As shown in the previous chart, they do not have the same importance. Incidentally, it would not be a good idea to embark on a joint discussion of both products, simply because the ideas to be considered in the analysis are not the same. One must, therefore, ASSESS THE IMPORTANCE OF EACH OF THE ASPECTS OF THE SAME TOPIC, as part of the **role to be played**.

- The topic "Estimate/Record the provision" was ranked as not very important. At first blush, this may seem surprising, since the bonus program is the most important distinguishing feature of the DFT case. One must, however, understand that the recording of the amount of bonuses to be paid does not involve any particular problem. There is no **uncertainty** here, since the bonus can be easily calculated, and then accounted for, as soon as the amount of the EBITDA will have been determined. It is an insignificant accounting topic, which is nevertheless very easy to resolve.

The sequence in which the topics appear in the case rarely coincides with their degree of importance.

- The chart contains the "new" topics arising during the fiscal year, which topics are essentially set out in Exhibit II (A5) that details "a number of events [that] have occurred since July". It is, among other reasons, because they occur near the year-end (**timeline**) that they must attract your attention. It would, therefore, not be useful, for instance, to discuss revenue recognition generally, since the type of products sold by DFT has not changed (A4). Instead, it is the manner of conducting business with certain clients that has changed (advance shipment of inventory to Indo-Tech, discount on sales of NRE (A5)). It is these specific and "new" circumstances which warrant a questioning of the accounting treatment to apply.

- Take the time to leaf through the case and to take into consideration the quantity of **information available** on each of the topics. You will quickly notice that the case provides more information on the more important topics, which makes sense. Since one of the goals of learning through case resolution is to enable you to incorporate your knowledge in the context of a scenario created for this purpose, there is no doubt you will require case facts to do so. Where there is no or little information on a topic, the analysis remains general in nature, which can only lessen its relevance. Hence, you can observe that the last three topics covered in the last three paragraphs of page A6 of the DFT case are of little significance.

  N.B.: I do ask, however, that you remain cautious with this criterion as to the quantity of available information. Do not rely only on this criterion, validate it by looking at any of the other criteria, and do so wisely!

POINT OF VIEW

You must be vigilant in your determination of what is important when examining financial data.
Be careful not to expatiate excessively on a topic by relying only on the presence of an important item in the financial statements.

Let us revisit an example set out in Part 1, namely that the item Receivables has doubled since the previous fiscal year although sales remained constant. During the reading of the case, you must be alert to any case facts with respect to the existence of doubtful accounts. Perhaps you will find these case facts, and perhaps not. In the absence of any case facts, it is useless to "speculate" and to embark on a discussion of the "potential" existence of a deficiency in the collection of accounts receivable.

IMPORTANT ITEM ≠ IMPORTANT TOPIC

Indeed, it is rather rare that a topic will be important if there is no qualitative information to go along with its quantitative aspect.

- When one examines the **available information** in Exhibit III (A7), one realizes that the amortization has been subjected to three adjustments (Notes 2), 3), 4)). One also observes that there is no separate item Amortization in net income. One could wonder: Why isn't amortization included in the list of accounting topics to be discussed? There are two reasons. First of all, one must recall that the calculation of the bonus is based on the EBITDA, which, by its very definition, excludes amortization. This reduces its significance. Secondly, one can easily notice the **absence of information** on this topic in the case. There is nothing to suggest that the amortization is erroneous, hence its absence from the list of accounting topics to be discussed.

  One could most certainly imagine that the amortization expense has been overvalued with a view to increasing the EBITDA and, accordingly, the amount of the bonus. This is plausible; however, once again, case facts are lacking. The possibility that the amortization may have been miscalculated may substantiate, for instance, the potential bias of management or the increase in audit risk. However, this point should be made succinctly: one sentence or two. Be especially aware that the case contains other information, both concrete and complete, allowing for a greater expansion on this type of comment. The recording as revenue of the $800,000 in grants although 75% of the related development costs still remain in deferred development costs is a much more revealing example.

POINT OF VIEW

Among the various case facts, one sometimes notices the presence of an opinion issued by the client. Thus, a shareholder could tell you: "First of all, we must calculate the redemption price of my shares". It is likely his priority..., however, it is not necessarily the priority as part of the duties as advisor, which have been entrusted to you by the President. It may be, for instance, that the decision to repair or replace an item of equipment is more important, since the frequent production shutdowns are very costly. Obviously, when your immediate supervisor makes his various requests, such as those made by Kin in the DFT case (A3), you would have to have very good reasons for not carrying them out!

Crafting One's Answer

The template for an answer to a case is relatively standard. Following a succinct presentation of the content, *via* an appropriate heading, the various problems and issues are analyzed. The topics are approached based on the order of importance previously established. The schedules, which appear thereafter, basically contain the calculations necessary to providing a complete answer. Under certain circumstances, a chart or table referred to more than once in the answer can be appended as a schedule. For instance, it could contain the list of strengths, weaknesses, threats and opportunities of the entity, the list of advantages and disadvantages of a business opportunity, or large sections of an implementation plan (who, what, when, cost). The format created by the use of software, such as *Excel*, simplifies the structured presentation of this type of information.

ANSWER TO A CASE

Heading
Issue #1 – Topic A, Topic B, Topic C, ...
Issue #2 – Topic A, Topic B, Topic C, ...
Issue #3 – Topic A, Topic B, Topic C, ... Etc.
Schedules
Reading Notes or Draft (if necessary)

The use of sections – Date, To, From, Subject – is especially effective when starting the answer to a case. While enhancing the professional appearance of your text, you recall the fundamental parameters. Since it is not always easy to start drafting an answer, preparing a heading is a good starting point. First of all, you must ensure that you properly determine the **Date** of drafting of the report, **To** whom it is directed (e.g.: Board of Directors, employer, client, partner, colleague) and the role (**From**) you have been assigned (e.g.: management consultant, auditor, comptroller, tax specialist). These sections, which you generally add as you read the case, inform the drafting. For instance, the contents of a report on a business acquisition will not be the same if the financial statements of the vendor are recent or were drawn up a few months ago, if one is directing one's comments to the vendor or the purchaser or if one is playing the role of a tax specialist or a management consultant.

EXAMPLE OF A HEADING TO AN ANSWER (DFT CASE)

MEMO

Date: September 12, 2012
To: Kin Lo, Partner
From: CPA
Subject: – Accounting issues
IMPACT on earnings
– Audit planning AND procedures to be performed
– Potential management bias

POINT OF VIEW

I frequently insist on the fact that the contents of an answer flow directly from the case parameters (context, role, requirement). Indeed, it is important to realize that the case facts could be used for several purposes. Up to a certain point, the author of a case "selects" the topics to be resolved, in light of the learning goals sought to be achieved. Let us return to the example of the case bearing on a business acquisition. Using the same basic information, the list of risks and opportunities will not be the same if one acts from the perspective of the purchaser or the vendor. Realizing this fact, which is inherent to the resolution of cases, reinforces the need:

to properly determine what needs to be done from the outset
and
not to lose sight until the last minute of the drafting of the answer.

READING

↓

PLANNING

↓

DRAFTING

The **Subject** section should contain, from the start, one or two sentences summarizing the essence of the work to be performed. I suggest that you take the time to write down the basics of what is required, using, as much as possible, the same words as those set out in the case. For instance, if you are asked for your opinion on each of the proposed options, the word "each" must draw your attention. It is an efficient reminder that you must set out your findings, maybe even your opinion, following an analysis of each option. Similarly, writing "IMPACT on earnings" reminds you of the need to finish the analysis of each of the accounting topics by indicating the impact on the EBITDA figure.

POINT OF VIEW

Under certain circumstances, it is useful to place a more complete list of the topics to be discussed in the Subject section. As far as I am concerned, writing down the important topics is an integral part of the process of evaluating their importance. In other words, I write down in this section any important topic as soon as it has been identified. That way, I make sure not to forget anything fundamental. This is especially useful where the issue is less explicit or where the assignment I have received is unusual. Moreover, it is efficient to "cut/paste" the topics to be discussed from the Subject section as the drafting progresses.

However, I stress – adamantly so – the need for succinctness in the presentation of the heading. Although necessary, such a heading is not considered, or very little, in the assessment of your answer. Finally, remember that the level of detail in the Subject section mainly depends on your personal needs.

The Subject of a case can be the outline of your answer.

The resolution of a case most often requires the submission of a report per se. If he or she so wishes, the candidate can simply write the word REPORT at the very beginning of his or her answer. He or she will do the same when the assignment to be performed is in the form of a letter, an internal memorandum, a memo or a summary. In the event of a letter, for instance, the candidate can revamp the sections – Date, To, From, Subject – in order to show that he or she is adapting to the situation. The date, the name of the recipient, a very short address as well as the Subject of the letter therefore appear in the heading on the first page. The candidate may then place his or her signature below a brief introduction or at the end of the letter.

Just before starting to draft your answer, I suggest you plan the time you have left. For a 70-minute case, such as the DFT case, you should have 45 to 50 minutes remaining to allocate between the major segments of your answer as you have outlined it. In the course of this exercise, you must ask yourself about the ordering of the topics, since the analysis of one may be required prior to the analysis of another. For instance, it is preferable to discuss revenue recognition prior to discussing inventory or the cost of sales. In addition, it goes without saying that the resolution of accounting topics must precede the analysis of their impact on the audit (A3). On the one hand, your immediate supervisor has asked you to proceed in this manner and, on the other hand, the audit procedures to be performed are directly related to the critical aspect of the various accounting topics. We will revisit this point a little later on in the volume.

POINT OF VIEW

By not adequately determining the importance or the sequencing of the topics, the candidate may spend too much time on aspects of lesser importance and not enough time on what is important. Incidentally, from experience, I can tell you that the simplest topics or the easiest ones to analyze are rarely among the most important. There is also a natural tendency to discuss the initial topics that appear at too great a length and the latter ones too little. Finally, one must be aware of another natural tendency, namely that of delving deeper into topics one masters or prefers. Need I even comment?

As mentioned above, to my mind, it is crucial to plan the apportionment of time between the various problems or issues, quite simply to ensure a reasonable coverage of the requirements. I have very often marked answers that provided an excellent analysis of the first point, but neglected the others due to a lack of time. It then becomes very difficult – if not impossible – to reach a passing standard. One must constantly be aware of the time limit inherent in any simulation or examination and act accordingly. Furthermore, one must leave sufficient time to conduct a quantitative analysis, if need be.

DFT CASE

The requirement clearly sets out two main issues to be analyzed: Accounting and Audit. As for the implications of the bonus program, they form part of a third issue, which coexists with each of the other two.

A candidate has about 50 minutes to draft an answer to the DFT case. At first blush, one must devote approximately the same amount of time to the two main issues, although the Accounting issue usually requires a bit more time than the Audit issue. On the one hand, one must anticipate having to explain or calculate the impact of the recommended accounting adjustments on the EBITDA in order to assess whether it is below or above the target of $14M. On the other hand, the analysis of the accounting issues requires more explanations than the review of the planning and the development of the audit procedures to be performed.

A candidate therefore has about 25 minutes – maybe 30 – to conduct an analysis of the accounting topics, 5 of which were determined to be important.

The drafting tempo is set.

When I prepare the heading to my answer or when I am about to resolve one of the issues in the case, I try to determine the analytical structure by asking myself what the end result of the discussion will be. In other words, I wonder what kind of answer the recipient of the report is expecting to receive. While it is not necessary to know in advance all the ideas that will be written down, nevertheless one must know the direction they will take. Assume, for instance, that you must respond to the inquiry from the financial advisor as to whether the CFE division is viable. The analysis, in the end, will need to determine "YES or NO" whether the CFE entity is solvent. It is easier to remain concentrated on the fundamentals when one does not lose sight of that fact. In the same vein, keeping in mind that one must determine if the preliminary materiality must be revised is a constant reminder to spend time discussing the factors that may warrant such a revision (A23). I will expatiate further on analytical structures in Part 10.

POINT OF VIEW

Instead of fleshing out the topics to be discussed, and structuring their answer accordingly, some candidates try instead to anticipate how the case will be graded. For instance, a candidate who thinks – or hopes – that the "Integration" skill will form part of the assessment (enabling competency) might decide to conduct an analysis on this topic. On the one hand, integration is a professional skill, which is proven by way of an expression of links all throughout one's answer; devoting a separate section to it is rarely appropriate. On the other hand, the level of integration to perform varies from one case to the next.

Personally, I do not attempt to anticipate how a case will be evaluated. Instead, I try to fully grasp the work to be done, as part of the role to be played, and to properly focus on what is important. I am convinced this is the best way of succeeding. Of course, you can ask yourself if interrelations or links exist between the various problems or issues set out in the case, but it is useless to insist where there are none.

Part 3
Drafting Relevant Ideas

Taking Into Account The Case Facts
Adopting A Systematic Approach
Integrating Ideas To The Case

"I know from experience that one of the major weaknesses of the responses proposed by candidates is quite simply that they did not answer the questions asked or dwelled too long on secondary issues at the expense of primary issues."

© Deslauriers Sylvie, *CGA = COMPETENCY*, AB + Publications, 2012, page 14.

Part 3
Drafting Relevant Ideas

Responding to the various requests made by an employer or a client is unavoidable if one wishes to succeed. Each case presents a unique scenario in which the candidate must call upon his or her knowledge with a view to resolving specific problems or issues. The answer to a case must essentially be made up of ideas that stay within the bounds of its parameters (context, role, requirement). In point of fact, the employer or client hires you to meet his, her or its particular needs. Hence, one must focus and provide the latter with what has been requested.

Unfortunately, some candidates exceed this scope, "decide" what is "good" for the client, and then embark on a discussion, which does not fall within the parameters of their assignment. Other candidates will instead show off their knowledge rather than focusing on, and using, only the concepts that are useful under the circumstances. Never lose track of the fact that successfully completing a case essentially depends on your capacity to draft relevant ideas.

UNIQUE CASE

↓

ADAPTED ANSWER

Taking Into Account The Case Facts

As one is about to draft an answer to a case, it is crucial to take into consideration the information, both qualitative and quantitative, that has been provided to you. While this is obvious, it is not always easy to do. First of all, one must constantly take into account the environment created by the case scenario. It happens too often that the scope of the work to be performed is understood or determined at the outset, but neglected thereafter. Hence, a candidate may be aware of the need to mention the impact of the bonus program (management bias) on the first or perhaps the first 2-3 accounting topics, and forget to do so for the latter ones. By losing sight of this important aspect as the drafting progresses, the analysis of the Accounting issue, as well as of the ensuing Audit issue, may turn out to be incomplete.

POINT DE VIEW

It is important to maintain one's concentration and not to get sidetracked along the way. Personally, I regularly re-read the description of the Required section, in the case itself – the text I have highlighted in green – or in the Subject section of the heading. When a candidate is about to write a sentence starting with words or expressions such as "Yes, but if …", "Perhaps …", "In the event that it were possible to do this …", "If the entity could change that …", the text that follows is rarely useful.

One must be wary of embarking on a hypothetical tangent that is not supported by the case facts provided.

One must also know when and how to use case facts in the course of the identification and analysis of the various problems or issues. For example, let us take the paragraph with respect to Zeus' inventory (A6). One might be inclined to think that the "measurement of cost" is the topic to be analyzed, in particular because DFT ran into unanticipated technical difficulties. However, the pending problem essentially relates to the "net realizable value" of the inventory of products manufactured. In reality, the case facts identified point to a questioning of the capacity to sell this inventory and not of the capacity to manufacture them or to properly determine their cost.

One must therefore understand the information provided, and then use it wisely in the analysis.

INFORMATION IN THE DFT CASE WITH RESPECT TO ZEUS' INVENTORY

Information in the DFT case (A6)	Comments
– "unanticipated technical difficulties" – "development of the new product, Zeus, was delayed"	– There is an explanation here as to why the development of the product was delayed. This information is not truly useful, since DFT overcame the problem and started producing inventory. Consequently, this has no influence on the reporting of inventory as such. – The information reveals that there were deficiencies in the planning of the technical feasibility of the Zeus product. However, the analysis of this issue does not fall within the case parameters.
– "DFT will likely only realize total sales of $200,000 for Zeus by year-end" – "likely have $400,000 of units in inventory at year-end"	– This information relates to the future and raises uncertainty as to the amount of sales for the current fiscal year. As such, it is not really sufficient to warrant a questioning of the value of Zeus' inventory. A delay in the fulfillment of the project does not automatically mean that its value has diminished.
– "a competitor was able to place a similar product on the market first" – "DFT isn't sure it can sell Zeus at the planned price."	– THIS IS KEY INFORMATION, information appearing at the very end of the paragraph. – The uncertainty with respect to the sales price is a critical aspect in the determination of the value of the inventory. **If** the price drops, it is then **possible that** the net realizable value may be less than cost. However, this is not a certainty and the analysis of this issue will have to take this into account.

In the absence of any valuable case facts, the discussion remains general or theoretic.

The chart on the preceding page fleshes out two fundamental items. First, it is important to properly identify what must be analyzed from the outset in order not to waste time. A discussion of the "cost" of inventory will not be considered in the assessment of the answer whereas a discussion of its "value" will be. Personally, I try to identify as precisely as possible the nature of the topic to be analyzed, which I write down as a title in my answer. Secondly, ideas making up an answer may be "correct" without being relevant. Some candidates erroneously believe they will be rewarded for any "good" idea they hatch in one of the issues forming part of the case.

**NOT ALL IDEAS COUNT,
ONLY RELEVANT IDEAS DO.**

POINT DE VIEW

You have probably already realized that the words and expressions used in a case are important. One also observes that "useless" items of information are few in number. This is true, in particular, so as to not burden down the task of reading or restrict the already limited time frame devoted to a reading of the case.

One must also understand that there is an unalterable nexus between the case facts and the ultimate resolution of the case. Where the author of the case wants a candidate to call upon his or her knowledge with respect to responsibility centers, for instance, he or she will design a requirement to that effect. If, more specifically, he or she would like the candidate to analyze the issue whether a profit center or an investment center is involved, he or she will provide case facts accordingly.

When time comes for preparing the proposed solution or the evaluation guide, constant reference is made to the case facts in order to ensure that the link does in fact exist. You must do the same when drafting your answer.

The above comments are also valid in the case of figures. The financial data supplied in the appendices or elsewhere in the text is, unfortunately, too often overlooked. It may be useful to **buttress the importance of a topic** or to **support the analysis**. Be careful, however, not to change the case data or to make arbitrary hypotheses for the purposes of calculations. The DFT case, for instance, contains no case facts with respect to the scope of an ultimate writedown of the inventory. Consequently, it would be futile to issue a hypothesis such as the following: "I assume that the obsolescence provision with respect to inventory is 50% of the year-end balance, namely $200,000". Whether one considers such a hypothesis or not makes no difference to the value of the answer.

The concepts relevant to the analysis do not need to be supported by an arbitrary figure.

As you undertake case simulations or examinations, I would like to encourage you to develop your intuition. It may seem somewhat paradoxical for me to insist both on the need for you to consider the case information while urging you to rely on your intuition. In reality, one must consider factual information while being alert to all that points towards a given result or a particular behavior. Some words, comments or expressions can, in and of themselves, signal the conclusion or the recommendation "you should reach".

On their face, they are case facts that color the analysis.

DFT CASE

Assume you have just read, and planned the resolution of, the DFT case. Immediately prior to starting your drafting of the accounting issues, what would your answer to the following question be?:

Do you believe that the adjusted net income figure, computed following the analysis of the accounting issues, will be less or greater than $14M?

I am practically sure you already know that it will be less than $14M.

Indeed, the case refers to several events having a "negative" impact on net income, since they have the effect of reducing income or increasing costs: (A5 and A6)

- inventory sent to warehouse on June 30, taken up by Indo only on August 2;
- sales discount to NRE in order to secure the contract;
- production delay with respect to the new Zeus product;
- a competitor was able to place a similar product on the market first;
- discontinuance of the development of the Ares product;
- reassessment by the State;
- impairment loss on production equipment.

Now answer the following question:

What events occurred during the period had a "positive" impact on DFT's net income?

The answer is not as obvious and you will likely have to re-read the case to be able to tell me that sales of the NRE product exceeded expectations (A5) or that government funding was secured (A6).

Hence, one observes that there are more case facts pointing towards a drop in net income. In addition, one must consider the weight of the various events heading in opposite directions.

Nevertheless, in spite of the above, "management is anticipating a more profitable year than previous years" (A3) and "Anne believes that everyone in the program will receive a bonus." (A6). A healthy dose of skepticism is in order!

You will notice later on, as the drafting of your answer progresses, that the appropriate accounting treatment is constantly at odds with that of management. You will then understand why, in the specific context of the DFT case, you must end up questioning management's integrity (A33, A34).

It is the accumulation of case facts heading in the same direction that brings about such a questioning.

CONSIDERATION OF THE CASE FACTS

↓

ADDED VALUE IN THE ANSWER

Adopting A Systematic Approach

With a view to arriving at a complete and appropriate draft of an answer to a given problem, issue or topic, I suggest that you adopt the following approach. As mentioned shortly above, it is very important – if not crucial – to quickly and precisely IDENTIFY the relevant problem. This **informs the drafting**. For instance, considering that the problem relates to "the absence of internal controls" as opposed to the "compensation method for salespersons" does not channel the analysis in the same direction at all. (Part 2, p. 17)

I suggest that you **clearly identify what the focus of any discussion or analysis is.** In most situations, stating it in title form is sufficient. However, on occasion, it may be necessary to justify its existence or to explain the root cause. This occurs when the problem is not clearly established in the case or where the issue is less explicit or non-explicit.

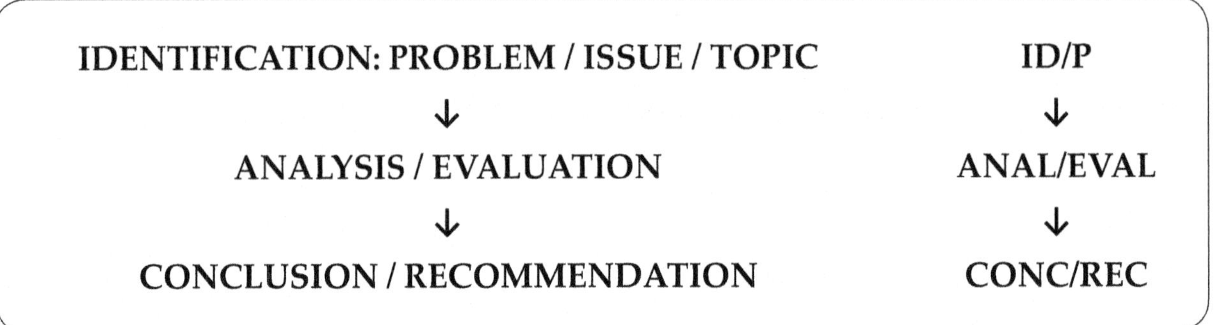

The ANALYSIS or EVALUATION section can take several different forms, in light of the circumstances and needs. What solutions ought to be contemplated? How does one account for a particular event? What is the impact of the deficiencies identified? How should one plan the transaction in order to minimize tax consequences?, or: What are the threats and opportunities relating to the capital project? **Your role is to contribute to the improvement of the current situation by resolving the issues and problems experienced by your employer or client.** It is crucial to determine how to conduct the analysis in order to reach your goal.

Every analysis must end with a CONCLUSION or a RECOMMENDATION – sometimes more than one – OR both. One must answer the following question: **What is the ultimate rationale of the analysis?** Incidentally, as I indicated previously, in Part 2 (p. 28), I ask myself questions, as soon as I start planning my answer, as to what the goal sought to be achieved is. An analysis of the factors to consider in order to justify the status of employee vs. self-employed, for instance, must lead to a conclusion as to the nature of the relationship set out in the case.

Determining the finish line helps you remain focused on what is important.

The chart on the following page provides examples illustrating the systematic approach to drafting.

It is better to write four or five relevant ideas, than ten that are not at all relevant!

EXAMPLES ILLUSTRATING THE SYSTEMATIC APPROACH TO DRAFTING

IDENTIFICATION **problem / issue / topic**	**ANALYSIS / EVALUATION**	**CONCLUSION / RECOMMENDATION**
Deficiencies in internal controls *Case facts:* Employees have access to all the data in the system.	Flesh out the impacts of the deficiencies identified E.g.: Confidential or sensitive information (e.g.: employees' salaries) could become common knowledge.	How can one mitigate or eliminate the deficiency? E.g.: Employees ought to be able to access only the information necessary to the discharge of their duties.
Substantial decline of the gross profit *Case facts:* The comptroller has the duty of explaining the deterioration of the financial state to the members of the Board of Directors.	Comment the current situation based on quantitative data E.g.: The contribution margin of each of the products is calculated, then commented.	What are the causes of the substantial decline of the gross profit? E.g.: For certain products, the cost of materials has doubled, due to a shortage on the ADC market.
Accounting issues of significance (A3) *Case facts:* $800,000 in grants (A6)	Discuss the appropriate accounting treatment E.g.: One must recognize the grants based on related costs: 75% to deferred development costs and 25% to R&D costs. (A12, A13)	What is the recommended accounting treatment? E.g.: "Therefore, revenue needs to be reduced by the full $800,000." (A13)
Inadequate preparation of receipts for charitable gifts *Case facts:* The volunteer for the organization handling the bookkeeping writes the amount requested by the donor on the receipt issued.	Indicate what the tax implications are of not proceeding in an adequate fashion E.g.: The government expects the organization to be able to justify the amounts appearing on the charitable receipts.	How should one proceed? E.g.: Works of art received from a donor must be subjected to an external valuation with a view to validating the amount to appear on the receipts.
Procedures to be performed (A3) *Case facts:* $800,000 in grants (A6)	Identify the assertion or the specific risk E.g.: "Risk that terms and conditions of the grant are not met and funds should be returned to government." (A28)	What procedures ought to be performed? E.g.: "trace these to the products in deferred development costs, to ensure the appropriate amount is deferred, and the appropriate classification – either expense or capital." (A28)

To help you provide a complete answer, I suggest that you regularly ask yourself three essential questions. From experience, I know that certain candidates – often out of ignorance – do not follow their ideas to their logical conclusion. I am also aware that one frequently runs out of ideas while drafting one's answer.

It is very useful to know how to ask the right questions at the right time.

QUESTIONS TO CONSIDER WHILE DRAFTING

Think of:	QUESTIONS	Examples
Justifying an idea, a problem, an issue, a topic, a conclusion or a recommendation.	**WHY? BECAUSE...** since… in order to… as… given that… due to... based on... in light of…	– "**Because** DFT cannot be certain that the courts will allow the money to be returned, virtual certainty does not exist, and **therefore** no asset should be recorded." (A15) – **Since** the services will be performed in 2OX4, the related costs will have to be expensed during this period.
Mentioning the impact or the consequence.	**CONSEQUENTLY?** therefore… I recommend... I conclude… as a result... then... hence… **AND SO?**	– "**Given that** DFT's products generally have a 40% gross margin, a decrease in the planned selling price, while reducing DFT's margins, would likely not result in a net realizable value that is below cost, and **therefore**, no writedown would likely be required as of September 30." (A13) – The working capital of 1.2 is less than that required by the bank, which can **therefore** decide to recall its loan.
Explain in concrete terms what to do. How can one go about this? What is the suggested action to be taken?	**HOW?** Who? What? When? How much? Where?	– "**As a result** management is likely expecting to be well above the threshold of $14 million required for the bonus, and that appears to be why Anne has indicated she will accrue a $300,000 bonus." (A33) – Emily should approve, on a monthly basis, all write-offs of bad debt.

Aside from the foregoing, here are a few additional comments to consider in the drafting of a relevant answer.

➢ *Essentially, one must discuss WHAT IS WRONG or WHAT NEEDS TO BE CHANGED.* By contrast, a discussion of what is working, only where it is useful to do so, need not be so in-depth. One or two sentences per topic are then sufficient to indicate what is adequate, and why, before moving on to something else. For instance, in the qualitative analysis of a capital project, one must focus more on the disadvantages or risks, describe them, and then suggest, if possible, means for mitigating or eliminating them. As for the list of advantages or opportunities, it is usually more succinct.

DFT CASE

A brief glance at the analysis of DFT's new bonus program confirms most of the statements above. The text of the proposed solution is divided into two parts. First of all, comments are made on the deficiencies of the current plan, followed by a description of the suggestions for improvement. (A37, A38)

Upon reading this part of the proposed solution, you can easily observe that there are practically no ideas – actually none at all – on the merits of the current program.

➢ *It is often useful to qualify the idea put forth.* Is it superior or inferior? Is it positive or negative? Is it a risk or an opportunity? Is it better or worse? Is it beneficial or not?

Incomplete drafting	Appropriate drafting
"Based on these calculations, overall materiality should be **revised**."	"Based on these calculations, overall materiality should be **decreased**." (A23)
"In the acceptance of this agreement, the fluctuation of the exchange rate is a factor to be considered."	"In the acceptance of this agreement, the fluctuation of the exchange rate is a **risk** to be considered."
"Risk: that inventory will be improperly recorded."	"Risk that inventory is **overvalued** and needs to be **written down**." (A29)

➢ *Adapt to the circumstances.* Flexibility and adaptation are skills to be honed. Your client tells you he does not wish to invest in corporations that are not in compliance with environmental legislation? You must respect this position. You do not understand the merits of a debt covenant required by a creditor? Your employer must nevertheless comply with it and you must take it into account in your analysis. Finally, a partner tells you that he "has completed the client acceptance procedures"? (A3) It would be futile to revisit this aspect on the grounds that you think of it systematically each time you are hired as the "newly appointed auditor". Your knowledge on this aspect may be very good, however, since you are not required to discuss it, it is useless to insist.

➢ *Use the time allotted as best you can.* One must be aware that it is very difficult – if not impossible – to provide a perfect answer.

Rather, the goal is to provide an adequate or reasonable answer.

Try to follow the outline of the answer you established, in particular because it contains the list of the important topics to be discussed, within the case parameters. If necessary, place this outline in a visible location throughout the drafting of your answer.

POINT DE VIEW

One of the greatest challenges in drafting a case in a limited time frame is to adequately balance DEPTH and BREADTH.

To this end, one must acquire experience in case simulations, by trying to consistently meet the following objectives:

Perform the work required, in light of the role to be played, taking into account the specific context of the case.

+

Analyze all – or nearly all – the important topics and, if possible, part of the topics of lesser importance.

Integrating Ideas To The Case

One must definitely submit an answer that is continuously integrated with the case and its specific parameters. Your analyses, arguments, advice, conclusions and recommendations must therefore directly meet the needs expressed by the recipient of the report. This is the very essence of learning through case resolution. In other words, you must develop this professional skill until it becomes an integral part of your way of drafting. One should also note that it is rare that the resolution of a case will require a straightforward theoretical presentation of your knowledge.

Instead of summarizing them willy-nilly, one must learn to IDENTIFY WHICH THEORETICAL CONCEPTS ARE RELEVANT under the circumstances.

One must use theoretical concepts wisely, and at the right place.

For example, let us take the topic "Research and Development". Assume that the case requires, more specifically, an analysis of whether an intangible asset arising from development shall be recognized (IAS 38, para. 57). The accounting standard requires six criteria[1] to be met for an entity to be entitled to recognize its development costs as an asset. In developing one's answer, one must ask oneself what are the criteria to be analyzed.

All six? THAT DEPENDS on the importance of the topic and on the available information. If no information is provided as to the ability to measure reliably the expenditure attributable, for instance, what can we conclude?

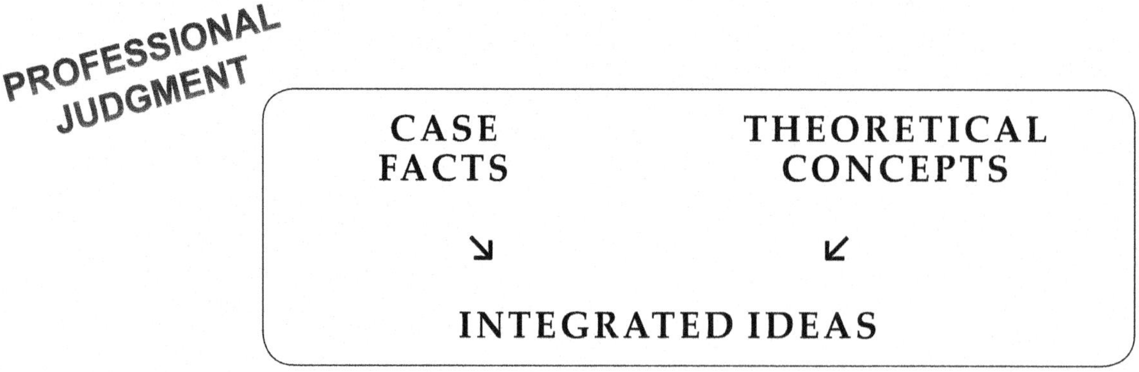

PROFESSIONAL JUDGMENT

CASE FACTS	THEORETICAL CONCEPTS
↘	↙
INTEGRATED IDEAS	

1 Succinctly put, the six criteria to be met for recognition as an intangible asset are the following: technical feasibility, intention to complete, ability to use or sell, probable future economic benefits, availability of resources (technical, financial), ability to measure reliably the expenditure. (IAS 38, para. 57)

In order to submit an integrated analysis, one must therefore link the case information or the case facts **TO** the appropriate theoretical concepts, or *vice-versa*. You will surely understand that the performance of such a task assumes that the concepts involved have been understood and remembered. Unfortunately, it is not always that obvious. Developing a good technique in case resolution is undoubtedly an asset, but it cannot make up for a lack of knowledge (standards, rules, laws, principles, etc.). It is always possible, of course, to use one's general knowledge, to rely on one's intuition or to call upon one's "good judgment". However, "managing" or "getting by" in this manner does not always lead to the development of sufficiently precise or complete ideas.

In Parts 9 and 10, I will present various means of remembering theoretical concepts.

DFT CASE

Let us take the topic "R&D costs" with respect to the Ares product in the DFT case. There are, all in all, a little less than four lines of information regarding the deferred development costs of $450,000. The purpose of the analysis is to determine whether or not to expense the costs. In light of the case facts, here are the relevant theoretical concepts, as they appear in the official solution to the case.

Case information (A6)	**Relevant theoretical concepts** (IAS 38 para. 57) (A14, A15)
– "DFT has now **abandoned** development of one of its products, Ares…" – "DFT's R&D manager **believes** that the development **can be** leveraged for a new product, Hades..."	*(a)* "**technical feasibility** of completing the intangible asset so that it will be available for use or sale." *(b)* "**intention to complete** the intangible asset and use or sell it." *(d)* "how the intangible asset will generate **probable future economic benefits**."

This example clearly fleshes out the fact that it is not always necessary to recall the six requisite criteria for the recognition of deferred development costs. Rather, one should identify WHICH ARE THE CRITERIA FOR WHICH INFORMATION EXISTS IN THE CASE.

Integration is an interactive activity, meaning that it establishes a nexus between theory and the case in one broad stroke. Some candidates tend to summarize the theory in their first paragraph and, in the next paragraph, to discuss what is going on in the case. This manner of proceeding does not always achieve the desired goal. Indeed, the connection between the theoretical concepts and the case facts is often lacking in fluidity and precision. Where several theoretical concepts are discussed together, it becomes difficult to determine which is the one that sparked any one of the ideas in the following analysis. Unless one includes an express link to one of the concepts appearing in the previous paragraph, it is more difficult to assess if integration has been achieved. The best way to show one's competence is

to learn how to simultaneously integrate the theory to the case, in the same sentence or the same paragraph.

POINT DE VIEW

It is sometimes permissible, during a simulation or an examination, to consult one of the core reference materials in our field of expertise: the accounting standards or the tax rules. You are sometimes even authorized to "cut" an excerpt in order to "paste" it in your answer. Straightaway, it must be noted that the mere fact of including such an excerpt does not demonstrate, in and of itself, your capacity for integration. At most, it enables you to have on hand the theoretical concepts relevant to the analysis. You must, therefore, make sure that you SHOW EXPLICITLY how they integrate with the specifics of the case.

Some candidates carry out the integration to the case by inserting their ideas at the appropriate locations within the text of the standards or rules they have copied. If you proceed in this manner, ensure that you highlight your personal ideas by using a different font, for instance.

Show off one's theoretical knowledge? NO

Leverage it by integrating it to the particulars of the case? YES

EXAMPLES OF INTEGRATION OF IDEAS TO THE CASE

- Since William is the son of the majority shareholder of the business, he is considered to be related to LP Inc. For tax purposes, he shall be deemed to have acquired the automobile at its fair value of $11,000.
- "Under IAS 2, *Inventories*, a writedown would be required if the net realizable value of inventory is below the recorded cost. Given that DFT's products generally have a 40% gross margin, a decrease in the planned selling price, while reducing DFT's margins, would likely not result in a net realizable value that is below cost, and therefore, no writedown would likely be required as of September 30." (A13)
- I recommend a transfer price equal to that of the market, since the two divisions are profit centers and there is an active external market.
- Capitalizing expenses — Continuing to defer development costs related to a specific product no longer under development, and recording the GST reassessment as a prepaid expense. (A34)
- "The construction of a new restaurant is risky in light of the great number of establishments closing in the area."

  To be preferred to: "Projects of this type are risky."
- "The Website development costs are capitalized as intangible assets, because sales will increase dramatically."

  To be preferred to: "There should be recognition as an asset, because there are future benefits."

Reminder: Theoretical concepts are highlighted in orange, whereas case facts are in yellow.

Where an idea, a sentence or a paragraph applies as such to all cases or to any entity, this means that the answer is not sufficiently integrated.

POINT DE VIEW

To the extent possible, one must take into account the particulars of the entity and of its environment by demonstrating one's ability to apply one's knowledge in a concrete manner. Since one sometimes has limited work experience, it is not always obvious to exhibit realism. Certain industries are harder to visualize than others.

Trust your knowledge and your practical sense.

Make analogies with what you already know.

Hence, your personal purchasing experience on an E-commerce Website, such as *Amazon,* can certainly guide you in developing internal controls for an employer wishing to enable his clients to do the same.

In order to enhance the integration of your ideas, I also suggest that you do the following:

- use the names of the stakeholders in the case, of the entities, of the products, etc. Customize your ideas by directing your remarks to the right person.

  E.g.: The list of receivables outstanding for more than 90 days can now be generated directly by the new CX system. Olivia can approve their writing-off and a different person, for instance Nicolas, can record the write-offs in the books

- to the extent possible, use the exact words and expressions appearing in the case. To be properly understood, one must avoid references that are too brief or using synonyms.

  DFT CASE (A29): "Risk that unanticipated technical problems cannot be solved and that Zeus cannot be brought to market and that costs can no longer be deferred."

  For instance, the reader of your answer might consider that the words "problems encountered with the product" are not the equivalent of "unanticipated technical difficulties".

- add a few words in brackets in order to insert the particulars of your case in your text. As well, one can simply add examples.

  E.g.: In a business valuation, non-recurring items (vast advertising campaign, flood loss, unusual write-off of a significant receivable) are set aside in order to make comparisons easier and to simplify the determination of the going concern value.

When one is about to resolve a problem or issue, it is generally preferable to analyze one single topic – or sub-topic – at a time. For instance, in respect of the issue "Management of ongoing operations", the two following topics: "Hiring a new salesperson" and "Preparation of submissions" should, normally, be tackled individually. In other words, each of them should have a separate analytical section devoted to it. This is the best means of ensuring that one submits a complete answer containing a minimum amount of relevant ideas. When topics are lumped together, it is more difficult to guarantee that one has devoted sufficient depth of analysis to each.

A little later on, one must ask oneself it there are links or relationships existing between them. Thus, one could consider that the "hiring of a new salesperson" will enable the sales manager to devote more time to the "preparation of submissions".

1- analyze the topics individually

2- flesh out the interrelations between the topics

Some candidates group topics together, for discussion purposes, either because certain case facts are useful in more than one location or because they involve the same skill. This is rarely a good idea, unless the analysis of each topic is essentially the same, which is rather rare. Incidentally, one must remember that the context of the discussion is a significant dimension to consider in the resolution of a case. By more clearly singling out the topics, it is easier to remain focused on the context that is specific to each requirement.

ONE TOPIC/ASPECT AT A TIME

I remind you as well, as I indicated in Parts 1 and 2, that the analysis of any of the problems or issues can influence any of the other issues in the case.

POINT DE VIEW

However, on occasion, it is more efficient to draft an answer to two issues concurrently. The DFT case provides such an opportunity. Indeed, it may be easier to develop the audit procedure to be performed as you resolve the accounting issues. Once the accounting treatment has just been analyzed, the specific risk and the appropriate procedure can easily be determined.

When drafting an answer – at least in part – to more than one issue at a time, pay attention to two things.

First, make sure that you have tackled all the aspects of an issue. Merely writing a procedure or two for each accounting issue is insufficient. The "audit planning" aspect, which is easy to forget under the circumstances, must also be discussed. Secondly, make sure you correctly differentiate each of the parts, by writing "PROC" (which stands for "procedure") next to the ideas in question, for instance.

POINT DE VIEW

The comments above ought to make you take stock of one fundamental fact, namely that it is quite possible that you may have to backtrack while you are drafting. If you deem that your answer will be enhanced as a result, do not hesitate to add an idea or a link to the analysis of a previous topic.

Part 4
Drafting New Ideas

Minimizing Repetitions Of The Case
Diversify The Ideas Put Forth In The Answer
Knowing How To Submit Recommendations And Conclusions

"Would I be prepared to pay for this idea? And for this report?"

Part 4
Drafting New Ideas

As seen in the previous Part, an appropriate answer to a case is essentially made up of relevant ideas. While complying with this requirement, one must also make sure to submit new ideas, namely ideas that give added value to the answer. In other words, successfully completing a case depends on your ability to draft a **reasonable number of relevant and new ideas on the main problems or issues**. An idea that does not have these characteristics is quite simply not even considered in the assessment of the answer.

Minimizing Repetitions Of The Case

A new idea is one that is unknown to the employer or client. Whether it takes the form of an argument, an explanation, a comment, an option, a conclusion or a recommendation, the idea must not have been previously put forth in the case. For example, if the case states that there are deficiencies in the organizational structure, a candidate who indicates that decentralization may be a solution brings a new idea to the table. On the other hand, if the case states that decentralization has already been considered by senior management, repeating this option will not be a new idea. The analysis of this option will, however, be one. Similarly, an idea repeated more than once throughout the answer represents only one new idea.

POINT OF VIEW

One must pay particular attention to any comment, opinion or request on the part of the employer or client. Where the client makes a suggestion or is considering proceeding in a certain manner, this must be discussed, even if you know ahead of time that this is not a good idea. The employer or client is definitely expecting to receive a reply from you on this aspect, within the case parameters.

It is not the idea originating from the client that is new, but rather the way in which you deal with it.

I frequently notice that some candidates systematically summarize the contents of the case prior to resolving it. At times, it is a verbatim summary. They thus state the current situation before moving on to the resolution stage. This kind of summary contains **no new idea**, which, per se, makes it useless. Instead, one ought to consider that the recipient of the report – in this case, the person grading it – is fully aware of the case facts.

RELEVANT AND NEW IDEA

↓

APPROPRIATE IDEA

EXAMPLE OF DRAFTING THAT NEEDLESSLY SUMMARIZES THE CASE FACTS

> At our last meeting, the Chief Executive Officer of the entity indicated that the bank had required debt covenants at the time of renewal of the mortgage. The agreement provided to me states that at least 5% of the total assets must be maintained in cash and cash equivalents, and the debt/equity ratio must not exceed 1.25.
>
> One must, therefore, determine if the required ratios have been complied with at year-end, in light of the reporting errors identified.
>
> Furthermore, it will be necessary to obtain the calculation formula used by the bank.

In the above example, the entire first paragraph is pointless. The reader of the report does not need this information, since he or she already has it. There are no new ideas stated. You will surely understand that the employer or client retaining you does not need for you to tell him what he already knows.

In certain circumstances, you may have to put things in perspective. The information originating from an external source, such as an excerpt of a newspaper article appended to the report, might not be known to its recipient. In such a case, the information reiterated is a new idea.

EXAMPLE OF APPROPRIATE DRAFTING

> Audit Procedures
>
> Clauses required by the bank
>
> - determine if the two ratios have been met at June 30 (5% of assets and maximum debt/equity of 1.25), in light of the reporting errors identified.
> - obtain the calculation formula used by the bank.

Obviously, not summarizing the case speeds up the drafting of your answer. A clear and precise title situates the reader properly as to the contents of the discussion. It is then possible to move straight on to the analysis in order to best use the restricted time frame allotted for the resolution of the case. Note, as well, that a brief reference to the ratios in brackets allows you to focus the discussion. Finally, since it is an action "list", each idea can quite simply start with a verb in the infinitive.

POINT OF VIEW

Some candidates consider that summarizing the case facts prior to embarking on their analysis enables them to better understand what is going on. This is an understandable point of view, since one must always make sure that one has correctly identified the problem involved.

There is no time available to re-write the case facts.

An acceptable compromise would be to go through this process in your mind or, for a complex situation or topic, to do so briefly *via* your Reading Notes.

A clarification is necessary here since the previous statements may appear to contradict the undeniable fact that an answer must consistently be integrated to the case, which will always be true. Therefore, there is a difference between summarizing or repeating the case facts, and using them.

Repeating the case facts needlessly weighs down the drafting of the answer.

Using the case facts provided is crucial to your success.

Personally, when I draft my answer to a case, I rarely start a sentence or paragraph with any of the information provided. It is an effective drafting tip in order to minimize useless repetition. When you think about it, it makes sense, since the case facts essentially serve to substantiate, explain or evaluate an idea that is put forth. They are there to go hand in hand with your analyses, not to be put forth in and of themselves.

EXAMPLES OF THE APPROPRIATE USE OF CASE FACTS

Incomplete Drafting	Appropriate Drafting
The manager tells me that product quality is a key success factor in the industry sector. I recommend that you not source your supplies from MIX.	REC.: No procurement of supplies from MIX, because the quality of the material is inferior to that currently used. It just so happens that quality is a key success factor in this sector.
Your objective is to diversify your activities. I recommend the acquisition of XYZ, since the ask price is less than the going concern value calculated.	I recommend the acquisition of XYZ, since the ask price is less than the fair value calculated and this coincides with your objective of diversifying your activities.
No repayment terms are provided in the agreement. The note payable to the shareholder must be allocated to Shareholders' Equity.	The note payable to the shareholder must be allocated to Shareholders' Equity, since no repayment terms are provided in the agreement.

By perusing the left-hand column, one realizes that the nexus between the case facts appearing at the beginning and the recommendation that follows is not clearly or directly established.

In other words, the reader must "assume" the existence of this nexus. In the first example, it "appears" that the recommendation not to do business with MIX is warranted by the lesser quality of its products. However, this is not so obvious, since the link between the two sentences is not systematically established. Some words are missing. In the right-hand column, there is no doubt as to the usefulness of the case facts in the analysis. Be aware going forward that one cannot ask the reader of an answer to add words or links, much less extrapolate the meaning of the statements made. We will revisit this aspect in Part 8.

USING CASE FACTS ≠ SUMMARIZING CASE FACTS

Diversify The Ideas Put Forth In The Answer

As mentioned in Part 2, one must attempt to analyze **all** – or nearly all – the important topics and, if possible, **part** of the topics of lesser importance. To this end, one must ensure balance in one's answer in order to provide sufficient depth of analysis with respect to the aspects that matter, while providing sufficient coverage. A candidate who deals in depth with two important topics whereas the case contains five of them will probably not achieve the passing standard. The answer must, therefore, cover a certain number of topics. On the other hand, covering the important topics too quickly is insufficient.

The analysis must be "reasonable", neither too short nor perfect.

POINT OF VIEW

From experience, I can tell you that it is not always easy to "let go" of a topic and move on to the next one in order to make the best use of the time allotted. This is even more difficult for candidates who are perfectionists and who aim at providing a complete answer. Generally speaking, let us say that the last ideas developed with a view to perfecting an analysis are usually less crucial to successfully completing a case that the first ideas of the next topic. Referring to the concept of a cost/benefit analysis, you will easily be able to convince yourself to diversify your answer.

The scope of analysis of a topic generally hinges on its importance.

In other words, an important topic requires consideration of a greater number of various arguments or aspects. One can also state that a larger quantity of available case facts makes the consideration of a greater number of DIFFERENT IDEAS in the analysis easier.

POINT OF VIEW

Not infrequently, certain candidates submit an incomplete analysis on an important topic. This can be explained by a poor assessment of the number of valid ideas. Because they have filled up a whole page on a topic, some candidates believe they have submitted a sufficiently in-depth analysis.

It is not the length of the analysis that matters,
but rather the number of relevant and new ideas.

This fact can also be explained by the natural tendency to curtail analysis of a topic when the conclusion or recommendation is known in advance. For example, a candidate may decide, upon reading the case, that the deferred development costs must be expensed. In so doing, he or she will perhaps essentially focus his or her analysis on the justification for this write-off, while omitting to consider what factors might justify a different accounting treatment. Certain ideas, which are crucial to the submission of a complete analysis, are then unfortunately set aside.

It is not always necessary to submit arguments that go exclusively
in the same direction as the conclusion or recommendation made.

A candidate may, for instance, be of the view that not meeting any one of the six requisite criteria for the recognition of development costs as an asset is sufficient to warrant a write-off. This is true. However, as part of the resolution of a case, one must demonstrate one's ability to take into consideration all the information provided in order to justify one's point of view. (A14 and A15)

Throughout the drafting of an answer to a case, one must diversify the ideas submitted in the answer. An idea or concept that is repeated rarely counts more than once. For example, it is not a good idea to suggest resorting to an expert by way of an audit procedure for all items that are fraught with a specific risk with respect to the "valuation" assertion. Rather, one must determine where – no more than two locations – this suggestion will be most useful, and find something else for the other occurrences. Moreover, do not be surprised if the accounting treatment of two buildings held by the entity, for example, is different. You are drafting an answer to a case, the purpose of which, among others, is to assess your ability to integrate your knowledge with practical situations.

What would be the use of asking you to repeat twice the same ideas in the same case?

EXAMPLE OF INAPPROPRIATE DRAFTING

> Revenue can be recognized if one considers that the transfer of ownership occurred during the current period.
>
> Revenue can be deferred if one considers that the transfer of ownership will occur during the next period.
>
> I recommend recognizing the revenue immediately, because I consider that the transfer of ownership has already taken place.

This example, which I will admit is slightly exaggerated, shows how the same idea can be reused from various angles. Nevertheless, it is a repetition of the same concept. Instead, one must vary the type of arguments made and use each only once, at least per topic, and where it is most appropriate. It is tempting, in the statement of the recommendation, to repeat an argument made in the course of the analysis, usually the one deemed to be the strongest. This is not necessary. Diversification is the key.

EXAMPLE OF APPROPRIATE DRAFTING

> The revenue can be recognized, since the transfer of significant risks and rewards of ownership has taken place. The buyer is responsible for paying the insurance on this inventory.
>
> Nevertheless, since the probability of returns of goods is difficult to estimate, the comptroller is not sure that the amount of revenue can be measured reliably. In such a case, the revenue recognition would have to be deferred.
>
> REC:
>
> Recognize the revenue immediately, since there is no doubt that the economic benefits associated with the transaction will flow to the entity.

The person grading your answer will not consider the useless repetition of the same idea or the same concept. The argument on the transfer of ownership, used three times in the example of inappropriate drafting, will most certainly not be considered three times in the assessment. Surely, that should be reason enough to avoid repetitions. In order to minimize the repetition of the same ideas, I suggest that you keep an argument in store for the recommendation. The example of appropriate drafting illustrates the situation that occurs where more than one option must be considered in the analysis. This type of situation, especially when it involves an accounting issue, occurs frequently. One can ask oneself, for instance, whether or not the inventory ought to be depreciated or whether or not the development costs ought to be recognized as intangible assets.

Things are not always so, as discussed below.

DFT CASE

Let us take the agreement entered into between DFT and Indo-Tech. It states as follows: "ownership of the inventory transfers to Indo once it is taken" (A5). Since the situation is evident, and there is no uncertainty, the accounting treatment to recommend is easy to determine. The other information supplied in the case, incidentally, does not allow for a questioning of any of the other conditions to be satisfied with respect to revenue recognition (IAS 18, para. 14). The analysis with respect to the shipping of $1.85M in components will, therefore, essentially serve to explain why the revenue must not be recognized during the current year (A12). It would be futile to consider the possibility of proceeding otherwise and "compelling" the analysis of more than one option.

One must diversify one's ideas,

but the presence of case facts supporting another position is necessary.

The answer to a case must contain ideas having an added value.

Frequently, the case facts are useful more than once. For example, let us take the information from the DFT case with respect to the Zeus product (A6). The development of the new product has been delayed, a competitor has been able to place a similar product on the market first and DFT isn't sure it can sell Zeus at the planned price. At first blush, since the case essentially refers to inventory, this information can be used to discuss whether a depreciation is in order. However, one must note that the same information can also be used to assess whether one should write-off the deferred development costs for this product. In this situation, there is no repetition of the same ideas, since the information is used in the analysis of two separate topics.

The analysis of a specific concept may also pop up in two different problems or issues. For instance, the impact of a related-party transaction can be analyzed under the Accounting issue, and then under the Taxation issue. Incidentally, the definition of a related party is not exactly the same. Since the context in which the concept is applied is different, it is useful – if not necessary – to tailor the analysis accordingly.

Under other circumstances, it will be possible to group certain topics that are to be developed together. For example, the expenses incurred for the construction of a new building (architect's fees, construction permit, excavation costs, carpenters' wages, etc.) are all direct construction costs that will be recorded under the Property item. There is no need to submit a separate analysis for each of them.

PROFESSIONAL JUDGMENT

↓

ADAPTING TO THE CIRCUMSTANCES

Where more than one option is to be analyzed, it frequently happens that the type of argument that can be put forth is of the same nature – at least in part – for any of the options. This occurs especially where competing options are involved and only one of the two is to be kept. The choice between two financing options or the decision to purchase or lease an item of equipment are examples of this. This type of analysis generally requires a consideration of the advantages and disadvantages of each of the options. No doubt, you will appreciate that the advantages inherent in one option may mirror – at least in part – the disadvantages of the other.

One must not lose sight of the fact that the same idea repeated – even in reverse – will not necessarily count twice. You can certainly "cut/paste" the same idea very quickly. However, in order to enhance your analysis, I suggest that you do the following:

1- *Flesh out the differences between the two options by comparing their features.*

Example:

debt financing

"The interest rate net of tax of 5% is far less than the dividend rate of 11%."

To be preferred to: "The interest rate net of tax is only 5%."

Note that it will not be necessary to write the reverse side of this idea under the heading "equity financing". You will agree that stating "The dividend rate of 11% is far greater than the interest rate net of tax of 5%" is merely a repetition of the same concept. The idea of comparing the financing costs is relevant, but it will only be considered once in the assessment of your answer.

2- *Submit first and foremost the items common to both options before tackling any differences.*

ANALYTICAL STRUCTURE OF COMPETING OPTIONS

Option #1 <u>and</u> Option #2
Pros...
Cons...
Option #1
Pros...
Cons...
Option #2
Pros...
Cons...

This manner of laying out your analysis minimizes needless repetition of the same ideas. It also allows for a better assessment of the situation by fleshing out more obviously the criteria to be considered in making the decision. Let us assume, for instance, that the two sources of financing cover all cash requirements. This advantage, that is "common" to both options, will not be the distinguishing feature when time comes to make a recommendation. One can definitely include it in the analysis, while taking stock of the fact that the final decision will essentially be based on those features that distinguish the two options. The fact that a creditor is requiring, for example, a personal endorsement from the shareholders would represent an important criterion in the decision to opt for debt financing or equity financing.

Aside from the need to diversify your ideas, I remind you that you must not lose sight of the importance of a topic and of the number of case facts available. It is, as I have stated, useless to "stretch" one's analysis when a topic is easily resolved or is of lesser importance.

EXAMPLE OF UNNECESSARILY STRETCHED DRAFTING

There is a writedown of inventory, because the net realizable value of $125,000 is less than its cost of $140,000.

I recommend the recognition of an inventory depreciation, because the net realizable value of $125,000 is less than its cost of $140,000.

EXAMPLE OF APPROPRIATE DRAFTING

I recommend the recognition of an inventory depreciation,

because the net realizable value of $125,000 is less than its cost of $140,000.

In this example, there is only one acceptable option: accounting for a writedown. It is, therefore, unnecessary to first discuss this only possibility, and then to revisit the same idea in the form of a recommendation.

I am often asked if writing down a wrong idea has a negative influence on the assessment of the answer. Let us say that, generally speaking, there is no "negative grading" per se. At least not directly. You will appreciate however, that an idea that is contradicted a little further in the answer will not be counted in the assessment, either the first or the second time. You will also appreciate that writing down a wrong idea clearly and directly shows your misunderstanding of the advanced concept. If it is a major error or where several ideas dealing with the same topic are erroneous, this seriously restricts your access to the passing standard. In other words, the influence of an error on the assessment of an answer depends on the materiality of the error, on its frequency, as well as on the quality of the remainder of the analysis.

POINT OF VIEW

From experience, I know that several candidates hesitate to write down their ideas. They are afraid of being wrong, or worse yet, of appearing ridiculous. On the one hand, let me tell you that you do not really have the time to weigh the pros and cons prior to writing down your ideas. It is also generally acknowledged that one must write down a great many relevant and new ideas. Aside from the time you stop to plan your answer, there is really no break in the drafting of ideas.

On the other hand, the persons grading your answers have just about seen it all. Reading an idea that is slightly "stupid" or "erroneous", while written under pressure, will not really shock them.

I suggest that you write down your ideas, even if you are not sure of yourself.

One must proceed in this manner, especially during the first few case simulations, where the number of ideas written down is generally not sufficiently high.

Knowing How To Submit Recommendations And Conclusions

As seen in Part 3 (p. 34), the systematic and structured resolution of any problem or issue concludes by the issuance of a recommendation or a conclusion – sometimes one, sometimes the other, at times both. This culmination of any analysis is essential, because it demonstrates that you use your professional judgment. You must appreciate that, in the absence of an appropriate recommendation of conclusion, it is difficult – if not sometimes impossible – to achieve the passing standard.

A recommendation is an **action to be taken**
that flows from the previous analysis. It is sometimes necessary to submit more than one.

A conclusion is an **overall comment**
that encapsulates the essence of a situation or highlights a particular item.

Assuredness must flow from the tone you use

Writing a recommendation or a conclusion requires the candidate to make a decision or issue an opinion. He or she must project assuredness in his or her drafting.

TRUST IN YOUR IDEAS.

Some candidates draft their text in such a manner that their answer appears to be right, regardless of the perspective considered. This is a true shame, because, in so doing, they miss out on the opportunity of showing that they understand the end result of the analysis.

EXAMPLE OF AN IMPRECISE RECOMMENDATION

I arrive at a positive net present value although another accountant might reach a different result. In any event, the new product appears to me to be profitable; however, other assumptions could change that assessment.

I recommend that you take the time to further reflect prior to embarking upon the project. Ultimately, you could proceed with it though.

N.B.: Need I even comment?

I suggest you start making your recommendations by using a verb in the infinitive or in the imperative form. This contributes to a more precise drafting of any action to be taken, while ridding your text of unnecessary words such as these: "In light of the foregoing, I feel that it is interesting to recommend that you expand the ...". Starting one's recommendations with a verb in the infinitive is an effective drafting tip, since you "appear" to know exactly what needs to be done!

POINT OF VIEW

Under certain circumstances, one might think that the responsibility for making the final decision is incumbent on the employer or client. Let us take the example of a management decision, such as deciding between making or buying (outsourcing). Some candidates use this a pretense for quite simply taking no position at all. They duly prepare their analysis, and then deliberately omit to recommend anything at all. In the resolution of a case, one must consider that orienting the employer or client forms an integral part of the professional skills that need to be demonstrated.

One must nevertheless take a position and tell oneself that the employer or client is, of course, free to decide otherwise if he so chooses.

Be precise

Be sure to express your ideas clearly at all times; however, one must be especially precise in making a recommendation or reaching a conclusion. To this end, you must concretely state WHAT NEEDS TO BE DONE or HOW TO PROCEED. It may even occasionally be necessary to state WHO, WHEN and HOW MUCH. Suggestions for improvement of internal controls, for example, are enhanced when direct reference is made to persons whose names appear in the case. Remember this as well: recommendations are often simpler than you think.

EXAMPLES OF VAGUE AND GENERAL DRAFTING

- By way of conclusion, changes are really in order with respect to the receipt of cash donations.

  (N.B.: What changes?)
- I recommend that you change the manner of allocating production overhead.

  (N.B.: How? What options can be considered?)
- Procedure for Indo-Tech: obtain a confirmation.

  (N.B.: Regarding what? From whom?) (A27)

Where the text is too vague or too general, it is next to impossible to identify the path to follow. To me, it seems to be preferable to clearly suggest solutions and to make mistakes than to remain vague and non-committal. Incidentally, I remind you that only those recommendations that are complete and precise, that flow from the analysis and are connected to the case facts, are considered in the assessment of an answer.

Recommendations that are made must also resolve the problem or issue involved, in a clear and direct line. A suggestion to the effect that the Board of Directors must now meet once a month solves the following problem: "Delays in the approval of material decisions". On the other hand, if the problem relates instead to the "Lack of expertise of the Board members", the implementation of monthly meetings will change nothing.

Finally, I suggest you avoid expressions such as "It appears that ...", "Perhaps one could ...", "It would be possible to consider that...", etc.

DO NOT TEMPER YOUR POSITION!

EXAMPLE OF APPROPRIATE DRAFTING

- REC.: Prepare immediately an amended tax return in order to avoid the payment of penalties and so as to reduce the amount of interest to be paid.
- "My revised estimate, calculated on the same basis but taking into account the accounting adjustments noted (5% of $8,457,000) is $422,850.

  Based on these calculations, overall materiality should be decreased." (A23)

"WHAT TO DO and WHY"

POINT OF VIEW

Some candidates try to absolve themselves of the duty to submit a recommendation or conclusion on the grounds that they do not possess all the requisite information. For instance, they will write: "I will have to gauge the reaction of the union before recommending that you contract out." I can tell you, from the outset, that it is rather rare that you will be in possession of a complete set of information as part of the resolution of a case. The missing information quite often relates to a future situation, which, by its very nature, is fraught with uncertainty.

You must nevertheless take a stand based on the information that is available, subject to briefly stating what additional information you would like to obtain, or specifying the assumptions you would like to validate.

EXAMPLE OF APPROPRIATE DRAFTING

- "Instead of booking as a prepaid, the amount should be posted where the reassessment indicated the errors were. Either way, expenses will be increased.

  The $125,000 is treated as an increase in general and administrative expenses for now." (A15)

In this example, the item Expenses to be debited cannot be specified, since it is unknown what the $125,000 assessment relates to. In the current circumstances, the General & administrative item is the most appropriate.

It is definitely possible to issue an opinion without having all the necessary information in one's possession.

Justifying one's conclusions or recommendations

This is self-evident. It is not only what you suggest that matters, but also WHY you are making the suggestion. Incidentally, in most cases, it is the analytical method that is assessed, not necessarily the conclusion or recommendation as such. The evaluation guides for a case are usually flexible enough to accept any logical, coherent and substantiated suggestion. Take into account the strength of your arguments when the time comes to make a comment. Some candidates jump a little too quickly to the conclusion that an employee ought to be dismissed, for example. Or they will emphatically recommend the acquisition of a new system based solely on subjective impressions or information found on the Web. Be realistic.

Finally, refrain from repeating the same argument or summarizing the analysis in order to reach your conclusion or to make your recommendation. In the absence of the submission of a new idea, a conclusion or recommendation that flows logically from the previous analysis may be a justification per se.

Any recommendation made must be precise, realistic, concrete, and take into account the particulars of the case.

If this has not already been done in the course of the analysis, the drafting of a conclusion or of a recommendation is an opportune time to PRESENT LINKS FOR INTEGRATION PURPOSES. Here are two manners of proceeding as such:

1- *Establish links with the most significant particulars appearing in the context:* the size of the entity, the industry, the significant dates, the key success factors, the strengths, weaknesses, threats and opportunities, the objectives, needs, biases and behavior of the stakeholders, the practices and policies of the entity, as well as any constraints.

EXAMPLE OF APPROPRIATE DRAFTING

– I recommend not investing any further in Pulse Ltd. In my opinion, this risky investment does not coincide very well with Christian's investor profile (in light of his age and financial position). At this stage in his life, he should instead seek to protect his existing capital.

2- *Establish links with other sections of the answer.* This is an opportunity to ask oneself if there are interrelations with other problems, issues or topics. For example, one can take into account the new features added to the computer system under the issue Governance when time comes to develop arguments on the type of reporting to be provided to the Board of Directors. Yet again, the redemption price of the shares of the selling shareholder can be considered in the analysis of the financing requirements. These interrelations, which demonstrate your capacity for integration, can generally be expressed in short sentences.

EXAMPLE OF APPROPRIATE DRAFTING

– "The reduction in revenue is significant, although not material on its own, in terms of the financial statements audit (see recalculation of materiality). The net reduction will have a direct impact on the bonus calculation." (A11)

(N.B.: In addition to the nexus established between the Accounting issue and the Audit issue, the idea is also tied into one of the significant particulars of the DFT case, namely the bonus program.)

POINT OF VIEW

One must not lose sight of the fact that the evaluation guide for a case is the same for all concerned. This means that the recommendation or conclusion for a given section does not alter the work to be done. Assume, for instance, that you conclude, from the outset of your answer, that there is a significant doubt about the entity's ability to continue as a going concern. This should not prevent you from analyzing a management decision, if such a request has been made. Assume, as well, that the case asks for the assessment of a capital project. Based on their respective analyses, two candidates may definitely arrive at opposite positions as to the merits of the project. However, whether or not the project is recommended does not obviate the need for conducting an analysis of the financing options available, when this is required.

You must resolve each important problem or issue requested.

Of course, one can establish a nexus between the results of the various analyses by underscoring their mutual influence, however, the result arrived at in one does not detract from the need to analyze the others.

Be constructive

When resolving problems or issues, it is preferable to do so in a positive and constructive manner. Admittedly, one must first of all identify the problem, the weakness or the deficiency, and then underscore, if need be, the impact or consequences thereof. Your duty is then to find useful and concrete solutions for your employer or client. Too often, some candidates will employ a negative drafting style which does not adequately serve the goal sought to be achieved.

Stating what one must not do does not amount to stating what one must do.

EXAMPLES OF INAPPROPRIATE DRAFTING

- Due to the loss of data and to the turnover in the accounting staff, I cannot consider the audit risk to be low.

  (N.B.: Therefore? Is it high?)

-

I cannot recommend that you not depreciate the inventory.	≠	I recommend that you depreciate the inventory.

- The central computer should not be placed in an open room next to the cafeteria.

  (N.B.: OK… what should one do then? And why?)

One should also observe that a sentence ending with a question mark is not particularly helpful. This is especially true if a recommendation or conclusion is involved. Definitely, one must ask oneself questions throughout the resolution of a case. However, remember that **your role is precisely to respond to these questions** by writing relevant and new ideas. When faced with a sentence in the interrogative form, the reader cannot know if this is an argument, a conclusion or a recommendation

EXAMPLES OF INAPPROPRIATE DRAFTING

- Since all the accounting policies chosen have been favorable to management, should one question the latter's integrity? (DFT case)
- Should one recognize a provision for restructuring costs?

N.B.: Need I even comment?

Flag the presence of a recommendation <u>or</u> conclusion

Make sure the reader knows this is indeed a conclusion or recommendation. Indent it from the margin or write a short title, such as "REC.:". This is especially useful when you insert recommendations as you analyze a problem or issue. For example, suggestions for improvement of the governance function can be made as the deficiencies, as well as their impact, are identified.

Part 5
Expressing One's Ideas Efficiently

Prioritizing Substance Over Form
Use An Appropriate Drafting Style
Exhibit A Proper Attitude

"One must draft one's response in simple, clear, precise and concrete terms."

Part 5
Expressing One's Ideas Efficiently

It is important to realize that it is not the number of lines or pages that guarantees the successful completion of a case, but rather the number of ideas submitted. An appropriate answer, which achieves a passing standard, must contain a minimum number of relevant and fresh ideas. And, if an important topic is involved, one must provide more depth, that is to say more ideas. In this Part, I would like to make you aware of the need to express your ideas efficiently, so that you are able to write down more of them.

Prioritizing Substance Over Form

Allow me to illustrate the statements that follow by relying on a well-known accounting principle: the precedence of substance over form. In other words, it is the quality of the ideas submitted that takes precedence, namely reality over appearance. It is obvious that an answer that is very well written, but lacking in ideas, will not have the upper hand over an answer that is not as well structured but that makes several good points. Therefore, one should not waste any time unduly worrying about the appearance of one's answer. Some candidates place so much importance on this aspect that they run out of time to draft a complete – or even reasonable – answer, containing ideas of sufficient QUALITY and in sufficient QUANTITY.

In light of the foregoing, I suggest that you:

- *minimize needless statements.* Aside from the sections of the heading of the answer, as discussed in Part 2 (p. 25), it is useless to lengthen the text by resorting to sentences used for courtesy. I understand that it may be tempting to do so, since, most of time, one is required to submit a "report" to an employer or client. However, the fact that a case must be resolved in a limited time frame greatly reduces the necessity, and especially the possibility, of proceeding in this manner.

EXAMPLE OF A NEEDLESSLY LONG INTRODUCTION

> Dear Mrs. Deslauriers,
>
> You will find appended hereto the report that the manager of our consulting firm tasked me with preparing following the pleasant meeting she had with you last week.
>
> You have been a client for a long time and I hope the analyses and recommendations that follow will be adequate and in keeping with your expectations.
>
> I remain at your disposal should you require any further information.
>
> Signature

N.B.: The text is very well drafted, but it contains no relevant and new ideas.

- *not abuse the options available in the software used.* Some candidates draft the entire text in capital letters, in italics or in boldface, for example. Others liven their text up by using colors or text attributes, such "shadow" or "outline". Moderation is in order. The person grading the report is definitely able to recognize an appropriate idea without it being made to stand out. All in all, I ultimately suggest that you use a standard font, without any frills (size 11 or 12, regular font style, black).

One must focus on the quality of the ideas put forth while attempting to find means of increasing their quantity.

- *flag each of the parts of the answer.* As shown in the examples contained in Part 4, a clear and succinct title quickly situates the reader of the answer. In addition, as discussed in Part 3, it is an excellent means of precisely identifying the problem or issue under discussion. Personally, in order to structure my thought process, each of the aspects analyzed is identified by a succinct sub-title. Of course, it is useless to write, for instance, "Preliminary Report" or "Draft" on each page of an answer.

- *not discard any text "deemed to be" useless.* Some candidates erase too easily those ideas that they deem to be inappropriate, although they may be good. Instead, I suggest that you use the "cut/paste" feature in order to place the discarded text at the very end of the answer. One never knows: you might change your mind several minutes later. Other candidates take the time to eliminate everything that is not directly part of their answer upon conclusion of the case. This is not necessary. Place the excess verbiage at the very end of your answer beneath a title such as "Reading Notes" or "Draft".

POINT OF VIEW

I often observe that the manner in which the answer to a case is drafted can make a difference to the outcome. Some candidates find it difficult to achieve the passing standard, quite simply because they do not know how to express their ideas appropriately.

If a candidate require 10 lines to express an idea, whereas another candidate can do so in only 5 lines, that makes a difference.

However, the value given to this particular idea by the person grading the answer will be same for both. However, when the time allotted for completion of the case runs out, the second candidate's answer will likely contain twice as many ideas. He or she will not necessarily have a mark twice as high as the first candidate, but the submission of a more substantive content is an undeniable advantage.

Use An Appropriate Drafting Style

One of the great challenges in drafting is to make sure one expresses one's ideas clearly and succinctly. Personally, I consider that you must, for the most part, build complete sentences with a subject, a verb and an object. These sentences must convey in a simple way the ideas expressed and not be cluttered with pointless words. Paragraphs must be short and generally deal with only one aspect at a time. The "debit" aspect in one paragraph and the "credit" aspect in another, for example. Or the "impairment" aspect in one paragraph and the "amortization" aspect in another. And, finally, "revenue recognition – 1.5M" in one paragraph (A11) and "revenue recognition – 1.85M" in another (A12).

ONE IDEA

ONE COMPLETE SENTENCE

Some candidates write sentences that are too short or excessively point-form. It then becomes difficult to understand the meaning of the ideas put forth, quite simply because too many words are missing. Other candidates develop their ideas in detail using long sentences. Aside from the futility of repeating the same thing more than once, it occasionally happens that the essence of a text becomes difficult to grasp due to over-explanation.

Essentially, one must focus on what contributes directly to the resolution of the case.

THE CHALLENGE CONSISTS IN WRITING COMPLETE IDEAS IN A SUCCINCT MANNER.

EXAMPLE OF DRAFTING IN AN EXCESSIVELY POINT-FORM STYLE

Mexico Subsidiary (RC)

cost: ensure regular procurement

profit: 60% 3rd

investment: decision parent co.

THEREFORE profit center

The text of this example does not submit ideas in an appropriate format. To be able to understand the meaning of the discussion, the reader must start by guessing the nature of the topic discussed, and then complete each line he or she reads. He or she can definitely imagine what the candidate wants to say; however, that is insufficient. The ideas put forth are not sufficiently explained and the recommendation is not substantiated.

POINT OF VIEW

When assessing an answer, the person grading it tries to fully recognize all the relevant and new ideas submitted by the candidate. However, he or she can neither extrapolate nor add words to make the answer make sense.

In the example above, the point-form style used requires the person grading the answer to relate the type of responsibility center (e.g.: profit) to its justification (e.g.: 60% 3rd). This is asking too much. To fully understand the basis of the argument, the person grading the answer must add too many words to what is written, which he or she will not do.

THE PERSON GRADING YOUR ANSWER CANNOT ASSUME THE EXTENT OF YOUR KNOWLEDGE.

When drafting your answer, you must, therefore, express your ideas clearly and fully. You will not have the opportunity of meeting with the person grading your answer to explain to him or her what you meant.

EXAMPLE OF NEEDLESSLY LENGTHY DRAFTING

Determination of the type of responsibility center of the new subsidiary in Mexico (This title is too long.)

I have conducted an examination of the features of the subsidiary that you own in Mexico. (Too long an introductory sentence; needless repetition of the title.)

It must be determined if it is a responsibility center that is a cost center or a responsibility center that is a profit center. (Pointless to repeat the words "responsibility center" twice.) After due consideration, I believe it may be a cost center, since the investment decision-making originates entirely from the parent corporation and is effected by a team of eight persons under the direction of the manager, Mr. Cameron. (This sentence is a useless preamble; too long a description of the management team, reiterating the wording of the case verbatim.) (Observation: The argument is intended to discard a third option, namely the "investment center". Instead, arguments supporting either of the options put forth ought to be submitted at the outset of the paragraph: cost center or profit center.)

Furthermore, the establishment of the subsidiary is intended to ensure a regular procurement of raw materials to the parent corporation. My first thought was that the responsibility center could be an investment center, however the Mexican managers do not make any investment decisions. (Repetition of ideas already put forth; pointless to emphasize this third option so much, since its is discarded from the outset.)

Hence, I believe one could consider the Mexico subsidiary to be a profit center as opposed to a cost center, since the subsidiary sells close to 60% of its production to third parties. (Useless beginning. It is preferable to get straight to the point. Writing "I believe" does not express sufficient certainty. It is pointless to reiterate that the subsidiary is in Mexico. We already know that. It is unnecessary to state what one is discarding in setting out the conclusion.)

One must not forget that, in Mexico, pesos are the currency. This will complicate matters for you. (What is the purpose of this comment? You have been asked to determine the type of responsibility center that is best adapted to the circumstances and not to discuss foreign currency translation. This statement is beyond the scope of the requirement. In any event, saying that this will "complicate matters" adds nothing relevant to the text; it is an empty statement!)

This means that the financial performance of the Mexico subsidiary will be assessed based on current net income. (The conclusion is more clearly stated here, but this useless repetition could be avoided by being more precise the first time around.) The profit may have to (The words "will have to" are preferable to the words "may have to".) take into account the costs directly related to the operation of the subsidiary as costs of raw materials, labor costs, power, plant maintenance costs, managers' salaries, etc. (The repetition of the word "costs" is useless; too many items listed.)

Items that are not controllable by the subsidiary are not to be taken into account, such as the sharing of common expenses (advertising costs, research and development costs, administrative costs, etc.) allocated by the head office. (The repetition of the word "costs" is useless; too many items listed.)

N.B.: My comments appear in blue.

The text of this example was not drafted efficiently, because it contains several pointless items. It is, however, important to understand **that everything that is written in this text is right** and that it does not contain **any wrong idea**. It is the drafting style of the candidate, which is needlessly cumbersome, that eats up too much time. In other words, it is the form or manner of expression of the ideas that is inappropriate, not the substance or the validity of the ideas in and of themselves. By improving his or her manner of writing, this candidate will be able to develop a greater number of ideas in the same time frame.

EXAMPLE OF APPROPRIATE DRAFTING

Type of responsibility center – Mexican subsidiary

It could be a cost center, since the primary mission of the subsidiary is to ensure a regular procurement to the parent corporation.

It could also be considered a profit center, since 70% of the production is sold to third parties.

REC

Set up as a profit center since the market is experiencing strong growth.

The subsidiary will be valued based on the profit it controls (costs directly related to operations: raw materials and labor).

The allocations by the head office (advertising, research and development) should not be considered, since these expenses are not controllable by the subsidiary.

N.B.: The goal is to show you an example of appropriate drafting. One must appreciate that the number of ideas submitted in order to discuss the type of responsibility center of the Mexican subsidiary is probably insufficient.

This example illustrates the drafting style that one should aim for. The title orients the discussion. The options to be considered are clearly fleshed out and supported. Each sentence is complete: subject, verb, and object. The theoretical concepts (in orange) are adequately integrated to the case facts (in yellow). The recommendation is justified. The use of brackets, adding examples taken from the case, is efficient. We will discuss this a little later, but note that some words or expressions can be abbreviated, such as "R&D" instead of "research and development" or "SUB" which stands for "subsidiary".

With a view to expressing your ideas efficiently, I also suggest that you:

- *choose to be brief.* Several candidates needlessly lengthen their answer by writing words that perhaps make the reading more pleasant, but which are nevertheless useless. The objective ought to be to try constantly to shorten the text without impinging on the essence of the ideas put forth. In this manner, more time is freed up for drafting, which time is available to write additional ideas that – we all hope – will be relevant and new.

EXAMPLE OF A POORLY EXPRESSED IDEA

The corporation could have earned three times more profit if it had not invested in the natural resources sector which could have generated more dividends but which were unable to live up to the promises. After due consideration, I believe you ought to have consulted me earlier.

N.B.: Need I even comment?

It is preferable to get straight to the point and not waste time with expressions or sentences that add nothing to the text. An introductory sentence such as "I will now impart to you my opinion regarding the new computer system." is unnecessary. The same goes for the linking words, such as "In light of the foregoing ..." or "I will pursue the discussion of this topic by adding that ...". One must arrive at the drafting of relevant and fresh ideas as soon as possible.

POINT OF VIEW

I suggest the occasional use of brackets in the course of drafting in order to shorten the length of the text or the sentences. This is especially useful when one wishes to add examples, to refer to another section of the answer or to a schedule, to justify an idea or supplement it by referring to a theoretical concept. For example, one can write the assertion "occurrence" in brackets next to a procedure dealing with the confirmation of the terms of an agreement. Brackets can sometimes also be used to express a personal opinion or to add a brief calculation. Under certain circumstances, this allows for the drafting of the idea in one single sentence as opposed to two.

Examples:

- "($1 million NRE plus $750,000 product)" (A11)
- "(event occurred after July projection)" (A27)
- "(based on 40% gross margin)" (A34)

➢ *use clear and precise language.* In point of fact, vague or general ideas are not very useful, in part because they are not integrated to the particulars of the case. At times, as well, some candidates quite simply forget to write what seems obvious to them, assuming that the person grading the answer will make the necessary inferences. Rather, one should try to use, as often as possible, the appropriate terms to do justice to the ideas put forth. Saying that "the project is interesting" or that "the system is effective" is not very helpful!

The person grading your answer should not have to wonder what you mean.

EXAMPLES OF CLEAR AND PRECISE DRAFTING

Vague and general drafting	**Comment** (review Part 3, p. 36)	**Clear and precise drafting**
One must consider the possibility that they are attempting to manipulate the financial statements to receive the bonus.	**Who** can do that? **Why?** **How** can they go about this?	"First, the existence of a bonus plan based on EBITDA increases the risk of error, since management may be biased to make decisions, or override controls, to increase EBITDA." (A24)
It is not right to leave her to do everything all by herself.	**Who? What? Why?** The expressions "not right" and "do everything" mean nothing.	The person in charge of the warehouse is in a position to pilfer inventory, since the internal control is deficient. In addition, no other person in the company has information that is that comprehensive with respect to the goods in inventory.
The inventory will have to be audited, since an audit will be required next year.	**What** will be done? **What is implicit** in the verb "audit"?	We will attend the physical inventory count on March 31, X3, since an audit will be required next year.

The choice of terms is particularly important when theoretical concepts are called into play. For example, an intangible asset must, among others, be "identifiable" (IAS 38, para. 11). It would, however, be inappropriate to use this notion in other contexts, such as: "Each identifiable part of property shall be depreciated separately." Here, one should instead refer to the concept of "cost that is significant in relation to the total cost". (IAS 16, para. 43)

Another example: writing "A physical count of the number of modems must be effected in order to determine their value." is not adequate. The physical count of the modems will yield their "quantity", not their "value". I will revisit the identification of theoretical concepts in Part 10.

A reference to key concepts in the standards, rules, laws, principles, etc.
must be as precise as possible
in order to demonstrate your ability to integrate your knowledge to the particulars of the case.

- *opt for a simple drafting style.* Do not lose sight of the fact that the objective is first and foremost to write ideas that will be understood by the reader of your answer. There is no need to draft in a fancy literary style. If, for example, you write the word "plan" twice in the same paragraph, it doesn't matter. Above all, do not take the time to look for a synonym so that the text will look nicer. I also suggest that you use a simple style of verb conjugation: present tense, past tense, and future simple. One must avoid any complicated form of drafting such as: "I could be led to believe that they could have advanced more money if they had been able to put their mind to it".

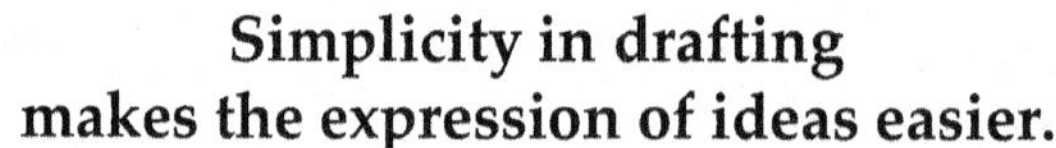

Simplicity in drafting
makes the expression of ideas easier.

POINT OF VIEW

Some candidates wonder about the importance of grammar and spelling in the drafting of an answer. From the outset, I can tell you that the restricted time frame in which to resolve a case does not provide you with an opportunity to re-read and tweak your text. Incidentally, I remind you that one must essentially give precedence to substance over form.

The goal sought to be achieved is not to arrive at a perfect form of drafting that is devoid of any mistakes. The omission of an "s", for example, in "the proceed", is not a serious error. Given the very nature of the resolution of a case, the presence of a certain number of mistakes is tolerated. Therefore, one should not, per se, expend any particular efforts for the sole purpose of arriving at an impeccable text.

However, if the number of mistakes is higher than usual, one must pay more attention when drafting so as to not distract the person grading the answer. Incidentally, it does occur that spelling mistakes cause ambiguity. For example, writing "takes money" as opposed to "makes money" can make a difference. Similarly, where the idea is nebulous or poorly expressed, it is sometimes impossible to know if it is a recommendation or merely another argument.

Under certain circumstances, it is possible to shorten the presentation of a part of the answer when one is able to identify a common point among several ideas. Hence,

- the same explanation can be used to reject two debt financing options;
- the same explanatory note can be used to justify adjustments to several items in the financial statements. (A18)

One can also do away with the beginning of sentences where the resolution of a problem or issue, for example, requires the presentation of a "LIST OF…":

- information to be provided in a note on the government grants received;
- advantages and disadvantages of incorporating the business;
- documents to be obtained to complete the tax return;
- steps to follow in the consolidation of the financial statements;
- information to provide in an offering prospectus.

POINT OF VIEW

It sometimes happens that one must draw up a list of information to obtain in order to complete the analysis of a problem or issue. At first blush, this situation might give the impression that one should use a question-type format, since the candidate must determine what information is missing (e.g.: What are the economies of scale following this business combination?). However, as indicated in Part 4 (p. 56), I maintain that drafting in a question format is to be avoided. Instead, I suggest the presentation in point-form of a list of items (e.g.: obtain the list of costs that will be reduced following the business combination).

It is preferable to suggest an action than to give the impression that one does not know what to do.

It is also possible that a part of the answer to a case can be presented in the form of a table or chart. Where such a situation arises, each column of the table should represent one of the aspects required in the work to be performed. A table allows for a better structuring of one's thought process and helps speed up the development of the answer while acting as a handy reminder. For example, writing the three main strategic objectives of the organization in the left-hand column reminds you that you must write down at least one performance indicator for each of them in the right-hand column.

EXAMPLES OF TABLES

Risks arising from the business combination	Means of minimizing negative consequences
…	…

Computed ratio	Interpretation
…	…

Finally, as indicated in Part 4 (p. 52), I remind you that it is very useful to express actions to be taken by starting with a verb in the infinitive or in the imperative. For example:

- audit procedures to be performed; (A25 to A30)
- suggestions of improvement to the receivables collection process;
- steps to take for the transition from the manual system to the computer system.

DFT CASE

When analyzing the impact of the accounting issues of significance on the procedures to be performed at year-end, the ideas set out in the answer can be placed in a table (A25 to A30), as follows:

Item	Assertion	Specific Risks	Procedures
...	...	...	...

The contents of this table could be presented differently. The topic in question could appear as a title and the assertion could be written in brackets following the procedure. The table would then look like this:

Specific Risks	Procedures
...	...

N.B.: It is not necessary to frame each column of text merely to improve its appearance. What is important is being able to easily distinguish each of the parts.

- *use professional language.* The answer must always be drafted using professional or business language. In other words, certain expressions, used in a casual conversation or which could be difficult to interpret, are to be banished. An idea that is not expressed using appropriate language is quite simply not taken into account in the assessment of the answer.

EXAMPLES OF INAPPROPRIATE EXPRESSIONS

- We cannot afford to cut corners and thereby sully the reputation of the firm.
- For several months now, inconspicuously, treasury management has become pretty shoddy.
- The core of the risk lies in the inventory!

N.B.: Need I even comment?

- *abbreviate certain well-known words.* The abbreviations must essentially form part and parcel of our field of competence or be widespread in everyday speech. They must be few in number and easy to recognize, for it is essential not to slow down the pace of reading of the person grading the answer. "RLY" in lieu of "really", for example, will not automatically be recognized by your colleagues.

The reader of your answer must quickly understand the gist of the ideas you put forth without having to search for the meaning of an abbreviation.

Skipping an article in a sentence doesn't matter, but skipping them all so as to leave only the other words, is going too far. Similarly, it is possible to shorten an expression by keeping the first letters of a word, such as "gov grant" or "rel parties". However, reading a sentence in which only the first letters of each word appear needlessly complicates the reading process.

Examples: "Inventories shall be measured at the lower of cost and NRV."

To be preferred to: "INV: + < C / NRV"

"The rev. may be undervalued." *To be preferred to:* "$ R not REC"

EXAMPLES OF ACCEPTABLE ABBREVIATIONS

MD&A	Management's Discussion and Analysis	EPS	Earnings Per Share
CCA	Capital Cost Allowance	ABM	Activity-Based Management
EDI	Electronic Data Interchange	WIP	Work In Progress
PUP	Personal Use Property	IPO	Initial Public Offering

I also suggest using the initials of the entity or the letters identifying a program or product. The result is truly shorter. No need to write "Inc." or "Ltd." each time. At times, it also possible to proceed in this manner with individuals' names (e.g.: Mrs. D).

Examples: "DFT" (A3) *To be preferred to:* "Digital Future Technologies"

"Crunch" or "CCP" *To be preferred to:* "Crispy Crunch Pack"

Finally, it is sometimes efficient to provide the abbreviation of a word – more often an expression – the first time one uses it. This enables you thereafter to use the abbreviation throughout the answer. For example, if the case requires you to consider "the impact on the management information system" of each item discussed, it is possible to use the abbreviation "impact MIS" or "MIS".

Exhibit A Proper Attitude

Throughout the development of an answer to a case, certain fundamental attitudes must be observed. In reality, in the manner of resolving problems or issues, the candidate's behavior must follow certain rules, whether implicit or explicit, that influence the expression of ideas.

Be a professional accountant

One of the objectives sought to be achieved by learning through case resolution is to develop your ability to apply your multi-subjects knowledge to various contexts. There is, however, a certain restriction to the diversity of requisite knowledge. In the DFT case, as in most accounting cases, one must appreciate that the problems or issues – if not all the topics – are essentially related to our main field of expertise. The notion of marketing or personnel management perhaps form part of the general education program, but they are "ancillary" fields. Expatiating on the marketing of the new Zeus product, for example, is not – **and will most definitely not be** – part of the topics to be developed.

Remain focused on the skills that essentially form part of our field.

Never lose sight of that fact so as to avoid embarking on irrelevant discussions.

POINT OF VIEW

As a professional, it is crucial that you remain objective towards the events with which you are confronted. You must examine the facts, and then interpret without bias. Easier said than done, since, unconsciously, your personal experiences and your personality may influence your perception of things. Take, for example, the situation where a disagreement erupts during the transfer of a family business to the next generation. From experience, I know that certain candidates are going to "lean" towards the parents whereas others will "lean" towards the children. A sentence to the effect that "They ought to consider themselves lucky that there is a succession to their business ..." is inappropriate. Such an attitude exhibits a lack of objectivity towards the current situation.

Personal, social, political or human opinions must not interfere with the resolution of a case.

REMAIN OBJECTIVE!

Play a leading role

Everything gravitates around you, since you are the only one who sees what is going wrong and what is changing, the only one who understands, assesses, analyzes and solves everything. True, there are other actors in the case, but they do not have the objectivity or the time needed to meet all the various demands. They are secondary actors. Consequently, one must not tell oneself: "Anne is the Chief Financial Officer of a public corporation with revenues in excess of $55,000,000; surely, she knows what to do!", or: "It is a private company established more than 20 years ago, in which there is a team of three managers who must surely be able to determine the transfer price."

If the request has been made or if case facts for problems or issues are provided, you must take this into account.

It is your assignment and, although it may appear strange at times that no one was able to solve some of the topics identified, you have no other choice but to respond to the work to be performed.

During the resolution of a case, YOU ARE the principal actor.

On the other hand, you will never become an expert in all disciplines. An accountant is neither a lawyer nor an environmental specialist or a computer expert. Therefore, it is not up to you to "assess the probability" of losing a lawsuit, but rather to "analyze the accounting for the contingent liabilities" following receipt of the assessment from legal counsel. In the same vein, your role is not "to assess whether damages were caused to the environment", but rather "to determine how to gather sufficient evidence".

Consider the financial aspect of the events

Throughout the resolution of a case, the consideration of the financial aspect of the events is ubiquitous, whether or not the case provides figures. At the heart of an analysis or in the development of a recommendation or conclusion, one must recall that the financial aspect is prevalent. Take the analysis of the impact of a deficiency in treasury management. It is preferable to focus on the risk of theft ($) than on the employee's job enrichment, for example. Similarly, a capital project with a positive net present value ought to be recommended. Human or social considerations may certainly be identified, as opportunities or risks, but they generally do not have much sway in the final decision.

POINT OF VIEW

In reality, in the resolution of a case, the direction of business decisions almost exclusively flows from the quantitative aspect. Although a list of qualitative factors is drawn up, it does not usually change the suggested decision as a result of a calculation. Succinct reference will be made to the loss of jobs following automation, for example. This qualitative factor will, however, not be sufficient to reverse the decision to automate. If need be, the costs of the termination of the employees will be incorporated in the calculation. In the same vein, one could indicate that it would be preferable to sell the plant to local buyers rather than to foreign interests. This will, however, not truly affect the determination if the latter offer a better price.

It is only on rare occasions that qualitative arguments become the reference point. This happens, for example, where two procurement options cost about the same price, where the net present value is nearly zero or where the difference between the prices offered by foreign buyers and local business people is minimal. It is also possible where the risks associated with the issue are extremely high or where the data used in the calculations is highly uncertain or very hypothetical.

Write your response for the benefit of a non-management employee

The person reading the answer to a case must understand what is written or be able to apply what is suggested **without need for any further clarifications**. The language used must, therefore, essentially be directed to the understanding of the ideas put forth (why), the resolution of the problems or issues (what to do and why) and the implementation of the recommendations (who, what, when, how much). On its face, this advice is valid, regardless of whom the recipient of the answer is: employer or client.

IT IS NECESSARY TO BE PRECISE IN THE EXPRESSION OF ONE'S IDEAS.

In order to assist you in the application of the above statements, I suggest that you pretend you are speaking to someone who has completed his or her first year of university education. It is not necessary to explain the difference between debit and credit; however, one may have to discuss the impact of the new lease on the financial statements. Incidentally, it should not be necessary to explain to the partner of an accounting firm why one must verify compliance with the contractual terms reached with Indo-Tech (A26). However, in the context of a case, it is.

Moreover, when one directs one's comments to a person outside our field of expertise, such as a lawyer or a notary, the definition of certain terms or more detailed explanations may be appropriate. You must take into account their degree of knowledge when determining the extent of explanations to provide.

Respect the management practices of the employer or client

During the resolution of a case, one must not lose sight of the characteristics and specific requirements of the employer or client. Essentially, the objectives of management (e.g.: stock market listing in three years), the preferences of stakeholders, risk tolerance (e.g.: do not exceed a debt/equity ratio – by 50%) and the policies of the entity (e.g.: no charging of interest on overdue accounts of less than 60 days) must be taken into consideration. Of course, you must fulfill your assignment and suggest, if need be, improvements to the current situation. However, one must take into account the wishes of the recipient of your answer and not overly disrupt or discard with impunity what matters to him or her.

POINT OF VIEW

In their answers, some candidates write comments such as "difficult topic" or "I just missed the boat!". **This is useless.**

Other candidates will write directly to the person grading their answer and, for instance, say: "If I had had the time to do so, I would have given you the procedures with respect to the inventory shipped to Indo-Tech." (A26). **This is pointless.**

Ultimately, one must do something rather than say that things ought to be done.

Be honest

It is imperative to demonstrate honesty in the resolution of cases while complying with the legislation, and exhibiting ethical and moral conduct. Hence, one must tell the owner of a small business that the personal benefits received from the business (e.g.: the car provided) are taxable and must be declared on his or her Statement of Remuneration. An accountant does not really have the power to prevent the owner from taking such benefits, since it is "his or her" business, but does have a duty to inform the latter of the applicable laws and tax rules. Similarly, it is acceptable and even recommended to side with the position taken by the employer or client while minimizing the tax consequences of the business transactions (e.g.: upon the disposition of assets), but this must be done in compliance with tax legislation.

Naturally, you must not agree to become involved in any fraudulent, illegal or shady transaction. No money laundering or bribes! Finally, you are under a duty to disclose to your professional association any conduct on the part of one of your colleagues that is unethical.

Be considerate

One must show consideration towards individuals, especially our colleagues. Personal, direct or drastic criticism is, therefore, to be avoided, particularly when the blame is directed at the person to whom you are directing your report! **Be diplomatic.** If you deem it necessary, it is always possible to voice your opinion about the attitude of the client in a separate memo directed exclusively to your immediate supervisor or to the Audit Committee, for example.

Personally, I prefer to criticize, or voice my opinion on, reports or ways of doing things rather than pass direct judgment on the individuals themselves. For example, stating that "The previous auditor was incompetent." does not appear to me to be appropriate. Instead, one should say: "The auditing standards were not followed". As well, one may "suspect the existence of fraud" instead of asserting that "The individual is a fraudster".

PROFESSIONALISM → COMPETENCY

Part 6
Making Proper Calculations

Determining The Calculation To Be Made
Using The Results Of A Calculation
Presenting One's Calculations Efficiently

"References accompany calculations; they do not replace them."

Part 6
Making Proper Calculations

The resolution of a short case occasionally requires one to do calculations. For example, a case may directly require you "to calculate the taxable income". In such a situation, there is no doubt that a quantitative analysis is in order. However, the situation is not always so evident and a candidate may have to determine if calculations are necessary to complete his or her answer. Hence, the inclusion or deduction of various items may require a qualitative analysis. One must then determine if it is necessary to submit a calculation in support of the ideas put forth.[1]

Determining The Calculation To Be Made

When called upon to make a calculation, I first take the time to DETERMINE THE INTENDED OBJECTIVE. What does one seek to accomplish? Personally, I express this objective in the form of an action to take, introduced by a verb in the infinitive. The idea is put forth in a short sentence, and added as a title to the calculation to be made. Precisely identifying the intended objective allows you to focus your efforts from the outset on what is essential. For example, "determine the warranty provision" or "determine if the debt covenant has been met" are clearly established objectives.

DFT CASE

Throughout the reading of the DFT case, one notes that figures are supplied for most of the accounting issues and that the projected net income has a whole exhibit devoted to it. As such, there are serious hints as to the merits of conducting a quantitative analysis. Nevertheless, one must validate the potential usefulness of any calculation prior to embarking on one.

Why compute adjusted net income?

To me, it appears to be necessary to justify making a calculation from the outset in order to ensure that one provides a relevant analysis. In one's need to carry out the work required, one must be aware of the time constraints involved. In the DFT case, the candidate has approximately 50 minutes to draft an answer. He or she certainly has no time to waste performing a useless calculation.

To bolster the qualitative analysis, two calculations can be considered: 1- determining the **adjusted EBITDA**, thereby enabling a comparison with the $14M target of the bonus program OR 2- determining the **adjusted net income**, thereby enabling a comparison or revision of preliminary materiality. Personally, in light of the pervasiveness of the bonus program, I consider that impact of the accounting adjustments on the EBITDA to be the most important aspect to consider.

Objective: Recalculate the EBITDA based on the accounting adjustments

One must appreciate that a candidate might instead decide to duly recalculate the net income. While this objective is indeed valid – and although this calculation is part of the official solution (A18) –, THE RESTRICTED TIME FRAME IN WHICH TO COMPLETE THE CASE REQUIRES YOU TO MAKE CHOICES AND TO FOCUS ON WHAT IS ESSENTIAL.

1 Before starting to read Parts 6 through 10 of this volume, I suggest you read the proposed solution for the DFT case (A9 to A39). Do not hesitate to refer to it as you read.

POINT OF VIEW

Certain candidates perform calculations that are not really necessary for the analysis. For instance, they will recalculate the total assets following a recommendation that certain costs be recognized on the balance sheet, or they will automatically calculate the tax consequence of each adjustment.
Even if they are short, these calculations are not to be performed and add nothing to the resolution of a problem or issue.

Make sure to determine "why" you are doing a calculation.

Once the objective has been determined, I suggest that you PLAN THE CALCULATION as such. How should one do it? What is its scope? What are the steps or its major portions? What are the specific and crucial components? Without losing sight of the desired end result, try to visualize how to proceed. For example, with a view to assessing if the debt covenant with respect to the minimum current ratio has been met, one must consider the adjustments to be made to current assets and current liabilities. To this end, the calculation could be set out in two columns indicating the adjusted total of each of the two parts of the ratio. These totals can then be connected in order to yield the current ratio.

When planning a calculation, one must take into account the importance of the components that may make it up. Using the nomenclature described in Part 2 (pp. 19 and 20), I suggest that you make a distinction between important components, components of lesser importance and not very important (insignificant) components.

One must **attempt to integrate all** – or nearly all – the **important components** and, **if possible, part of the components of lesser importance**.

In order to submit a "reasonable" calculation, consideration must be given to all the available data and one must DETERMINE WHAT IS IMPORTANT, IN LIGHT OF THE CASE PARAMETERS.

DFT CASE

Among the ten or so accounting issues in the case, six of them require an adjustment to net income. When performing a calculation, you must at least make sure to consider what is the most important. In light of the very nature of a quantitative analysis, the significance of the amounts involved is the criterion to rely on. We can add, for the DFT case in particular, that the adjustments that influence the EBITDA are, per se, more important than the others.

Important adjustments:
- Indo-Tech's revenues of $1,850,000 (including the cost of sales)
- government funding (grant) of $800,000
- R&D with respect to the Ares product of $450,000

Adjustments of lesser importance:
- discount of $225,000 in revenue on NRE

Not very important (insignificant) adjustments:
- GST/HST reassessment of $125,000
- impairment loss of $100,000 on production equipment

You will note, and this is not really surprising, that the important adjustments flow from the important accounting topics identified in Part 2 (p. 21).

As indicated throughout this volume, ONE MUST FOCUS ON WHAT MATTERS MOST: THE IMPORTANT COMPONENTS MUST BE PART OF THE CALCULATION. They require more depth or explanations, whereas components of lesser importance are, on their face, resolved faster.

DFT CASE – EXAMPLE OF AN APPROPRIATE CALCULATION (direct method)

Objective: Recalculate the EBITDA based on the accounting adjustments

	Amortization to be excluded	Unadjusted numbers	Note	Adjustments	Adjusted numbers
Revenue		59,224	*a*	- 1,850	
			b	- 800	
			d	- 129	56,445
Cost of sales (40%)	- 33,872 + 430	- 33,442	*a*	1,110	- 32,332
R&D	- 3,991 + 1,620	- 2,371	*c*	- 450	
			b	+ 200	- 2,621
Sales and marketing		- 2,622			- 2,622
General and administrative	- 7,924 + 2,995	- 4,929			- 4,929
EBITDA		**15,860**			**13,941**

This example of an appropriate calculation meets the requirements of the DFT case satisfactorily. It is not a complete, nor a perfect, but rather a "reasonable" calculation. It contains the three important adjustments previously identified (*a, b, c*), plus a fourth (*d*), of lesser importance. I considered the latter adjustment due to its unusual nature and its impact on revenue recognition. The fact that the adjustment that arises as a result brings the EBITDA below the $14M target, thereby changing the conclusion, is not insignificant.

Upon examination of the example of a calculation above, the following can be stated:

- The items Interest and Income taxes are not part of the analysis, quite simply because they are, by definition, excluded from the EBITDA.
- A column titled "Amortization to be excluded" is provided in order to highlight the fact that certain items of net income contain such expense. By excluding amortization from the outset, this allows for a more precise focus on the components of the adjusted EBITDA.
- The impact of the adjustment of the same accounting issue is recorded for all items involved in one single operation. For example, the "*b*" adjustment with respect to the $800,000 in grants results, among others, in an income reduction of $800,000 and a reduction of R&D expenses of $200,000. This latter part of the adjustment must not be "glossed over" on the grounds that the amount is of lesser significance. Where an adjustment is identified as important, each of the parts of the adjustment entry must be integrated to the calculation.

  Thinking "debit-credit" is an effective trick when one wants to make sure that one has considered the full impact of a given adjustment. Reconciling the entry in one's head also promotes an understanding of the most complex items. It is not, however, necessary to write it down in one's answer.

Adjustments that are integrated to the calculation are what matter.

When it is not easy to determine what to calculate, I suggest that you start with a simple calculation. In an uncertain situation, some candidates will waste time making calculations that are needlessly long, too complicated or quite simply inappropriate. Remember that it is easier to add figures than it is to recover time wasted performing a useless calculation. Other candidates will instead refrain from making a calculation altogether on the grounds that it will not be complete. Remember that it is possible for you to demonstrate – at least in part – your analytical ability by submitting an incomplete calculation whereas it is impossible if there isn't any! In order to provide a reasonable calculation, the consideration of those components of lesser importance may be useful.

It is preferable to do a simple and short calculation than none at all!

POINT OF VIEW

One must be aware that calculations can easily and quickly eat up time. From experience, I can tell you that it is very tempting – especially for an accountant – to want to make complete and proper calculations. This attitude is not bad per se, but one must never lose sight of the fact that minutes are ticking away.

As in the example of an appropriate calculation appearing on the previous page, to me, it seems to be crucial to ensure that one performs "**in a reasonable manner**" the calculations required as part of the case; nothing more, nothing less. I regularly read answers from candidates who unfortunately invested too much time in the preparation of the quantitative analysis, to the detriment of the rest.

Make sure you have properly determined the intended objective, and then plan the calculation.

DO NOT GET SIDETRACKED!

PROFESSIONAL JUDGMENT

QUALITATIVE ↘ QUANTITATIVE ↙

BALANCE

↓

APPROPRIATE ANSWER

The preparation of a calculation sometimes requires the positing of working assumptions. Under certain circumstances, the figure to use must be estimated or a choice must be made between two options. However, this is not a very regular occurrence in short cases and, if it does happen, the assumptions to be made are very few in number.

Make sure that the circumstances truly warrant the making of working assumptions.

CHARACTERISTICS OF WORKING ASSUMPTIONS

Characteristics	Examples
Assumptions **result from a choice**.	Where the data in the case is supplied as such, it is not an assumption! – The case states that the average margin of the product sales is 40%. (A4) No need to explain the source of this information in the calculation of the EBITDA or of net income.
Assumptions must be **reasonable**.	One's practical sense should be engaged, so as not to make unsound assumptions. – While taking into account the particulars of the case, the discount rate you decide on must be realistic. At first blush, 3% is too low and 20% is too high!
Assumptions are **based on the case facts**.	It is pointless to make an arbitrary assumption! – When called upon to allocate the discount between two periods, it is logical to use the sales figures provided in the case: $1,000,000 for 2012 and $750,000 for 2013. (A5) – When called upon to amortize $600,000 in grants, one must base one's assumption on the estimated life of the product of 3 years. (A6) – It would be pointless to assume an inflation rate of 2%, especially if the case makes no mention of it.
Assumptions must be **easy to work with**.	Since they are assumptions, one must make things simple, and not add useless complications. – By any standards, it is simpler to use the straight-line method than the diminishing balance method in order to depreciate an asset.
Assumptions are to be **substantiated briefly**.	Generally speaking, a sentence is sufficient to state which assumption is being made, and why. – "Since the useful life of the equipment required is five years, I will conduct the feasibility analysis over this period."

Of course, it may happen that a candidate will make a mistake and, for instance, take 60% to calculate the sales cost of the products of components whereas he or she should instead choose 40% (A4). One must appreciate that such a mistake does not invalidate the entire calculation made. In addition, as part of the assessment of an answer, it must be remembered that a mistake will only be penalized once. Moreover, the aim is not to arrive at a perfectly precise calculation, but to submit a reasonable one.

The person grading the answer assesses a calculation in its entirety,
as well as any underlying reasoning,
in light of the figures and assumptions used by the candidate.

POINT OF VIEW

Generally speaking, one must not change the information provided in a case, at least not initially. Some candidates question everything, and then arbitrarily change the financial data integrated in their calculation. Where a case, for instance, provides the sales forecast for a new product, one must use these figures, even if one "suspects" the owner of the business of being slightly too optimistic. At most, this will be a qualitative comment to be indicated as a risk associated with the project. A risk is not the same thing as an assumption!

One must have clear and concrete indicia to change the figures provided in a case.

On the other hand, if the manager of the Marketing Department, for example, states that "Forecasts are overvalued by 20%.", this is a case fact to consider. The reference to "20%" enables the calculation of a precise adjustment in the financial data. It is no longer strictly arbitrary.

Finally, note that the limited time frame in which to complete a short case does not usually allow for the submission of a detailed analysis in which various scenarios of a given situation are contemplated.

Using The Results Of A Calculation

Before moving on to the step of using the calculation made, make sure the result is credible.

HAVE THE REFLEX OF ASSESSING THE PLAUSIBILITY OF THE RESULT REACHED.

Too often, it happens that candidates mechanically juggle with figures without really seeing them. For instance, take the calculation of DFT's adjusted net income. Based on the existing income of $7,051, in light of the extent of the adjustments, it would be surprising to arrive at a higher net income or to end up with a loss! Before pursuing the drafting of your answer and interpreting an implausible number, take the time to validate the result reached. For example, you may have written "$8,150" instead of "$1,850" or written down "+ $1,850" in lieu of "- $1,850". Without needing official evidence that the calculation is correct, it is certainly possible to estimate an interval or establish a plausible benchmark that will validate it. Under certain circumstances, the case may even contain case facts that may guide you on the path of the results to come. (Part 3, p. 33)

It is crucial to INTERPRET ANY CALCULATION made. What is it used for? THE RESULT REACHED MUST BE USED. A calculation is rarely the crux of a problem or issue, especially in a short case. In other words, the calculation is part of a qualitative analysis, which encompasses it. It is not an outcome per se. The calculation of the estimated liability related to promotions, for example, may be used in the accounting discussion or the tax discussion. Moreover, determining whether the debt covenant has been met enables us to assess the solvency of the entity, for example. Personally, to ensure that I have not forgotten anything, I write a conclusion in the schedule containing the calculation itself, as soon as it is complete. Some candidates prefer to write it down in the body of the text of the answer; it makes no difference.

It is not the result one has arrived at that matters, but rather the quality of the interpretation that one makes of it.

At this time, I would like to bring to your attention the difference between a statement and an interpretation.

A **statement** expresses in words what the calculations show.

An **interpretation** relates to the **meaning** or **usefulness** of the calculation.

It is in the interpretation of the results arrived at that the candidate exercises his or her professional judgment and demonstrates his or her ability to use a calculation for specific purposes. In other words, a calculation forms an integral part of the resolution of the problems or issues of the case.

EXAMPLES OF THE INTERPRETATION OF THE RESULT OF A CALCULATION

Calculation of the current ratio

500,000/400,000 = 1.25

Statement: The current ratio is 1.25.

Examples of interpretation:

The ratio of 1.25 is higher than the minimum threshold of 1.0 required by the mortgagee.

OR

The ratio of 1.25 is higher than that of the industry that hovers around 0.80, which confirms the existence of an inventory overage.

OR

The ratio of 1.25 is lower than the objective set by the comptroller of maintaining it above 1.40.

The interpretation of a calculation requires a certain amount of analysis or of integration, which requires more effort. In the example above, stating that "The current ratio is 1.25." is not particularly useful. It amounts to saying in words, or summarizing, what the result of the calculation clearly shows and, in this respect, **it is not a new idea**, it is obvious!

POINT OF VIEW

In the example of the DFT case appearing previously (p. 74), the adjusted EBITDA of $13,941,000 $ is less – but not by much – than the target of $14,000,000. At first blush, such a result is easier to interpret, since it, to a certain extent, provides evidence of management's bias. However, one must be aware of the possibility that the result arrived at might be greater than the target of $14M. A mistake in the adjustment of an accounting issue can make a difference. Hence, the mere fact of not considering the adjustment of the discount of $129,000 increases the EBITDA to $14,070,000.

All results must be interpreted, even if they run counter to initial expectations.

A candidate who arrives at a figure of $14,070,000 can indicate that it is very close to the target of $14,000,000. He or she could even add that the majority of the adjustments for the period reduce the net income, and that it is possible that the target will not be met after completion of the financial statements. Arriving at such a result does not prevent one from making an observation as to management's bias in making adjustments that increase the EBITDA. (A33)

What is important is providing a valid interpretation, which takes into account the particulars of the case, regardless of the result reached.

In addition, the person grading the answer will focus on the contents of the "adjustments" column. Writing "XXX" or $0, for example, would not be very helpful. If need be, qualitative arguments generally appear in text portion of the answer.

ASPECTS THAT CAN ENHANCE THE INTERPRETATION OF THE RESULTS OF A CALCULATION

<table>
<tr><td>Comparison</td><td>With a view to discerning a pattern, a relationship or a trend, the results of a calculation can be compared from one period to another, be positioned as against the industry or expressed as a percentage of a benchmark. You can also demonstrate your practical sense, given the quantity arrived at, by proceeding with a calculation of the break-even point or with an interpretation of a payback period, for example.
E.g.: Over the past few months, Reacto's share price has fallen by about 20%. During the same period, the stock market index, considered on the whole, rose by approximately 3%.
For comparison purposes, it is essential to have available to you data that, per se, is comparable. The calculation of the after-tax rate, for instance, enables a comparison of various financing options.</td></tr>
<tr><td>Objective of the calculation</td><td>Reverting to the objective written in the heading of the calculation page (e.g.: recalculate the net income) is a good starting point for the interpretation stage.
E.g.: "Materiality was initially estimated in July to be $434,000 based on 5% of preliminary net income before tax of $8,681,000 (using CAS 320 A4 and A7). My revised estimate, calculated on the same basis but taking into account the accounting adjustments noted (5% of $8,457,000) is $422,850." (A23)
N.B.: A candidate who proceeded to calculate the adjusted EBITDA, as in the above example of an appropriate calculation (p. 74), will have to make additional adjustments. He or she will be able to quickly perform the following calculation:
Adjusted EBITDA — 13,941
Amortization (430 + 1 620 + 2 995) — - 5,045
Interest — - 314
— 8,582
Revised materiality (5%) — 429</td></tr>
<tr><td>Particulars of the context</td><td>It is sometimes possible to relate the various particulars of the case to each other, such as the objectives, needs, biases and behavior of the stakeholders, the practices and policies of the entity, or the constraints.
E.g. "However, based on the recommended accounting adjustments, adjusted EBITDA would be approximately $13,766,000, which is under the $14-million threshold. As a result, management will be very sensitive to any adjustments that are proposed since the bonus threshold is no longer met." (A33)
N.B.: Considering the example of an appropriate calculation shown above (p. 74), the amount of the adjusted EBITDA would be $13,941,000 instead.</td></tr>
</table>

OBJECTIVE

↓

CALCULATION

↓

INTERPRETATION

POINT OF VIEW

Some candidates scrap their qualitative analysis when the result arrived at in the quantitative analysis is not in keeping with their expectations. This is not a good idea. For example, they will drop the analysis of the advantages and disadvantages of the acceptance of a special order on the grounds that the sum of variable costs is greater than the price offered by the client. One could indeed state that it is a valid reason for rejecting the order.

Incidentally, I remind you, as seen in Part 5 (p. 69), that the financial aspect takes precedence when one is called upon to make a choice or a decision.

Regardless, ONE MUST SUBMIT A COMPLETE ANALYSIS ON THE TOPIC, even where the recommendation is known in advance. Besides, it is quite possible that the passing standard requires the candidate to prepare a reasonable qualitative analysis and a reasonable quantitative analysis in order to properly justify the recommendation.

Finally, I would like to draw your attention to the fact that a quantitative analysis obviously includes a strictly mathematical portion. For example, income must be multiplied by 60% in order to arrive at the adjustment of the cost of sales. However, it is not so much the multiplication that matters in the assessment of the answer, but the idea of adjusting the cost of sales and, thereafter, the items as properly established. I raise this point because one must appreciate that the mathematical aspect is usually correctly performed by the majority of candidates. This is, therefore, not what enables a candidate to stand out from the crowd.

Yet, it often happens that some candidates simply do not understand why they were not successful in the calculation portion of a case. On the one hand, it may be that the components used in the calculation were of lesser importance or insignificant. There are definitely components that require greater consideration than others.

To successfully complete a calculation, one must consider the important components.

On the one hand, it may be that a good portion of the work performed by a candidate was strictly mathematic or was essentially a repetition of the information already available in the case. Multiplying all the figures by 1.02, for example, to take into account inflation, is an essentially mathematical action, which is devoid of any real content. The candidate may have the impression that he or she devoted a reasonable amount of time to the calculations, although this is not the case.

Presenting One's Calculations Efficiently

As indicated above, one must first identify the objective sought to be achieved by doing the calculation, and then determine what the main components thereof are. One must also plan the extent of the calculation as well as the steps necessary to performing it. For example, when one needs to ensure that the current ratio meets the limit required by the bank, it is not, as a result, necessary to redo the statement of financial position (balance sheet) in its entirety. Rather, one should focus on those items or groups of items making up the current assets and current liabilities.

When called upon to restate part of the financial statements, there are two ways of proceeding: the direct method or the indirect method. The **direct method** involves redoing a financial statement, or a part thereof, starting with a list of existing, unadjusted items. The requisite adjustments are then recorded in order to extrapolate the adjusted balance of each of the items. The calculation of the desired result is then conducted. Using this method, we previously recomputed DFT's EBITDA (p. 74). This manner of performing a calculation is followed in most official solutions to cases.

On occasion, it may happen that the **indirect method** can be used. Depending on the intended objective, the starting point of the calculation is, instead, the total or sub-total of the target items, to which the requisite adjustments are applied. The result arrived at will be the same, but performing the calculation can be done in a shorter time period.

DFT CASE – EXAMPLE OF AN APPROPRIATE CALCULATION (indirect method)

To be compared with p. 74.

Objective: Recalculate the EBITDA based on the accounting adjustments

Income before taxes (A7)			10,501
PLUS: Interest			314
PLUS: Amortization		'=430+1620+2995	5,045
EBITDA before adjustments	Note		**15,860**
Indo – not yet earned revenue	*a*	- 1,850	
Cost of sales (40%)	*a*	+ 1,110	
Grants – not sales	*b*	- 800	
part in income	*b*	+ 200	
Write-off R&D – Ares	*c*	- 450	
Deferred discount	*d*	- 129	**- 1,919**
Adjusted EBITDA			**13,941**

Consequently, it is not always necessary to redo a statement completely and properly, in order to arrive at the desired result. All depends on the requirements and the number of items involved. Where the result of one single figure, in this case the EBITDA, is needed for analytical purposes, the indirect method meets the requirements. The situation would be different if one needed the adjusted balance of each of the important items of the statement in order to conduct a comparative analysis with the previous period, for example. **Where there are many adjustments, and the statement contains few items, the direct method is usually followed.** In the example of the calculation of DFT's adjusted EBITDA, most of the items under net income require adjustments. Consequently, the time required for performing the calculation, using either method, is approximately the same.

Finally, where the adjustments to be made involve few items, it is pointless to repeat the balance of the items that remain unchanged. In the calculation of the adjusted current ratio, for example, it would be useless to repeat each of the items making up the working capital if the only adjustment to be made relates to the item Inventory.

POINT OF VIEW

When called upon to adjust financial information, the indirect method is generally faster. It is, however, slightly more complex. Some candidates may experience difficulty in correctly identifying the sign of each of the adjustments. Others may need a more detailed picture of the situation in order to grasp all the implications.

One must be comfortable with the indirect method, because it is unfortunately easier to omit something or to make a mistake. Regardless, as we shall see in Part 7, it is useful to reconcile the calculations of a proposed solution by using the indirect method, just to validate one's understanding of what is going on. This also allows you to experiment with different ways of reaching the same objective.

The calculations are generally made using software such as *Excel*. They are, as a result, appended as a supplement to the text of the answer. I suggest that you use a different tab for each of the calculations performed, and then that you designate them individually (A, B, ... or 1, 2, ...). In order to enable the person grading your answer to assess the qualitative analysis and the quantitative analysis at one and the same time, **make sure you include an appropriate reference to the schedule containing your calculations**. Incidentally, I suggest that you briefly write down this reference at the outset of the analysis of the problem or issue involved. Remember, as well, that a short calculation can be included in the body of the text itself, in brackets.

Where the calculation comes along with explanatory notes or working assumptions, I suggest that you place them on the same page as the calculation to which they relate. Personally, I place them at the very end so that the calculation performed will appear upon opening of the file. A short explanation (e.g.: 30%) or a short assumption (e.g.: assume a constant) can, however, be inserted between two lines of the calculation without altering the professional appearance of the answer.

DFT CASE

When called upon to adjust financial data based on the analysis of various accounting issues, a candidate can do his or her calculation as he or she is performing the qualitative analysis, or upon its completion. For the sake of efficiency, I suggest that you first create the framework of the calculation to be made by listing therein the items involved.

This framework is then filled out as the qualitative analysis progresses. Upon completion of the discussion of a topic, one then carries over the requisite adjustment, as well as any related explanations, to the calculation contained in the schedule. This obviates the need for later having to backtrack in order to trace the impact of any of the accounting issues.

You would proceed in the same manner in respect of the calculation of the cumulative material effect of the misstatements, for example.

You have probably understood by now that the quantitative analysis is subject to the same imperatives as the qualitative analysis. It must be planned in order to include essentially the same relevant and new ideas, submitted in an efficient manner. The notions set out in the earlier parts of this volume therefore apply as well to the performance of calculations. Consequently, I suggest that you:

- *not perform useless calculations.* It is quite natural, for example, to calculate the gross profit in a statement of net income duly submitted. In the answer to a case, in light of the restricted time frame, such a sub-total is rarely useful. Similarly, calculating the Income before taxes, followed by the amount of Taxes in order to yield the Net income, can be performed faster. Taking the Income before taxes, and multiplying it by "1 - tax rate" yields the same result. Finally, if need be, add all the adjustments prior to calculating the tax consequences. This will save you the trouble of performing a calculation in each of them. The same reasoning applies where you are asked to update financial data.

- *specify the meaning of the figures used.* From experience, I can tell you that it is easy to get tangled up in the numbers and to make a mistake while performing a mathematical operation. Knowing in which direction to adjust an item is one thing, identifying it in such a way that the calculation software will consider it properly is another altogether. Personally, for the sake of simplicity, I write a " – " in front of all figures that are to be subtracted. For example, with a view to recalculating net income, everything that reduces this income will be preceded by the minus sign. In this manner, the "SUM" feature readily and quickly meets the majority of requirements.

- *abbreviate the sections used.* Out of reflex, most candidates take the time – too much time even – to write down in detail each of the sections. This is really not necessary, since the essence of the quantitative analysis relates to the calculation itself. Therefore, you may – and I strongly urge you to do so – further abbreviate your words than in the qualitative analysis. Hence, "G&A" is sufficient to convey "General and administrative" and "Tax" can replace "Income taxes". Incidentally, it would be pointless to specify that the numbers are expressed "in thousands of Canadian dollars" if such is indeed the situation in the case. (A7)

  Naturally, where the same sections are used for more than one calculation, one should contemplate including a table or chart in a comparative format. For example, the definition of a ratio may be used in the calculation of this ratio for two periods. The same would go for a calculation of cash flow over more than one year.

REMINDER: PRECEDENCE OF SUBSTANCE OVER FORM

POINT OF VIEW

One must take into account that the reader of your answer – namely the person grading it – generally receives the answer to be assessed in PDF format. In other words, **he or she only sees what is apparent.** Experiment with the printing of one of your quantitative analyses in order to see what the person grading your answer receives.

You will understand, as I do, that:

- pages are ordered from top to bottom, not left to right. Where a calculation is spread out over a great many columns, the part that is outside the margins of the current page will appear below. The pages of one and the same calculation will, therefore, not automatically follow each other sequentially.

  SOLUTIONS: – limit the number or width of the columns;

  – use the "landscape" format.

- the formulas used do not appear. Only the result arrived at is visible.

  SOLUTION: add a sign of some sort in front of the formula and place it in the cell next to it. E.g.: " '=430+1620+2995" (p. 81)

  N.B.: Only those formulas that are necessary to the reader's understanding need appear, such as the weighting of the normalized earnings in the determination of the value of a business. It is not necessary, for example, to show the basic formulas used in the calculation of DFT's EBITDA (pp. 74 and 81).

- the letters A, B, C… identifying the columns and the numbers 1, 2, 3… identifying the lines still do not appear. It is therefore useless to refer to them.
- the text of a cell exceeding the column width does not necessarily appear where it should.

- *not clutter the calculation made.* Figures can be rounded off and the "$" sign is not necessary. Admittedly, you may tell me that writing "000" at the end of each number doesn't take long. True, but letting the spreadsheet breathe more makes what is essential stand out. One must also avoid inserting explanations that are too long within the calculations.

  N.B.: Another unit of measurement than dollars, such as the number of liters, for example, should be pointed out, only once, at the beginning of the line or at the top of the column.

POINT OF VIEW

It can definitely happen that the resolution of one of the problems or issues in the case will bring to the fore an item that was not considered in a calculation previously made. Subsequently adding an additional component may even lead to a change of interpretation of the result arrived at.

Where the component is important, ideally you should take the time to make the change: calculation and interpretation.

Due to a lack of time, it is, however, not always possible to do so. You should know that you can insert a number in a calculation without, however, changing the final result. For example, by placing a " ' " in front of the number, the latter will simply not be considered by the computation formula. However, you will have incorporated the given adjustment in the quantitative analysis.

It is the understanding of the concept that matters, not the mathematical calculation.

- *avoid repetitions.* Incidentally, it is very easy to repeat things in explanatory notes or assumptions. Where the justification for an adjustment is in the text of your answer, it is not necessary to explain it once more in the schedule used for calculations. For example, the calculation of the discount amount of $129,000 (A11: $128,751) to be deferred to 2013 requires an explanation, which is to be developed directly in the qualitative analysis. There is no need to summarize the discussion once more in the schedule. Make a short reference, or quickly use the "cut/paste" feature. Personally, I use letters to refer to explanatory notes and assumptions, quite simply to avoid any confusion with numbers. By the way, the same reference must be used for all items or adjustments relating to the same topic.

  Furthermore, one must minimize the time devoted to copying information supplied in the case. Although it is crucial, the column setting out the unadjusted figures (p. 74) (A18) has no value as such when time comes to assessing the calculation.

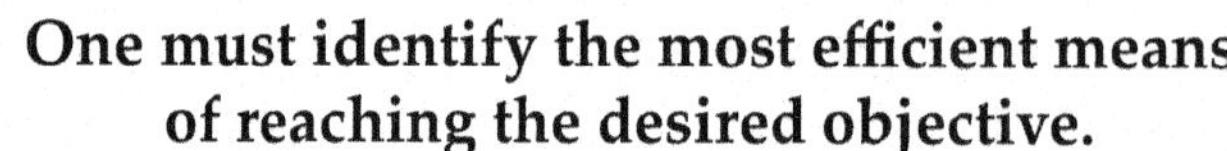

- *not overexplain what is obvious.* Writing out in words what the figures clearly show is pointless. For example, stating "I am going to add the amount of interest and of amortization to Income before taxes in order to arrive at the EBITDA figure." adds nothing to the calculation per se. As in the case of the example above (p. 81), the calculation is simple and easy to follow. Similarly, writing "40%" in brackets next to the item Cost of sales needs no further explanation. It is useless to explain the source of the figures that are provided as such in the case. Incidentally, you will note that the same figure is rarely used more than once, which makes tracking it down faster.

Part 7
Analyzing A Simulated Case

Do Not Lose Sight Of The Case Parameters
Understanding The Ideas Set Out In The Proposed Solution
Analyzing The Evaluation Guide

"There is always an explanation and finding it will help you develop your competency in the resolution of the cases."

Part 7
Analyzing A Simulated Case

For the purposes of continuous improvement, to me, it appears to be crucial to conduct an in-depth analysis of each simulated case. I personally believe that one must devote on average two to three times more time to the analysis of a case than to its simulation per se. For example, one should set aside a post-simulation perusal time of 140 to 210 minutes (2 to 3 hours) for a 70-minute case. I suggest that you conduct the analysis of a case as soon as possible after simulating it. It will still be fresh in your memory. In my view, ideally, you should at least read the proposed solution on the very day of the simulation; the rest of the work can ultimately wait a few days.

A case usually comes with a "proposed" or "official" solution embodied in an evaluation guide or introducing the latter as a separate document. This solution contains the essence of the relevant and new ideas that meet the various case requirements. As for the evaluation guide, it explains how to assess – or grade – a candidate's answer. Although these two parts are inherently connected, a little later I will conduct an analysis of the evaluation guide.

Do Not Lose Sight Of The Case Parameters

As stated in the previous Parts, the case parameters act as a guide and framework throughout the reading (p. 1) and the drafting of an answer (p. 30). When the time comes to analyze a simulated case – and then potentially mark it –, it is important to consider the influence of these particulars on the resolution of the problems or issues.

INFLUENCE OF THE CASE PARAMETERS ON THE PROPOSED SOLUTION

Case parameters	Examples (DFT CASE)
The context What basic information needs to be highlighted in order to better understand the environment in which the entity under study operates?	DFT is a technology company. (A3) Consequently, – The nature of DFT's industry is a factor to take into account in the assessment of the audit risk. (A24) – "Valuation" of the item Deferred development costs (A14, A15) and of the item Inventory (A13) is the critical aspect to analyze. – Government funding has been secured to assist DFT in developing new products. (A12, A13) – The deferred development costs are amortized over a short useful life, namely 3 years. (A13, A18, A20)

One must flesh out the particulars of the proposed solution.

INFLUENCE OF THE CASE PARAMETERS ON THE PROPOSED SOLUTION

Case parameters	Examples (DFT CASE)
The role From which perspective are the problems or issues to be approached? Which protagonist are you being asked to play in the case?	An auditor must assess the impact of the new bonus program on his or her audit engagement. – The existence of this program increases the audit risk. (A24) – The reliance of management for purposes of the bonus calculation suggests the setting of a separate materiality (at a lesser amount) on areas affecting EBITDA. (A23) – Additional procedures must be performed. (A25 to A30) The fundamental role of an auditor is not to question the merits of the bonus program. The "management" aspect of this program is, incidentally, deemed to be a secondary issue. (A37)
The requirement What is the work to be performed? What are the problems or issues? What are the important topics?	– As requested, the proposed solution contains two major sections: accounting and audit. – The significance of the amounts involved, as to the impact they have on the EBITDA, determines the importance of the topics to analyze. (Part 2, p. 21) – Aside from the reference to the appropriate accounting treatment, one must inquire about its financial IMPACT.

When confronted with the proposed solution to a case:

- Make sure you are able to explain the presence (or absence) as well as the importance of each problem or issue.
- Proceed to identify the critical aspect of each of the topics.
- Go to the trouble of retracing all the case facts justifying the presence of a less explicit issue, such as the questioning of management's integrity. (A34)
- Take cognizance of the level of depth of the various topics.
- Note the interrelations between the various parts analyzed.

Understanding The Ideas Set Out In The Proposed Solution

It is essential to read the proposed solution carefully in order to take advantage of the opportunity for perfecting your knowledge of the problems or issues involved. Each idea, each argument and each calculation must be understood, regardless of its importance in the case. You must have the reference documents, such as the accounting standards and the tax rules, on hand and you must consult them regularly. A candidate may have run out of ideas, made a mistake or not known, for example, how to adequately analyze the accounting issue of the government funding received. As you perform more and more simulations, you must take note of these topics that require additional study and write them on your agenda. One must also examine the manner in which theoretical concepts are applied to the specific context of the case.

POINT OF VIEW

Some candidates simulate a case, and go directly to the evaluation guide in order to mark their answer without delay. They do not read the proposed solution, or very little of it, only if necessary, in order to look at a calculation, or in order to clarify what is meant by "discuss some of the audit procedures" (A31).

By starting the analysis of a case with the application of the evaluation guide, the focus becomes the assessment of the answer. By "electing" to read only a part of the proposed solution, with a view to completing the evaluation guide, certain aspects, which could indeed be very useful, will just not be considered. Candidates who proceed in this manner do not take full advantage of all the solution can teach them, and thereby restrict their experiential learning.

I suggest that you start the analysis of a case by understanding the ideas set out in the proposed solution. On the one hand, this allows you to revise or to perfect notions you have already learned.

IT IS AN EXCELLENT SOURCE OF IDEAS.

Moreover, a topic of lesser importance in a case could very well be at the forefront in the resolution of another. On the other hand, a good understanding of the suggested solution will greatly facilitate the subsequent assessment of your performance in the answer.

One must not be content to merely "read" the proposed solution,

one must "meticulously study each component".

The reading you perform must be active, full of queries and questioning. It must also be undertaken in an interactive manner, along with the case facts or any other useful reference tool. Aside from an understanding of the ideas put forth, the analysis of the proposed solution must also enable you to develop your ability to resolve a case appropriately.[1]

Tie the solution to the case facts

The ideas put forth in the proposed solution are definitely not there by mere coincidence. They directly depend on, and derive from, information (case facts and parameters) supplied in the case. I suggest that you regularly embark on the exercise of selecting any of the ideas set out in the proposed solution and explaining how, based on the case, you could have come up with these ideas. In other words, you must track down the information that explains the presence of the idea in the solution. This will enable you to grasp how the ideas appearing in the answer originate from the simulated case, while helping you to improve the quality of your reading of the next case. In so doing, you will notice that the text of each case undeniably contains a wealth of information that is relevant to the resolution of the problems or issues.

CASE FACTS

↓

PROPOSED SOLUTION

1 Appendix A illustrates how to analyze the contents of the proposed solution of the DFT case. (A9 to A39)

POINT OF VIEW

Candidates are often surprised to discover to what extent the case contains information that sparks the drafting of relevant ideas. The connection is inextricable. In point of fact, the process is simple.

When a professor or an author wants a particular topic to be developed in the answer, he or she includes the requisite information in the case.

We previously stated the following in Part 3 (p. 31): in the absence of any valuable case facts, the discussion remains general or theoretic.

The use of the case facts is crucial to the development of an appropriate answer.

EXAMPLES OF CONNECTIONS BETWEEN THE PROPOSED SOLUTION AND THE CASE FACTS

Ideas appearing in the proposed solution	Case facts
The analysis of the break-even point establishes the minimum number of units to be sold to achieve a nil net income.	The fixed costs in the industry are high, especially in the case of a new product.
One must identify, and then analyze, those items in respect of which the variation is the greatest. The calculation of certain variances rounds out the discussion.	The President, Michael, would like to understand why the actual net income is less than the anticipated net income, although sales have increased.
– With a view to manipulating the EBITDA and increasing its bonuses, management might be tempted to "capitalize expense items". (A33) – "Continuing to defer development costs related to a specific product no longer under development..." (A34)	"It must constantly reinvest in research and development to ensure that its products remain relevant and can integrate with the latest technology." (A4)

You will notice that, at times, the case fact is clear and direct, such as the request made by the President. Under other circumstances, the case fact may be part of the information describing the entity in the case, such as the need for DFT to "constantly reinvest in R&D". It also happens that a given item of information for an issue may be useful in a different context. Take, for example, the situation where a GST/HST audit has led to a reassessment of $125,000 (A6). Aside from the accounting treatment of this reassessment, this event can lead the auditor to question the quality of the accounting and record-keeping (A24). Finally, you will sometimes need to connect two or three case facts located in different parts of the case to explain the contents of the proposed solution.

WHY?
That is the question to ask oneself during the analysis of a case.

Integration of theoretical concepts and case facts

All throughout your analysis, I suggest that you pay particular attention to notions and theoretical concepts referred to in the proposed solution.

What are the concepts (standards, rules, laws, principles, etc.) that were used to resolve the various problems or issues?

In the proposed solution to the DFT case, I regularly flesh out the concept underlying the analysis, such as the concept of "virtual certainty" for the topic Contingency (A15). Under certain circumstances, I prepare a chart illustrating the events (A12) or a table summarizing the notions (A16).

You will also notice that there are no – or very few – strictly theoretical statements in a case. The reminder of the accounting standards (in italics) is solely for educational purposes. As discussed in Part 3, one must **simultaneously integrate the theory to the case**, in the same sentence or paragraph. Personally, in order to assimilate the drafting process, I frequently highlight the case facts (in yellow) and the theoretical concepts used (in orange). The use of different colors allows me to easily observe the manner in which the ideas fit together. Of course, the use of underlining or another sign, such as an arrow or a bracket, can be just as effective.

EXAMPLES OF INTEGRATION OF THEORETICAL CONCEPTS TO THE CASE FACTS

- The cost of the owner's compensation is considered too high, because it includes bonuses totaling $500,000 this year. The payment of such compensation is not a usual practice of the entity, and the amount therefore ought to be excluded from the calculation of the normalized earnings amount.

Normalized earnings: earnings adjusted to remove non-recurring and unusual items

- As of now, Charity International has not yet received its status as a registered charitable organization. Your donation of $2,500 is therefore not deductible.

Registered organization → deductible donation

- Our colleague, Mr. Smith, did not comply with the Code of Ethics regarding confidentiality and security principles when he delivered the budget for the upcoming year to the potential buyer.

Colleague? → Think of Code of Conduct/of Ethics

The examples above illustrate how theoretical concepts are applied to the particulars of the case.

THE PROFESSIONAL COMPETENCE OF "INTEGRATION" IS SHOWN.

It is also possible to flesh out the essential ideas put forth. The definition of "normalized earnings", for example, is briefly referred to. As for causal relations, they are succinctly highlighted.

POINT OF VIEW

The observation of any proposed solution leads us to an important conclusion:

ONE MUST GRASP THEORY WHEN DRAFTING A CASE.

A candidate who, for example, does not remember that charitable donations are only deductible if made to registered organizations will not be able to provide an appropriate answer to this question.
In addition, one must know how to decide what the aspect involved in a given situation is. In the DFT case, for example, it is not the measurement of the cost of Zeus' inventory that is problematic, but rather the determination of the net realizable value (A13). The presence of a discussion of the first aspect cannot compensate for the absence of a discussion of the second.

One must identify the notions and theoretical concepts that apply to the case.

By way of conclusion, there are manners of proceeding or "techniques" that can help you improve your performance in the drafting of cases. However, they cannot make up for the lack of knowledge. In Part 10, we will revisit the issue of remembering notions and concepts with a view to promoting your success.

Fleshing out relevant ideas

You must learn to flesh out the relevant and new ideas contained in the proposed solution. Since the latter is drafted in the form of continuous text, and presented as a professional report, it is normal that the writing style will be fancier, and even lengthier. One must, therefore, reach a point where one is able **to identify the ideas that can be taken into account by the person grading the answer** in his or her assessment thereof.

The next page contains two examples where the relevant and new ideas of a proposed solution are underlined with a simple line. The drafting exercise appearing in the right-hand column is intended to flesh out the ideas in a more succinct manner, using an efficient drafting style.

POINT OF VIEW

Of course, there are other ways of fleshing out the relevant and new ideas appearing in an official solution. Some candidates will instead place each idea in brackets or put a checkmark in front of each of them. If it is possible to alter the text of the solution using word processing software, some candidates will remove the words, sentences or, more rarely, paragraphs that are useless. As a result, they end up with a series of ideas that they are better able to analyze.

The drafting exercise appearing in the right-hand column on the next page is not always easy to perform, especially when one is at the stage of one's first case simulations. However, I urge you to train by doing these exercises **in order to improve your ability to write a greater number of ideas in the same time frame**.

RELEVANT AND NEW IDEAS

↓

PASSING STANDARD

EXAMPLES OF RELEVANT AND NEW IDEAS EXCERPTED FROM A PROPOSED SOLUTION

Relevant ideas – identified by underlining – contained in the proposed solution	Efficient drafting of the ideas appearing in the proposed solution
Cash flows of LCA Ltd.: Over the past two years, LCA Ltd. has experienced significant losses on its ordinary activities. In 20X4, the losses amounted to 3.58 million dollars (5.88 million dollars in 20X3). However, net income was 1,94 million dollars and, even more important, the net cash outflows from operating activities were 1,19 million dollars (30 million dollars in 20X3). This means that the cash position is improving and that it is far less than the operating losses set out in the income statement. The cash flows from operating activities are an important aspect to take into consideration in the assessment of LCA Ltd.'s ability to continue as a going concern. The new share issue contemplated for 20X5 will have the effect of improving cash flows, but only in the short term.	**LCA cash flows:** – Oper. losses have been IMP for 2 years (X4: -3.58 and X3: -5.88). However, pos. net income of 1.94 in X4. – Imp. to consider cash flows from oper. in the assessment of LCA's ability to continue as a going concern. – Positive pt: cash flows from oper. improving for 2 years (X4: -1.19 and X3: -30). In X4, cash outflows (-1.19) are less than oper. losses (-3.58). – Share issue in X5 to improve cash, but only in ST.
Research and Development – Ares (A14-A15) "The abandoned development of the Ares product would normally indicate the need for a writedown. Under IAS 38, *Intangible Assets*, the conditions for recognizing an intangible asset include the technical feasibility of and intention to complete the intangible asset so that it will be available for use or sale, and the probability it will generate future economic benefits. These conditions must be met at a point in time, such as when evaluating the project. Although the related development may be at least partially transferable to the new product, Hades, DFT clearly has no intention of continuing with Ares. At some point in time there would need to be an assessment of Hades to determine whether the conditions of IAS 38 are met. It would not be possible to link the Ares costs to the Hades project, unless some of the costs had been identified as applying to both projects when first initiated. As a result, the related development costs of $450,000 should be written off. The write-off results in an increase in expenses of $450,000."	**Depreciation of dev costs – Ares** (past → future) – One can assume that the criteria for capit. (e.g.: technical feasibility, intention to complete) were previously met, since the amount of $450,000 was recognized as an asset. – However, no longer any future economic benefits for the Ares product, since DFT decided to discontinue its development. – Manager believes that the development can be leveraged for the Hades product, but this is uncertain. – Nothing implies that the deferred costs are common to both products. They should have been identified as such from the outset. (Ares → Hades) CONC: Write-off dev costs to $0 Record an expense of $450 (reduces EBITDA)

Observations: In the right-hand column, the sentences are complete, essentially written in the present tense. The ideas are expressed clearly, precisely and directly. There are not really any useless words. The abbreviations are kept to a reasonable number. The use of brackets is very useful to specify, for example, that this is a loss situation. The integration of the theoretical concepts to the case facts is constant. Finally, the conclusions are clearly indicated. The use of bullets (–) highlights the various ideas. However, it is not necessary to proceed in this manner in the answer.

Until now, you have understood the ideas appearing in the solution, connected them to the case facts, called upon theoretical concepts and identified the relevant ideas.

Also highlight the manner in which the ideas are expressed.

part 3 page 36

Personally, all throughout the reading of the proposed solution, I highlight the following items:

- *the justification for an idea, a problem, an issue, a topic, a conclusion or a recommendation.* To this end, I underline, among others, the following words: "because", "since", "in order to", "as", "given that", "due to", "based on", "in light of". In so doing, one notices that a great many ideas contained in the proposed solution can be explained in this manner.

  The word "BECAUSE ..." greatly facilitates the integration of ideas to the case.

- *the reference to the impact or consequence.* In this respect, I underline, among others, the following words: "therefore", "I recommend / I conclude", "as a result", "then", "hence", "and so?". The places where the impact is expressed in numbers are also flagged.

  The word "THEREFORE" is a constant reminder that one must adequate complete any analysis.

- *the concrete explanation of what must be done.* In this respect, I flag the places where answers, among others, are provided to the following questions: "How can one go about this?", "What is the suggested action to be taken?", "Who?", "What?", "When?", "How much?", "Where?".

POINT OF VIEW

All of the above comments apply equally to the quantitative analysis and to the qualitative analysis. One must take the time **to understand the calculations set out in any proposed solution**. When performing this activity, here is a list of questions to be answered.

- What is the usefulness of the calculation in light of the resolution of the problems or issues?

  E.g.: The objective is to recalculate the EBITDA based on the accounting adjustments in order to determine if the target of $14M used in the calculation of the bonuses has been met.
- What are the assumptions made and why?

  E.g.: The estimated life of DFT's products is three years or less. (A18)
- What are the means used or the steps followed in the performance of the calculation?
- What is the source of the information used?

  N.B.: One must distinguish the figures provided directly in the case from those generated as a result of the analysis.
- How was the result that was arrived at integrated to the qualitative analysis?

  E.g.: The calculation of the adjusted net income or of the adjusted EBITDA is used more than once in the proposed solution. It forms an integral part of the analysis of management's bias in the selection of accounting policies (A33 and A34) and is also used to justify the need for reducing materiality (A23).
- What are the important components, as well as those of lesser importance? How can one submit a reasonable and appropriate calculation within the restricted time frame allotted for resolution of the case?

  E.g.: refer to the discussion in Part 6 (pp. 73 and 74)
- Is it possible to reconcile the result arrived at in another manner, by using the indirect method, for example?

  E.g.: refer to the discussion in Part 6 (p. 81)

Examine the components of the solution

Beyond understanding the ideas contained in the proposed solution, as previously explained, I suggest that you examine how it is structured.[1]

Take a step back.

Get an overall picture of what has been presented to you.

Here are examples of what you could look at.

- *The sequencing of the topics.* One must make sure that one understands, at least ex post facto, the positioning of each of the topics, in light of the particulars of the case. Try to determine what represents a "reasonable" answer based on the proposed solution. I also suggest that you draw up an "ideal" outline of an answer to the case, within the allotted time frame. What are the topics that must absolutely be tackled? And how much time does one have to analyze the various problems or issues?

Item to look at	Examples (DFT case)
Sequencing of topics Must the resolution of one topic precede that of another?	– PRIOR to determining if inventory should be included in the cost of sales in net income, one must determine when revenues are recognized. (A11, A12) – One must know if the research and development costs will be recognized as an asset PRIOR to tackling the topic of amortization. (A13)

- *The systematic approach of the analysis.* The abbreviation "ID" can indicate the topic to analyze. As well, as appears frequently in Appendix A, one can highlight the critical aspect or the intended objective. To me, it appears to be especially important to determine what lies at the heart of any analysis ("ANAL/EVAL"). What should one do? Any conclusion ("CONC"), opinion or recommendation ("REC") must stand out.

Item to look at	Examples (DFT case)
Steps in the approach (or aspects considered) What is the analytical logic?	– R&D Ares/Hades: Critical aspect: criteria to capitalize – writing-down 1- expenses allocated to Ares product only 2- transfer of costs to Hades product N.B.: The drafting example at p. 92 clearly fleshes out the presence of these two aspects. – As part of the analysis of the impact on management's bonuses of the adjustments to DFT's EBITDA, one must explain how the financial data was manipulated. One must first know how such a manipulation can happen, then explain, using examples taken from the DFT case, what happened with respect to the $14M target. (A33, A34)

1 This activity can, of course, be performed – at least in part – while any of the other activities previously described are ongoing.

- *The presentation of the proposed solution.* The purpose is to take note of different and efficient ways of presenting ideas.

Item to look at	Examples (DFT case)
Presentation of ideas Is there a more efficient way of presenting the answer?	– Table titled "Procedures and Planning for Key Risk Areas Identified". (A25) – Listing of the various ways of manipulating financial data. (A34) N.B.: This is a "LIST OF…", along with examples taken from the DFT case.

PROPOSED SOLUTION

↓

REASONABLE ANSWER

↓

PASSING STANDARD

Analyzing The Evaluation Guide[1]

The assessment of the performance of a candidate in a case is closely related to the competencies he or she must demonstrate. Each evaluation guide, therefore, contains a list of competencies (or assessment opportunities), most of the time assessed on an individual basis in light of their own criteria. Their name and number vary in light of the particulars of each case. One can understand, for example, that the assessment opportunity Finance appears in the evaluation guide of a case where the client is wondering "what selling price to ask for in order to recover all his direct costs". Similarly, the competency Assurance can appear twice in the same case, for two different aspects. Of course, since the grading criteria are generally presented in a succinct text that only indicates the major assessment criteria, one must regularly refer to the proposed solution.

It is crucial to find the justification for each component of the evaluation guide.

For each of the components to be assessed, the guide specifies the requisite criteria for achieving each of the various levels (or categories) of performance. With such a measurement scale, achieving a given level usually implies that all the requisite criteria for the lower levels have been met. Note, as well, that the assessment criteria are usually expressed in such a way as to enable the person grading the answer to reward any relevant and new idea. In other words, as part of the case parameters, two candidates may achieve the passing standard by submitting different answers. For example, in the DFT case, the "Competent" level requires, among others, a discussion of some of the audit procedures (A31). It goes without saying that various combinations of the procedures set out in the proposed solution can make up an appropriate answer. We will revisit this point in Part 8.

1 Appendix A illustrates how to analyze the evaluation guide for the DFT case (A21-A22, A31-A32, A35-A36, A39).

POINT OF VIEW

It appears to me to be clearly preferable to adopt a constructive attitude towards the evaluation guide. However, I know that some candidates are quick to criticize its contents, making statements like: "If the guide had been done properly, I would have been successful in the case!" or: "Insufficient importance was given to management in this guide; they do not understand the situation!".

THIS IS A WASTE OF TIME.

One must try to understand and explain

– HOW and WHY –

in order to avoid repeating the same mistakes from one case to the next.

When examining an evaluation guide, the first step is to **look at the structure**. Hence, one focuses on the organization of the guide by noting, first of all, the various competencies assessed. In light of the previous analysis of the proposed solution, one must make sure one understands the presence of each of the competencies (or assessment opportunities) contained therein and, under certain circumstances, that one is able to justify their absence. You will notice, for example, that ethical considerations are sufficiently important to represent a separate competence. Incidentally, one must constantly flesh out the nexus between the case facts (including the parameters), the proposed solution and the evaluation guide.

Analytical objective	Examples of observations
Establish the **nexus** between the structure of the proposed solution and the evaluation guide.	– Besides referring to a deficiency and its impact on the governance of the entity, the proposed solution contemplates one or two improvements for each of them. It will not be surprising to note that the passing standard requires the presence of solutions that eliminate or mitigate the deficiencies identified. – The proposed solution constantly mentions the impact of the treatment of the accounting issues on the EBITDA. To achieve a passing standard, one must, therefore, refer to the impact on the financial statements or on the bonus calculation – qualitatively or quantitatively –, at least for the important topics. (A21)

Thereafter, one must make sure that one **understands how each of the assessment criteria applies**. As with the analysis of the proposed solution, I remind you that it is vital to find the justification as well as the meaning of each component of the evaluation guide. In my opinion, none of them must be neglected, even if you believe it is a point that is too complex or that does not appear important to you. Some candidates sometimes skip over such and such part of the evaluation guide on the grounds that they completely blew it or, conversely, that they breezed through it. The examination of an evaluation guide is not only intended to assess an answer. The outcome is not the only thing that matters.

A GOOD UNDERSTANDING OF THE BASIS OF THE ASSESSMENT PROCESS PROMOTES THE DEVELOPMENT OF YOUR ABILITY TO IDENTIFY WHAT IS IMPORTANT.

POINT OF VIEW

Many observations made during the analysis of a case ought to be kept for future reference.
I will revisit the manner of recording your observations in Parts 9 and 10.

Analytical objective	Examples of observations
Pay attention to the **words used** in order to be able to explain each criterion in the evaluation guide. The action to be performed has its own meaning: "address", "assess", "attempt to", "calculate", "compare", "discuss", "estimate", "explain", "identify", "prepare", "provide", "recognize", "reconcile", "restate", etc.	– Merely **addressing** the choice between selling the assets or the shares allows the candidate to barely avoid achieving the lowest assessment level. To achieve the level just below the passing standard, one must tackle either of the two choices by putting forth a few relevant arguments. – **Recognizing** the potential for management bias toward a higher EBITDA allows one to achieve the level "Reaching competence". To achieve the passing standard ("Competent" level), one must **discuss** this bias in light of the adjustments to be made to the financial statements. (A35)
Identify the **interrelations** between the sections.	– One must determine the sale price of the business before calculating, for comparative purposes, the tax consequences of the sale of the shares or assets. Without this connection, it is impossible to achieve the passing standard in the Taxation competence. – There is an undeniable nexus between the critical aspect of the accounting issue and the objective of the audit procedures to be performed. (A25 to A30)
Noticing the use of two conjunctions – **and** – **or** – in several locations.	– To achieve the passing standard, one must analyze the various options open to a financially troubled entity wishing to continue as a going concern – **and** – examine possible courses of action to rectify the situation. – How the Assurance competence in the DFT case was graded clearly shows this aspect. The "Reaching competence" level can be achieved in one of three different ways (A31, A32). A candidate who submits a weak answer in either one **or** the other of the two parts of the requirement can, therefore, achieve this level. However, to achieve the "Competent" level, one must provide a reasonable answer to **both** of the parts of the requirement.

One must understand what to do to achieve the passing standard.

When you examine the contents of an evaluation guide, I suggest that you PAY PARTICULAR ATTENTION TO ANYTHING THAT CAN MAKE A DIFFERENCE BETWEEN SUCCEEDING AND FAILING.[1] One must be able to identify, in a reasonable manner, what the ideas are that are necessary to achieving each of the competencies set out in the guide successfully. It is also noteworthy that most of the answers submitted by candidates fluctuate between the level just below the passing standard ("Reaching competence") and the passing standard ("Competent"). Consequently, one must pay particular attention to the assessment criteria for these two levels. I urge you, of course, to aim for a level above the minimum passing standard. From this point of view, an examination of the requisite criteria for achieving the upper level ("Competent with distinction") must also be performed. Who knows? One of these criteria may be a crucial criterion for achieving success in the next case.

Analytical objective	**Examples of observations**
Identify the presence of a **decisive**, **crucial** or **unusual** assessment **criterion**.	– The passing standard requires an analysis of the advantages **and** disadvantages of the **three** financing options. N.B.: Since more than two options must be analyzed – which does not occur very frequently –, one must review the case facts in order to understand why this is so. – The "Competent with distinction" level requires the candidate to acknowledge the fact that certain events beyond DFT's control, such as Indo-Tech taking inventory out of the warehouse, could make a difference between the payment or non-payment of bonuses to management. (A21) N.B.: Any section of the guide focusing on professional skills/enabling competencies (e.g.: A33 to A36) must be meticulously analyzed.
Examine the requisite **graduation** criteria from one assessment level to the next.	– To achieve the "Reaching competence" level, one must **identify some** tax issues, and then **discuss one** of the **important** issues. To achieve the passing standard, one must **discuss some** – more than one – tax issues. – The passing standard requires an analysis of **some significant** accounting issues. To achieve the upper level ("Competent with distinction"), one must perform an analysis of **several significant** accounting issues. (A21)
Consider the **comments on the performance** of the candidates or the comments from the persons grading the answers.	– "The candidates did not provide any discussion on the level of assurance that could meet the requirements of the users". Observation: In other words, one must consider these requirements to achieve the passing standard. – "... strong responses included a more thorough discussion of the procedures and a concise explanation as to why they would be required." (A30) Observation: In other words, the procedure to be performed must derive from the risks identified.

1 The achievement of the various analytical objectives of an evaluation guide can result from an individual analysis of each of them or from a joint analysis of all of them together.

Part 8
Assessing The Performance Of An Answer

Distinguishing Relevant And New Ideas
Determining The Performance Level Achieved
Appreciating One's Performance

"The challenge is to correctly assess a case response, without under-evaluating or over-evaluating it."

Part 8
Assessing The Performance Of An Answer

The assessment of the performance of an answer takes place once the analysis of the proposed solution and of the evaluation guide is complete. From the outset, I would like to draw your attention to two things. First, the proposed or official solution of the case is an "excellent answer", nearly perfect, if not outright so. It easily achieves the passing standard – or the higher level – in all primary competencies. All the topics are analyzed, be they important or of lesser importance, and the calculations made are complete, as if there were no time constraints. No important item has been omitted. It goes without saying, for example, that a candidate cannot compete with the proposed solution of the DFT case (A9 to A36) in only 70 minutes!

ONE MUST DETERMINE
WHAT IS NECESSARY TO ACHIEVING THE PASSING STANDARD.

Secondly, a candidate must adopt a constructive attitude towards his or her own answer. The goal is to determine the value of the ideas written down, in a given time frame. HIGHLIGHTING YOUR STRENGTHS AND WEAKNESSES IS A CRUCIAL STEP IN THE IMPROVEMENT PROCESS.

Distinguishing Relevant And New Ideas

When marking or assessing your answer to a case, you must, first of all, bring out the ideas that are appropriate, namely those that are relevant and new. As discussed in the previous parts, ideas falling outside the case parameters are not relevant (or are, at most, secondary). For instance, the DFT case requires a listing of procedures to be performed. Where the inventory has made its way to India, a relevant procedure would be to "...confirm with Indo-Tech what it believes the amount in the warehouse is..." (A27). On the other hand, explaining what physical controls ought to be implemented for this inventory would not be relevant. Improvements to internal controls are quite simply not part of the requirement. Ideas must also be conveyed in the appropriate context. One cannot, for example, read an idea written under the issue Financial risk as if it formed part of the issue Audit risk, and *vice-versa*. Remember, as well, that repetitions, introductions or case summaries are not new ideas.

It happens on occasion that an idea that is relevant and new is not expressly mentioned in the proposed solution. A candidate may certainly, for instance, put forth an audit procedure that does not appear in the list supplied in the official solution (A25 to A30). However, as one knows, evaluation guides are usually sufficiently flexible to allow for a consideration of such ideas. Do not lose sight, however, of the fact that the essence of what needs to be said on a topic appears in the proposed solution.

An idea put forth within the framework of the case parameters is an appropriate idea.

I suggest that you start by first highlighting the ideas in your answer that will be taken into consideration in the assessment. Also refer to the part of the evaluation guide – problem or issue, assessment opportunity, indicator, or competency assessment criterion, etc. – to which they relate.

It is not always easy to know when an idea conveyed is considered appropriate. A sentence written during a simulation is rarely identical to any appearing in the official solution to a case. The ideas in a candidate's answer are also often incomplete or poorly stated.

The question arises as to whether the idea written down has the same meaning as the one conveyed in the proposed solution, even if the words used are not the same.

EXAMPLES OF IDEAS THAT MAY (OR MAY NOT) BE TAKEN INTO ACCOUNT IN THE ASSESSMENT

Idea set out in the proposed solution	**Idea put forth by the candidate and NOT accepted in the assessment**	**Idea put forth by the candidate and accepted in the assessment**
"Any indication that a cheque has been forged must be investigated."	"All cheques issued must be examined."	"Cheques on which the name or amount have been changed must be given closer scrutiny."
The principal idea relates to the fact that forged cheques were issued and must, therefore, be subjected to a specific investigation.	The idea of investigating the forged cheques is not there, since the reference is to all cheques whatsoever. The idea of examining the cheques is good, but not sufficiently adapted to the circumstances.	The idea of investigating the forged cheques is there, since the candidate specifically defines what he or she is looking for. The important idea is therefore stated.
"A statement of cash flows will have to be submitted to the bank."	"The bank will have to be notified of the financial situation."	"A statement of receipts and disbursements will have to be submitted to the creditor."
The principal idea relates to the statement of cash flows. The candidate must show that he or she has understood the relevance of this information for the bank.	The idea of cash flows is absent. The expression "financial situation" is imprecise. The idea of providing the information to the bank is valid, but it is not the most important aspect.	The expression "receipts and disbursements" is an acceptable synonym for "cash flows". The important idea is therefore stated. Referring to the creditor instead of the bank makes no difference.
"The predecessor auditor must be contacted regarding the dispute."	"The previous auditor must be contacted and any critical issue must be discussed with him."	"The previous auditor must be contacted and his position regarding the intangible assets must be discussed."
The principal idea relates to the dispute. The candidate must demonstrate that he or she understands the need to discuss it with the predecessor auditor.	The idea of discussing a current dispute is absent, since the expression "any critical issue" refers to nothing in particular. The idea of contacting the auditor is valid, but it is not sufficiently justified.	When referring to the position of the previous auditor regarding the intangible assets, the candidate directly refers to the dispute. The important idea is therefore present.

Observation: The use of synonyms is acceptable, so long as the principal idea is set out in the text.

POINT OF VIEW

When assessing their answer to a case, some candidates do not sufficiently distinguish between **what they know, what they thought** and **what they wrote**. I constantly run into candidates who claim to have successfully completed a case ... without having even re-read their own answer! They base the determination of the outcome solely on the "memory" of what they did during the simulation! In proceeding in this fashion, the candidate often overestimates his or her grade or leaves room for excuses to justify a poor performance such as: "This is what I wanted to say ...", "I thought about it, but I forgot to write it down ..." or "I'll be sure to write it down next time!".

It goes without saying that I do not endorse this manner of proceeding. First of all, it seems to me to be difficult to remember everything one wrote down. Secondly, it is frequently the case that the idea written down does not convey the thought clearly enough. Knowing an idea and knowing how to express it appropriately are two different things. Finally, the interpretation of such a result, which is lacking in objectivity, is not particularly useful. During the official assessment of a case, the candidate does not have the opportunity of explaining what he or she meant, of supplementing his or her ideas or of demonstrating the entire scope of his or her knowledge to the person grading the answer.

Only the ideas that are written down will be assessed, regardless of what the candidate thought or knew.

When identifying the relevant and new ideas in your answer, I suggest that you emphasize any potentially useful comment. For instance, one can pick up on what is missing to complete an idea, cross out any useless wording, establish causality, draw a diagram or observe that the conclusion is too general. In this respect, using the "Track Changes" feature of a word processing software is especially helpful.

EXCERPT OF A CANDIDATE'S COMMENTS ON THE ANSWER

DFT CASE

grant for R + D
↓
so discuss both!

800K grant

useless intro

- The grant applies directly to research expenses incurred.

  I must determine if the acct is correct, since they were directly recognized as revenues.

  Misidentified problem!
  What needs to be analyzed is the grant, not the R&D acct.

- The acct of the grant must only take place if the business is sure to comply with the 6 requisite criteria. THEORY

- 1- A grant can be record either by setting up the grant as deferred income or by deducting the grant in arriving at the carrying amount of the asset. OK

incomplete impact ↓ think EBITDA!

- Since 2- the grant has been directly made for development costs that have been rec as assets, and therefore meet the 6 criteria, 3- the grant must be deducted from assets so that reality is fairly presented to users. GENERAL

  credit OK
  debit?

  PROC: Obtain the grant agreement in order to validate compliance with its terms and therefore ensure proper acct treatment. OK

N.B.: there are three relevant and new ideas in the Accounting section (1-, 2-, 3-), one idea in the Audit section.

Here is a list of abbreviations or symbols that can be used in order to facilitate the analysis of your answer, or to speed up the marking of one of your colleagues' answers.

- "b/c" (because) for the justification of an idea. It is useful to flag the existence, but especially the lack, of any such justification.
- "CONC" for conclusion and "REC" for recommendation. The intent is to designate ideas that are overall comments or actions to be taken. One could also use the word "therefore".
- "cont" for contrary or contradictory. With this, one flags those places where the candidate contradicts an idea previously put forth.

POINT OF VIEW

Candidates often wonder if writing a "wrong" idea is prejudicial during the assessment of an answer. For example, a candidate might write something like: "You have no need to borrow, because your retained earnings balance is very high.". However, as we know, this balance has next to nothing to do with cash flow levels.

First of all, one must recognize that we are all somewhat nervous when we simulate a case. It happens to everyone – even candidates who achieve the superior performance level – to write an idea, let us say, that is a little strange.
One must appreciate, as well, that the presence of one or two unfortunate ideas will not truly throw off the assessment of the person grading the answer, who will just not take them into consideration.

However, if the number of these odd ideas shows that the candidate is lacking in knowledge or professional judgment, this will probably influence the assessment of the opportunity in question.

- "INC" for incomplete. With this, one can indicate that the analysis is not sufficiently in-depth, that an idea is incomplete, or that the argument is overly subtle.
- "+/–" for more or less clear or accurate or "W" for "*weak*". These allow you to flag ideas that will likely not be considered in the assessment, due to a lack of specifics or consistency.
- "GEN" for "general" or "dump" for "*dumping*" of theory without any application to the case specifics. As you already know, one must simultaneously integrate the theory to the case.
- "Ⓡ" for repetition of the same idea. An idea that is repeated, even using different words, is not taken into account twice in the assessment.

POINT OF VIEW

Each competence must be subjected to an individual assessment.
A candidate may very well be successful in the Finance competence, but experience a lot of difficulty with the Governance and strategy competence, or *vice-versa*.

One must pay attention to the context in which the ideas are written in order to identify which part of the evaluation guide they relate to.

- "+" or "pro" and "–" or "con" can be used to flag arguments that are advantages or disadvantages. This simplifies the assessment by showcasing the contents and balance of the arguments put forth in the analysis.
- 1-, 2-, 3-, etc. or a, b, c, etc. These annotations are used to indicate the number of ideas (e.g.: audit procedures) or the number of arguments put forth on a given topic (e.g.: p. 102).
- "NP" or "N/A" for "not pertinent" (irrelevant) or "not applicable". This means that the idea, the sentence, the paragraph or the page is useless, in light of the case parameters.

Determining The Performance Level Achieved

Most evaluation guides succinctly set out the criteria to meet for each of the categories of performance. Where the guide is very summary in nature, it is not easy to dig out a *modus operandi*. One must then determine what is sufficient, if not "reasonable", for achieving each competence. A little earlier (Part 7, p. 92), I set out an exercise in order to flesh out relevant and new ideas from the proposed solution. This is definitely useful here. Generally speaking, to achieve the passing standard, one can say that a candidate must have written in his or her answer a majority – if not all – of the important ideas appearing in the proposed solution. This is the measuring stick by which to determine the level of depth required.

With a view to determining as accurately as possible what is required to achieve the passing standard, I suggest two steps. One must, first of all, have on hand the list of topics or aspects included in a given assessment opportunity or indicator, ranked in order of importance. Then, one must make sure that one has fleshed out the analytical approach followed (ID/P – ANAL/EVAL – CONC/REC) for the resolution of each of them.

One must identify the critical aspects and key concepts, and then flesh out the steps, if need be.

The passing standard requires the appropriate consideration of what is fundamental to the analysis.

APPROACH TO THE DRAFTING OF THE "MATERIALITY" TOPIC IN THE DFT CASE

MATERIALITY (A23, A24)

ID:	determine if the preliminary calculation of materiality is still appropriate
ANAL:	assess the need for revising the materiality
	– impact of the accounting adjustments on net income / EBITDA
	– users: reliance by management for purpose of the bonus calculation
REC:	revise materiality / set separate materiality on some areas / revisit materiality after year-end

Although it is not necessary to submit an answer as complete as the proposed solution, one must nevertheless consider the nature and number of ideas contained in it. For the "Materiality" topic, two aspects appear in the analysis: the impact of the accounting adjustments AND increased reliance on the part of the users, in this case management, on EBITDA. It is clear that a certain depth of analysis is required. In my view, a "reasonable" answer must at least cover each of these two important aspects. While it is true that a good analysis of one aspect could make up for a certain weakness in the analysis of the other, I remain adamant in my position that both aspects must be tackled for the "Materiality" topic to be considered successfully dealt with. In other words, merely stating that "The materiality must be lowered in light of the new bonus program based on EBITDA." is insufficient.

For each of the topics or each of the parts of a given competence (assessment opportunity), I suggest that you answer the following question by YES or NO:

"Have I written a reasonable number of relevant and new ideas on the crux of the topic?"

If in doubt, refrain from answering "yes".

Where all the important topics and aspects have been assessed individually, one must then take a step back and consider the entire requirement in the given assessment section. Personally, when I am asked to grade a competence involving the analysis of several topics or aspects, I prepare a succinct performance report.

REPORT ON THE ASSESSMENT OF THE "ASSURANCE" COMPETENCE IN THE DFT CASE

Assessment Opportunity: Audit and Assurance (A23 to A32)

√ : succeed

AUDIT PLANNING:	ID	ANAL (theory/case)	CONC
– Materiality	√	____	√
– Risk Assessment	√	√	√
– Approach	√	____	

PROCEDURES TO BE PERFORMED:	Assertion/Risk(s)	Procedure(s)
– NRE — revenue	____	____
– Indo-Tech — revenue	√	____
– Indo-Tech — inventory	√	+/–
– Government funding	____	____
– R&D — ARES	√	____
– R&D — ZEUS	____	____
– Zeus — inventory	√	√
– GST/HST audit	____	____
– Impairment — equipment	____	____

The Audit and Certification (Assurance) issue in the DFT case includes two parts: the planning of the audit and the procedures to be performed. Thereafter, based on the proposed solution, a list of topics that can be analyzed appears. The most important topics/aspects are highlighted in blue.

Being able to have a comprehensive picture of what has been successfully done or not, for a given competence makes the assessment of the performance easier.

In the above example, one observes from the outset that the candidate correctly identified most of the important and specific risks (or assertions). However, one can see that he or she was unable to determine what procedures needed to be performed. He or she neglected this part of the requirement or simply had difficulty articulating concrete and precise procedures.

However, such a report on the assessment must be used with discernment. **The assessment process is not the sum of a simple mathematical addition of the number of checkmarks obtained.** Those persons grading the answers often are faced with ideas that are "+/–" complete, "+/–" clear or "+/–" accurate. One must never forget that it is the "quality" of the candidate's answer that is taken into consideration. A candidate who provides very good procedures for two topics among the most important ought to achieve a better assessment that the one who provides a great many inappropriate procedures. Where the person grading the answer wonders if each of the procedures he or she is reading is sufficiently good to be considered, this no doubt has an influence on the final assessment.

EXCERPT OF THE ASSESSMENT OF THE "ASSURANCE" COMPETENCE IN THE DFT CASE

Assessment Opportunity: Audit and Assurance (A31, A32)

...

well done

Reaching competence — The candidate identifies some of the audit planning issues (materiality, risk, etc.) and attempts to develop audit [INC] procedures to address them [OK], OR discusses the audit planning issues, OR discusses some of the audit procedures.	43.0%
Competent — The candidate discusses some of the audit planning issues and some of the audit procedures. [INC]	48.3%

The two parts of the requirement are incomplete.

...

ASSESSMENT: "Reaching competence"

DFT CASE

The above excerpt taken from the DFT case – and the same would go for any other case – raises a very legitimate question. What is the meaning to ascribe to the word "some"? Besides, most candidates will ask themselves "How many procedures must one write down in order to achieve the passing standard?".

I will tell you outright that there is no set answer.

There are admittedly a minimum amount of procedures to provide, but one must take into account the circumstances. I can tell you that the procedures that matter are those that are concrete, precise and flow from specific and relevant risks. There are five significant risk areas. Personally, if I were grading this case, I would require about four "appropriate procedures" in three different sectors. However, a candidate submitting three excellent procedures instead of four could also achieve the passing standard. It is a matter of professional judgment.

The basic question is the following:

"Is the candidate demonstrating his or her competence sufficiently (in terms of quantity and quality) when analyzing the impact of the accounting issues on the procedures to be performed?".

Various combinations of procedures can enable a demonstration of this competence!

A good understanding of the proposed solution makes the application of the evaluation guide easier.

POINT OF VIEW

I regularly insist on the fact that one must focus more on the important problems, issues or topics. One might wonder how the relevant and new ideas on topics of lesser importance are considered in the assessment. By definition, they are worth less. Such ideas may contribute to success by supplementing or enhancing the quality of an answer. At most, they may warrant achievement of a performance level below the passing standard. The resolution of topics of lesser importance cannot, however, be a substitute for the need to develop important topics more in depth.

Ideas do not all carry the same weight or have the same value in the assessment.

IT IS ESSENTIALLY THE PERFORMANCE IN THE RESOLUTION OF IMPORTANT PROBLEMS OR ISSUES THAT DETERMINES SUCCESS IN A CASE.

I suggest that you start the assessment of the performance in an answer by examining the criteria for the level below the passing standard. Since the majority of candidates achieve at least this level, it is more encouraging. Then, after having fully understood the meaning of each of the criteria making up the passing standard, one can examine if they have been met. Personally, I underline any part that has been successfully completed or partially so, whether the passing standard has been achieved or not.

In the application of the evaluation guide, I also suggest that you do the following:

- ***take into account the objectives of the assessment opportunity – expectations.*** Most evaluation guides will state rather tersely what the indicator (or competence) basically wishes to measure. This allows for a quick determination of what is fundamental to success. For example, we could find a statement such as this: "The candidate is to advise his clients about tax planning opportunities." It is then clear the "opportunities" are what will be assessed. A candidate who, instead, refers to the tax consequences of the new transactions during the period cannot hope to achieve the passing standard for this particular competence.

- ***take into account the performance level in question.*** You already know that the passing standard ("Competent" level) is the critical, make-or-break level. It is most certainly wise to adopt a harsher attitude during the assessment of the criteria at that level. Ideas that are "+/–" clear or accurate, for example, will be given no, or very little, consideration. One can afford to be slightly more generous when assessing a lower level, but not when success in a competence lies in the balance.

Climbing from a lower to another level can be slightly easy to achieve.

Therefore, one must be strict in the assessment of the passing standard.

TO ACHIEVE THE PASSING STANDARD, YOUR ANSWER MUST OFFER ADDED VALUE.

Do the ideas put forth go beyond basic concepts?

Have you identified the critical or fundamental aspect at the heart of the analysis?

Does your answer contain sufficient depth?

A candidate who only states general ideas, who summarizes the case facts, who submits few ideas in his or her analysis, who lingers on aspects of lesser importance or who does not use appropriate concepts cannot hope for success in a competence.

In the application of the evaluation guide, I also suggest that you do the following:

- ***read the comments of the examiners and persons grading the answers***, where such information is available. Quite often, these comments clarify the evaluation guide by underscoring the weaknesses, omissions and errors of the candidates. For example, one might read as follows: "The candidates did not apply their knowledge to the specific context of a medical clinic." This mean that a candidate who submits an answer that is too general, that does no take into account the features specific to this type of entity, will likely not achieve the passing standard.

- ***take into account the performance of the other candidates***, where such information is available. In fact, and without prejudice, one must recognize that the performance of the other candidates has a certain influence on the assessment of your answer. For example, let us assume that most of the candidates did not pick up on the serious cash flow problem of the entity, whereas you dealt with the topic. The "value" of your ideas is enhanced as a result of the fact that few candidates thought of this problem. The reverse is also possible. In other words, the same idea, appearing in two different cases, will not necessarily carry the same value in the assessment.

POINT OF VIEW

Several candidates quite simply never go look at the criteria required to achieve the superior level. To them, the only thing that matters is the passing standard or they tell themselves "In any event, it is next to impossible to achieve!". Whether that is true or not doesn't mean that the exercise is pointless. Who knows? It may even be a criterion that is crucial for achieving the passing standard in the next case.

I have the same opinion in the event of a competence that is botched by most candidates. It would be useless for me to say: "Since no one tackled this competence, I don't need to study it."

The difficulty in achieving success in a competence does not detract from the usefulness of analyzing its contents.

QUALITY

+

DEPTH

↓

PASSING STANDARD

Appreciating One's Performance

Rightly so, the very first reflex of any candidate is to assess whether he or she was successful in the performance of the simulated case. It is undeniable that achieving the passing standard in the various competencies (assessment opportunities) of an evaluation guide demonstrates the quality of a performance. I would, however, like to remind you that drafting answers to cases is a continuous learning process that stretches out over several months. The results of the first simulations are usually weak. Not infrequently do candidates completely miss a competence, not target what is required or important, or outright forget relevant theoretical concepts!

I ask you to put your results in perspective, since the level of performance achieved does not reveal all. A successful simulation does not necessarily mean that one has understood everything and that it is useless to simulate other cases. It frequently happens that the passing standard is just barely achieved, sometimes a little inadvertently. **One should guard against excess optimism.** On the other hand, a weak grade does not mean that one knows nothing and that one will never be able to successfully complete a case. **This is being excessively pessimistic.** In fact, one should view one's result as a constructive message, with a dose of impartiality. The idea is to assess ideas and skills, not a person's value. Subtle difference.

POINT OF VIEW

I suggest that you **analyze the answer of all cases that you simulate**, whether or not you were successful. Of course, it is normal to conduct a more detailed analysis of cases that you found hard, especially if there are two or three in a row that threw you off. Do not, however, neglect the ones you were successful at.
Since there is always something that can be done better, their analysis will help you improve your future performances.

THERE ARE NEVER TWO IDENTICAL CASES:

EACH CONTAINS ITS SHARE OF SURPRISES AND NOVELTY.

In the appreciation of the performance of an answer, I suggest that you consider the following:

- *the specifics of the case.* Certain contexts, problems or issues are harder to resolve than others. From experience, I know that candidates find it more difficult to resolve a case dealing with non-profit organizations, for example. The same goes for unusual roles you are asked to play. Where one of the competencies of the case is difficult to identify or analyze, achieving a level below the passing standard may be a good result in and of itself.

- *the performance of the other candidates as well as the comments of the persons grading the answer.* Like it or not, the positioning vis-à-vis the group is an important benchmark in our field. For example, reading that "Candidates were generally able to provide clear and valid procedures to address the risks." (A30) is a piece of information to consider. A candidate who fails to answer appropriately this part of the requirement places the "Competent" level out of reach (review pp. 105 and 106).
  No doubt, one must progress in light of individual goals, but one must also aim for results that are above average.

➢ *your personal strengths and weaknesses.* Each case is unique and each individual has his or her own strengths and weaknesses. Hence, being personally comfortable when confronted with certain contexts, roles or topics may impact performance. A candidate may be very competent at auditing, but at a loss when asked to perform a review engagement, for example. In this situation, achieving the level just below the passing standard is not necessarily bad news. The reverse may be true for a colleague.

Once you have assessed the level of performance of each of the competencies of a case, I suggest you analyze your answer from various perspectives, examining what is included and what is missing. Candidates who have taken the time to annotate their answer while they are marking it, as suggested previously, already have a good idea of what can come out of this analysis. Seeing the word "general" appear at various locations, for instance, is indicative of a lack of integration. As for the abbreviation "REC", it is a reminder to the candidate that he or she found a way to adequately complete his or her analyses. I suggest you take the time to ask yourself questions with respect to each of the six themes corresponding to the first six parts of this volume.

The objective is to identify the weaknesses – as well as the strengths – of your answer in order to be able eventually to discover the means of mitigating or eliminating them.

EXAMPLES OF A PERFORMANCE ANALYSIS

Reading and annotating a case	*Were the case parameters properly identified from the outset?* E.g.: NOPE. The fact that the entity is running at near-peak production capacity is an inherent constraint in the analysis.

Was the outline of the answer properly prepared, and then followed? E.g.: +/–. Certain topics were analyzed in too great a level of detail regardless of their importance. An insufficient number of different topics were tackled.	**Planning the answer**

Drafting relevant ideas	*Are the theoretical concepts integrated to the specifics of the case?* E.g.: NOT ENOUGH! The relevant theoretical concepts are not sufficiently explicit (too many "Ws").

POINT OF VIEW

It is quite revealing **to calculate the number of relevant and new ideas in an answer**; not the number of sentences or paragraphs, but the number of ideas. If an answer contains, for example, only 8 or 9 "good" ideas, you will appreciate that it is difficult to successfully complete a 70-minute case. Of course, the number of ideas necessary to achieving the passing standard depends on the degree of difficulty of the case and on the quality of the ideas put forth. However, based on the proposed solution of the DFT case, to me, it seems difficult, if not impossible, to successfully complete this case without having submitted at least 25 to 30 "good" ideas. (Appendix A)

It is also interesting **to note where the relevant and new ideas appear**. A candidate could thus observe that, on average, he or she writes two good ideas per topic. That is not enough for important topics. He or she might also realize that a lot of time is wasted summarizing the case prior to analysis.

Did I waste time in the submission of my answer? E.g.: YES. The ideas are too often repeated (too many "Rs"), using synonyms.	**Drafting new ideas**

Expressing ideas efficiently	*Did I convey my ideas in succinct, but complete sentences?* E.g.: YES. Well-structured report. Organized presentation of the various topics.

Can the calculation be shown in a more efficient manner? E.g.: A WORK IN PROGRESS! The quantitative analysis is so detailed that the qualitative analysis was not completed. More balance is needed in the answer!	**Making proper calculations**

In the appreciation of the performance of an answer, the natural tendency is to shed light on "what went wrong". I suggest that you take the time **to flesh out the strengths AND the weaknesses**.

Personally, I start with the strengths, as a motivational tool. There are always some, regardless of the outcome. It is also a good idea to identify what has improved since the last time.

EXAMPLES OF "STRENGTHS TO REMEMBER"

- Excellent application of knowledge in the resolution of the Taxation issue.
- Less explicit problem of cash shortfall well identified from the outset.
- A few (or several) good integration links to the case facts.

The list of weaknesses identified during the analysis of an answer is often longer, especially for the first few case simulations.

One should focus more on the weaknesses that prevented achievement of the passing standard.

Draw up your list of weaknesses in the form of a listing of things to do during the next simulation. Thereafter, try to find how, concretely, you can improve the situation. What solution could counter such and such a weakness?, or, What exercise can one conduct in order to practice with a view to better resolving cases?

**It is not enough to "know what to do",
one must "be able to do it".**

EXAMPLES OF "WEAKNESSES TO BE IMPROVED"

- Provide fewer superfluous details in the list of arguments.

  Exercise: go through the text once more, striking out everything that is useless, and then calculate the number of ideas.

- Establish a proper sequencing of the topics, such as restating the income statement prior to commenting the financial performance of the company.

  Solutions: – take the time to plan the answer.
  – consider connections between topics.

- Provide greater depth for the most important topics.

  Exercise: add ideas to the current answer or rewrite certain parts of the case, within a restricted time frame, in order to grasp what an appropriate answer is.

WEAKNESS

SOLUTION / EXERCISE

POINT OF VIEW

It is stimulating and enriching to exchange answers between colleagues on a regular basis. Asking someone else to determine, and then to comment, the performance level achieved (e.g.: pp. 102 and 106), and offering in exchange to do the same for that person, leads to several advantages.

➢ *It allows one to become acquainted with a different manner of drafting.* The analytical approach of a colleague may be better structured or he or she may have a more effective drafting style. In addition, another candidate asked to grade your answer can point out his or her difficulty in understanding the ideas conveyed or in recognizing the figures used in the calculations.

➢ *The assessment is more objective.* When asked to assess their own answer, some candidates are either too harsh or too lenient. Instead, an independent person grades the answer and assesses what he or she sees written – BLACK ON WHITE – and not what the author of an answer knows or wanted to say. In this case, another person can raise different "Strengths to remember" and "Weaknesses to be improved".

N.B.: Where your answer is marked by someone else, I still suggest that you perform your own assessment so as to be able to compare the two results.

➢ *It allows for the constructive exchange of ideas.* Aside from grading an answer, the creation of a working group with a view to analyzing a proposed solution allows the candidates involved to exchange various points of view. The review of the case parameters, an understanding of the more complex aspects or the determination of what a reasonable answer is can be debated within a group format. In addition, a candidate might grade the answer to a case for all his or her colleagues, including his or her own, in order to better compare the various ways of successfully completing the same case. Each of the members of the group, in turn, could perform this exercise.

Part 9
Acquiring Knowledge And Experience

Fleshing Out The Fundamentals Of The Case(s) Simulated
Assessing One's Progress Over Time
Conducting A Comparative Analysis Of Simulated Cases

"There are no doubt weaknesses that I do not seek,
so I must at least take care of those that I do see."

© Deslauriers Sylvie, *Easy $uccess,* AB + Publications, 2012, page 20.

Part 9
Acquiring Knowledge And Experience

I consider that the resolution of cases is one of the biggest challenges in accounting studies. On the one hand, it requires the consideration of multi-subjects knowledge in a particular context, which context varies from one case to the next. On the other hand, the learning process extends over a long period, even several months, and ultimately leads to university exams or professional exams.

IT IS CRUCIAL TO DO A FOLLOW-UP OF CASES SIMULATED
IN ORDER TO CONSOLIDATE ONE'S ACHIEVEMENTS.

Fleshing Out The Fundamentals Of The Case(s) Simulated

In the process of learning through case resolution, one frequently returns to a case previously simulated. For instance, one would like to review how a topic was analyzed or one may wish to compare two different cases dealing with financially troubled entities. In this vein, taking a few minutes to flesh out the particular and decisive aspects of each of the simulated cases is time well spent. I, therefore, suggest that you collect your observations in a practical and succinct manner, in the same file, in order to be able to quickly track down the information you are looking for. Hence, one can rank the various cases simulated by category, according to the role to be played or the work to be performed.

"Case Information"

The following page sets out an example of what I call the "Case information" sheet. Of variable length, as needed, its contents are factual in nature, since it recalls the features of the case. The upper part contains basic information such as the **Date of the simulation** and the reference to the **Case** (name, origin or number). The **My Performance** section briefly indicates your results in each of the competencies of the simulation in relation to that achieved by the **Other Candidates** (if known).

The information sheet then sets out the case parameters: **Context**, **Role** and **Requirement**. The **Context** section lists the particulars of the case that impact the resolution of the problems or issues. It may list, among others, a key success factor, management's objectives or behavior, a policy of the entity or a constraint. The **Requirement** section more or less repeats sentences from the case specifying the work to be performed, as part of the **Role** to be played. To me, it is preferable to use the exact wording of the case in order to establish with the greatest possible objectivity the link with the proposed solution. In addition, as in the DFT case, one can highlight the fact that the auditor's role is "standard".

The **Structure of the solution** highlights the parts or steps involved in the resolution of certain problems or issues. In the example taken from the DFT case, it is stressed that the analysis of the procedures to be performed can be made using a table. Furthermore, one can flesh out the approach followed in the resolution (ID/P – ANAL/EVAL – CONC/REC) of unusual or more complex topics.

**Case information sheets recall
the fundamentals of the cases simulated.**

EXAMPLE[1] OF A "CASE INFORMATION" SHEET

Date of the simulation: 06/14/X2

Case: DFT (70 minutes)

My Performance:

Accounting: Competent (C)
Audit: Reaching competence (RC)
Enabling competencies: Reaching competence

Other Candidates: (A21, A31, A35)

RC: 36.7% — C: 61.5%
RC: 43.0% — C: 48.3%
RC: 16.0% — C: 52.9%

Context:

IFRS – bonus program – management's bias – technology company

Role:

Auditor – client acceptance procedures and initial audit planning completed

Requirement: "standard"

- ACCOUNTING (issues of significance)

  IAS 18: discount (single/linked transactions) – IAS 18: revenue recognition (transfer of risks and rewards of ownership, 60 days) – IAS 20: grants – IAS 2: inventories – IAS 38: research and development (writedown) – IAS 37: contingent asset (contingency) – IAS 16: impairment (equipment) – IAS 19, IAS 37: bonus (obligation)

- AUDIT (Y/E audit planning + procedures to be performed)

  Materiality (% NI, revision, performance, new users, unadjusted errors)
  Risk (new events, bonus program)
  Approach
  Procedures (occurrence, accuracy, completeness, cut-off, classification, valuation)

- LESS EXPLICIT REQUIREMENT — PROFESSIONAL SKILLS

  IMPACT of the adjustments and errors on management's BONUS
  (earnings manipulation, management's integrity)

- SECONDARY TOPIC (bonuses, compensation, balanced scorecard)

Structure of the solution:

Item	Assertion	Specifics Risks	Procedures

Analysis of management's bias:

ID: determine the existence of a potential bias on the part of management
ANAL: examine the accounting adjustments overall (manipulation)
CONC: reach a conclusion on management's conduct (impact)

Other observations:

MANAGEMENT BIAS: EBITDA > 14M

To be considered throughout the answer!

Public company: – IFRS (A9)
– presence of a Board of Directors (A34)
– management's compensation: stock options or shares (A38)

...

1 Many additional observations referred to in this volume could be added.

The last section of the Case information sheet allows for the addition of any **Other observation** arising from your personal analysis of the case. One could, for example, indicate any interrelations between the topics of the case, write down a reminder of an important criterion barring achievement of the passing standard (e.g.: impact of the accounting issues on the projected financial statements or on the calculation of the bonuses (A21), justification for the need to improve cash management), or refer to the repercussions of one case particular on the solution (e.g.: public company, combination with another organization within six months).

POINT OF VIEW

In filling out the Case information sheet, one must not lose sight of the fact that objective is to facilitate any potential revisiting of the simulated case. One must, therefore, be clear, concise and specific, and only note that which is essential. To this end, the example contained in the DFT case contains, among others, a reference to a standard underlying the analysis of each accounting issue. It also lists the aspects discussed as part of the Materiality topic.

The use of "key words" makes locating the information easier.

It is also preferable to rely on the same reference words from one case to the next, and, obviously, to choose words that are familiar to you. Some candidates will write down the word "provision", whereas others will prefer the expression "estimated liability". What is important is that it makes sense to the candidate. Incidentally, I suggest that, from your very first cases, you adopt a classification system that you find easy to apply and recognize.

Take the time to keep your Case information sheet up-to-date!

Besides preparing a Case information sheet, I also suggest that you reflect on your performance. As mentioned in Part 8, this is a crucial step in the process of improvement through practice.

"Case performance"

The next page gives an example of what I call the "Case performance" sheet. Of variable length, its contents are personal in nature, since it brings out the crucial aspects of your performance. This concise report enables you to gauge your progress over time in order to be able to set goals for improvement from one simulation to the next. Ranking these sheets in chronological order allows for a better follow-up.

From the outset, you should list the **Concepts requiring review**, because it often happens that not fully understanding theoretical concepts is prejudicial to the resolution of problems or issues. Thereafter, listing those **Simple ideas missed** will enable you to take stock of the appropriate level of language. The **Difficulties experienced** during the drafting process must be expressed in clear terms. A candidate may realize, for example, that he or she had trouble starting a calculation, and that he or she wasted precious time as a result. Resolving this difficulty may not be an easy thing to do, but recognizing it is already a good start. In fact, after simulating a case, always ask yourself the following question: "Where did I run into the most trouble?".

One of the significant aspects of this reflection is to flesh out the **Strengths TO REMEMBER** and the **Weaknesses TO BE IMPROVED**. Moreover, you can list in this report the means, exercises or tricks to implement in order to mitigate or eliminate any weakness observed. **Other observations** can also be added to this sheet, as needed. Finally, one can single out any **Outstanding Questions**, where some aspect of the proposed solution or of the evaluation guide, for example, has not been understood.

EXAMPLE[1] OF A "CASE PERFORMANCE" SHEET

Date of the simulation: 06/14/X2 | **Case:** DFT (70 minutes)

My Performance:

Accounting: Competent (C)
Audit: Reaching competence (RC)
Enabling competencies: Reaching competence

Other Candidates: (A21, A31, A35)

RC: 36.7% — C: 61.5%
RC: 43.0% — C: 48.3%
RC: 16.0% — C: 52.9%

Concepts requiring review:

IAS 18: separately identifiable components of a single transaction OR linked transactions

Simple ideas missed:

The grant! The case clearly indicates to which item (BS or IS) the grant relates. Easy to make the connection!

Difficulties experienced:

Allocation of time between topics. Too much time spent on accounting, not enough on audit.

Not obvious to identify the critical aspect to be discussed. E.g.: writedown of R&D or Zeus' inventory.

Strengths TO REMEMBER:

- All analyses end with a conclusion or a recommendation.
- The review of the audit planning takes into account NEW events.
- Good use of the case facts. Excellent integration.

Weaknesses TO BE IMPROVED:

- Better fleshing out of the important topics in order to have the time to provide a reasonable answer on each significant problem or issue.
- Learn to develop concrete and useful procedures. "Check if the $800,000 grant has been received" does not satisfy the audit risk specific to the situation.
- Properly identify the problem to be discussed (ID) before embarking on the analysis. With Indo-Tech, the problem is revenue recognition, not inventory!

Other observations:

Pay attention not to misread! The case describes the grant received for R&D without referring to a specific project or product. Therefore, do not assume that the grant relates to the Zeus product on the basis that this product is discussed in the previous paragraph, nor that it relates to the Ares product on the grounds that it is discussed in the following paragraph.

Do not question the fact that 75% of the costs are allocated to deferred R&D expenses!

It is important to identify and use appropriate accounting concepts in the analysis of the accounting issues. E.g.: "cut-off" in the recognition of revenues.

...

Outstanding questions:

Why discuss if DFT has a legal obligation or a constructive obligation to pay bonuses if it is clear that the EBITDA will be less than $14M?

---

1 Many additional observations referred to in this volume could be added.

POINT OF VIEW

By suggesting that you fill out a Case performance sheet, I basically want to bring home to you the need to take a step back to look at your performance. Some candidates take the time to fill out such a sheet – with even more details – whereas others go through this process in their mind.

What is important is to reflect on the performance, in an objective and constructive manner.

Assessing One's Progress Over Time

Following the analysis of each of your simulations, I suggest that you set improvement or learning goals for yourself. From experience, it appears that ideally one should establish no more than three objectives at a time. This allows for a better focusing of one's efforts.

ONE MUST BE REALISTIC IN THE DETERMINATION OF THE ASPECTS THAT REQUIRE IMPROVEMENT.

IT IS NOT POSSIBLE TO SOLVE EVERYTHING ALL AT ONCE.

What are the weaknesses hindering the improvement of your performance? What were the difficulties encountered during the simulation of the case? What prevented you from achieving the passing standard? In the determination of your goals, be aware that the weaknesses that you would like to mitigate are not of the same level of importance. Hence, understanding precisely what the words in the requirement mean or imply is definitely more important than curtailing the length of one's sentences. No doubt, one will eventually have to work on this latter aspect, but each thing in its own time.

POINT OF VIEW

The determination of objectives to attain requires both humility and detachment, while exhibiting a constructive attitude. One must, first of all, accept the fact that one cannot necessarily remember everything one has previously studied, that one may have difficulty applying one's knowledge at the right place or that one does not truly understand how to answer a case. It also happens that a weakness that does not show for two or three cases in a row will surface a little later on. This situation is not infrequent. For example, for no apparent reason, a candidate who had learned to submit recommendations that were more concrete may fail to do so in the next simulation.

It appears to me to be preferable to state the objective to aim for in the form of an action to undertake or to express with confidence the goal sought to be achieved. A sentence to the effect of "I am better at identifying audit procedures in light of the risks identified." is undeniably motivational. Incidentally, I suggest that you place such a sentence conspicuously on your message board or that you read your goals for improvement two or three times during the simulation of a case.

Persevere!, despite the stumbling blocks!

Once a candidate has a few simulations under his or her belt, it is normal that he or she would like to assess whether progress has been made. However, one must appreciate the fact that assessment though competencies makes this task difficult since a long time – sometimes several months – may elapse before a candidate is able to achieve the passing standard. It is not rare to witness a certain amount of progress for several simulations, followed by a period of stagnation.

It truly is not obvious to make a determination as to the existence of any improvement, even after several simulations.

In addition, each case is unique. The next case can come as a total surprise due to its contextual setting or the manner in which problems or issues are resolved. The drafting of an answer to a case is a slightly more complicated process than learning the technical aspects of a topic, such as the calculation of an exchange gain or loss. The ultimate success of a case simulation requires good training, which includes practicing cases and an objective assessment of each of one's performances.

POINT OF VIEW

THE LEARNING CURVE IN CASE RESOLUTION IS NOT THE SAME FOR EVERYONE.

Let us say that it is rather rare that progress will be regular or constant. For the majority of candidates, progress towards success takes place in increments. A series of cases where performance was mitigated will suddenly be followed by a certain degree of improvement. Then, a poor performance in the next case unfortunately shatters any idea of progress. In other words, a candidate may achieve – even comfortably – the passing standard in two cases in a row for the Assurance competence, for example, but achieve a lower level in the ensuing case. However, believe me when I tell you this, the achievements from previous simulations always end up bearing fruit.

The process is longer for some candidates, and shorter for others.

One should also recognize the fact that it is always possible to improve one's performance in case resolution. Achieving the passing standard at each assessment opportunity does not necessarily mean that everything is perfect.

There is and will ALWAYS be something that could be done better and it might make the difference in the next case.

Comparing one's performance from one case to the next allows for an identification of the contexts, roles or topics with which you experience greater difficulty. A candidate may realize, for instance, that he or she is not very successful in all cases involving a non-profit organization. Such a realization fuels the urgency of rectifying this weakness by reviewing the concepts specific to this type of entity and training to better apply them. Another candidate may realize that he or she is sloppy in his or her analysis of revenue recognition and thus canvass all cases containing this topic so as to study them all together.

One of the inherent features of assessment through competencies is that the number of levels of performance in the evaluation guide is not very high. In addition, as mentioned in Part 8 (p. 107), most candidates achieve either the passing standard, or the category immediately below. Consequently, it frequently happens that candidates have the impression of "stagnating" in the "Reaching competence" category for several months, and sometimes even all the way up to the official exam! It then becomes more difficult to remain motivated, especially when the candidate says that he or she is incapable of being "Competent". A consistent harping on the word "Competent" as an assessment criterion is pejorative in itself.

There are many different ways to assess any progress made in your performance. First, one could consider competencies as a whole and prepare a chart depicting your evolution towards success. One could, for example, place certain sections of the Case performance sheet in a comparative table that makes the profiles and trends stand out more.

One could also, for instance, calculate the following ratio per case, per group of cases or per period.

$$\frac{\text{number of assessment opportunities achieving the passing standard}}{\text{total number of assessment opportunities}}$$

The ratio thus arrived at ("Y" axis) would be placed in a chart containing each simulated case or group of cases ("X" axis), in chronological order.

Secondly, one could proceed to assess the progress achieved in the results, competence by competence or topic by topic. A candidate could focus more on those competencies deemed to be the most important, such as accounting and audit, or limit himself or herself to those that cause him or her more difficulty. For a given competence, this would, incidentally, enable him or her to compare the criteria of the evaluation guide for the various simulated cases.

By way of encouragement, I suggest you use a simple form of grading for those categories close to the passing standard, such as: low, medium or high. At times, there is very little difference between achieving a HIGH "Reaching competence" level and achieving a low "Competent" level.

EXCERPT FROM THE "RESULTS PER ASSESSMENT OPPORTUNITY" TABLE FINANCIAL REPORTING (ACCOUNTING)

Case	My Performance	My observations	My goals for improvement
BUMP 02/21/X2	RC – weak	– inappropriate presentation of the analysis. – difficulty in submitting my ideas in a structured manner.	→ review intangible assets! → submit my recommendations more clearly. Start with a verb in the infinitive!
MAX 05/3/X2	RC – average	– too long a summary of the standards. + proper and justified recommendations. – lack of time to deal with all important topics.	→ integrate simultaneously the theory to the case facts instead of summarizing in a separate paragraph. → minimize useless repetitions of the case.
DFT 06/14/X2	C – a bit weak	+ manner of analysis of a topic greatly improved! – imprecise as to the critical aspect to be discussed.	→ properly identify the problem (ID) before embarking on the analysis.

N.B.: The contents of the table vary from one candidate to the next, as needed.

POINT OF VIEW

Here is a testimonial from a candidate:

"For each simulated case, I followed up on my performance in respect of each of the assessment opportunities (or indicators) using software (*Excel*). This way, I was able to sort the data per competence. I especially highlighted those situations where I was below average or below the passing standard. This helped me a lot, because I was able to identify those competencies that were causing me more difficulty, and to observe my improvement over time. I was, therefore, able to step up efforts on critical aspects. Before doing all this, I could see that my results were adequate overall, but I could not clearly see where my weaknesses lay."

Finally, it is possible to imagine a table containing essentially a list of questions to be answered or a list of goals to meet. Each of the columns thereafter refers to a particular case, in chronological order. As the simulations pile up, the candidate, at least in the mid term, ought to be able to see improvement. As discussed previously in this volume, you will eventually have to identify the method you need to implement or the exercise you must perform in order to overcome any weakness you have identified or any goal you have not met.

WEAKNESS
↓
OBJECTIVE
↓
MEAN(S)

Telling oneself "I'll do better next time."

IS NOT AN OBJECTIVE THAT IS CONCRETE ENOUGH.

EXCERPT FROM THE TABLE "FOLLOW-UP ON LEARNING OBJECTIVES"

My goals for improvement	**BUMP** (02/21/X2)	**MAX** (05/3/X2)	**DFT** (06/14/X2)
Identifying all important problems or issues	no (2/4)	Nearly all	OK
Adequately allocating time between the various aspects or topics	+/–	Acceptable	NO! (audit section too short)
Not wasting time presenting calculations	fair (repeating figures from previous year is useless)	N/A	Waste of time explaining source of figures used
Integrating theoretical concepts to the case facts	NO (text too general)	BETTER	Well done (critical aspect better identified)
Not summarizing or repeating the case prior to the analysis	+/–	good	PERFECT!

N.B.: Do not hesitate to highlight what is going right. ***Account For Your Success!***

Conducting A Comparative Analysis Of Simulated Cases

Once you have completed several case simulations, it then becomes possible to compare the contents of one against the others **in order to highlight the similarities and differences**. Although the entire set of particulars of each case is unique, some contexts, roles, problems or issues resurface more than once. The objective of a comparative analysis of simulated cases is to take stock of what is repeated and what is distinctive, and why. There are reference points or rules of conduct, that are often implicit, and that must be recognized. The observations arising from any comparative analysis potentially ought to be kept so as to be re-read, augmented and remembered. We will revisit the creation of info-cards in Part 10.

Comparing roles

As discussed in Part 1, the role to be played determines the perspective from which the problems or issues are to be approached. It determines the personality or attitudes you are to take on, for the duration of the resolution of a case. In this vein, I suggest that you study the various roles assigned to you in the cases you have simulated. Let us, for example, take the typical cases that ask you, at least in part, to act as an external auditor. You will easily note that the accounting standards, the auditing standards, as well as the Code of conduct/of ethics are the basic reference materials. Unless told otherwise, you must refer to them and comply with them. It is to be noted as well that an auditor does not discuss management issues, unless a specific request to that effect is expressly made.

DFT CASE

This latter observation is easy to confirm upon a perusal of the proposed solution to the DFT case. Hence:

- It is inappropriate to mention or to discuss the fact that a margin of 40% on the components of the technology company with an estimated life of three years is low. One must use this percentage in the calculations, but not question it.
- The assessment of the new bonus program is a secondary issue. It is not necessary to tackle this issue to be successful in the case. (A37)
- The focus is essentially on the accounting for events, such as revenue recognition following the transfer of inventory to India. The merits of such a business practice are not to be discussed.

I would like to point out to you that what is suggested by the above statements is not wrong. It is quite simply not relevant based on the role you are asked to play – in light of the requirement – in the case.

A candidate writing down such ideas is not losing points.

He or she is wasting time!

ROLE

↓

ATTITUDES TO ADOPT

Aside from the typical or standard role of the external auditor, a professional accountant is called upon to assist his or her employer or client in various ways. For example, he or she may be tasked with issuing an audit report on compliance with agreements. His or her role can also be limited to preparing documents for the Audit Committee or developing internal controls. When unusual roles are involved, conducting a comparative analysis of the cases simulated is a slightly more difficult, but all the more useful, activity to undertake.

IDENTIFYING THE SIMILARITIES AND DIFFERENCES
ENABLES ONE TO UNDERSTAND HOW TO SHAPE AN ANSWER.

THIS EXERCISE BUILDS UP THE QUICKNESS OF YOUR REACTION
BY HONING YOUR ABILITY TO ADAPT.

EXAMPLES OF OBSERVATIONS
SIMILARITIES IN THE ATTITUDES TO ADOPT ACCORDING TO THE ROLE TO BE PLAYED

Role to be played	Similarities in the attitudes to adopt
Management consultant	– Think "business", namely cash flows, standard or real costs, contribution margin, etc. – One must take into account the needs or preferences of stakeholders, uncertainties or risks, as well as constraints. – The accounting standards are of little use, except where they have an indirect impact on a management situation (e.g.: impact of the accounting of a lease on the debt/equity ratio).
Specialist asked to arbitrate a dispute over the calculation of royalties payable to an author **OR** **Specialist** asked to assess the damages suffered as a result of a construction delay	– The terms of the agreement are the basic reference materials, clauses which may be in keeping with accounting standards or refer to another method of calculation. One must, therefore, be open to the use of other rules (e.g.: cash basis of accounting, standard cost, fair value) and demonstrate this in the resolution of the case. – If there is no specific clause or if there is one but it is vague, one must, first of all, see if one of the existing clauses can be used. For example, if the agreement states that no provision for sales returns is to be taken into consideration, one could infer that the same goes for sales discounts. – Under other circumstances, one must exercise one's professional judgment and search for the "spirit" of the agreement in order to establish a baseline. For instance, with a view to "assessing the damages suffered as a result of the postponement of the startup of activities", the advertising costs already incurred to announce the opening date of the restaurant can be claimed.

The analysis of previous cases promotes success in future cases.
On the other hand, there is no guarantee that the future will reflect the past.

POINT OF VIEW

One must conduct any analytical and comparative exercise in respect of cases **in order to understand what is going on.**
The goal is most definitely not to learn sentences "by heart" in order to repeat them as soon as a case "looks like" any of the previous cases.

Use your knowledge and your experience

by adapting, with discernment and flexibility, to each case.

EXAMPLES OF OBSERVATIONS
DIFFERENCES IN THE ATTITUDES TO ADOPT ACCORDING TO THE ROLE TO BE PLAYED

Role to be played	Differences in the attitudes to adopt
Member of the Board of Directors asked to comment on financial results	– He or she must conduct his or her analysis from an external point of view, taking into account the various parties present, such as shareholders and creditors. – He or she must explain the terms used to other members (lay members) who are not from the accounting field or have no management experience.
Comptroller asked to comment on financial results	– He or she must conduct his or her analysis from an internal point of view, taking into account the objectives and preferences, such as improvement of productivity. He or she highlights the evolution of the financial performance. – If he or she is directing these comments to people in-house, there is no need to explain certain accounting terms. Besides, it can be assumed that the latter have management experience.

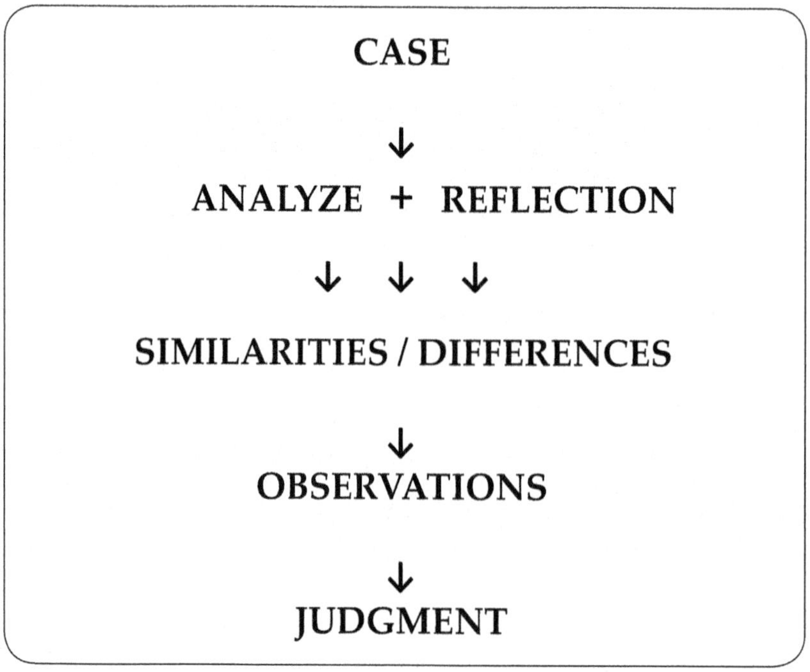

CASE

↓

ANALYZE + REFLECTION

↓ ↓ ↓

SIMILARITIES / DIFFERENCES

↓

OBSERVATIONS

↓

JUDGMENT

Comparing requirements

Throughout this volume, I have regularly stressed the need to limit oneself to what is required. As you will no doubt have understood, it is a fundamental condition to success in a case. As part of the comparative analysis of simulated cases, it is crucial to ask oneself whether a connection exists between the requirement and the contents or structure of the proposed solution.

When I want to highlight the **similarities** from one case to the next, I often express my observations in the following manner:

"WHERE THERE IS (ARE)..., ONE MUST THINK OF..."[1]

The recognition of this "causal" relation will enable you to detect that which resurfaces frequently in cases in order to remember it for upcoming simulations. Moreover, this will also enable you to determine faster the impact of the requirement or of the work to be performed or to consider the influence of case facts on the drafting of the answer.

EXAMPLES OF OBSERVATIONS
SIMILARITIES IDENTIFIED FROM ONE CASE TO THE NEXT

Where there is (are)...,	**one must think of...**
an investment to analyze	the pros and cons of the investment.
a due diligence to plan	setting materiality at a very low level, nearly "dollar for dollar".
non-controlling shareholders	what could be detrimental to them (e.g.: related party transactions).
a creditor threatening to recall a loan	– the fact this may cast doubt on the appropriateness of the going concern assumption; – posting the loan in current liabilities.
a financially troubled entity	cash flows.
a management bonus program	– the possibility of financial data being manipulated; (A33) – controllable factors. (A37)

POINT OF VIEW

Such a list of observations, which is easy to draw up, can quickly grow in length as you perform your simulations. I suggest that you sort them from the outset. It is thus possible to single out causality per topic (e.g.: management accounting, taxation) or to separate out the causal relations that arise from the particulars of the case (e.g.: service business, foreign transactions).

1 Other similar formulations can be just as effective, such as "IF..., THEN...", "Where one notices/observes that..., one must not forget to... ", or "The presence of... means that... ".

To me, it appears especially useful to identify, and then to explain, any difference in the make-up of the relevant ideas set out in the proposed solutions. For example, it may be that the analytical approach is not the same for both cases, although, at first blush, the requirement or the information supplied appears to be similar. One must then TRY TO FIND OUT WHY THIS IS SO, which is not always an easy exercise to do. First of all, it requires an excellent understanding of simulated cases. In addition, one must be alert to any difference resulting from a comparison of two or more cases sharing similar features. Finally, it is not always so obvious to find an explanation for the **difference** that was identified. At times, it is a mere nuance that could be buried anywhere in the text.

EXAMPLES OF OBSERVATIONS – DIFFERENCES IDENTIFIED BETWEEN TWO CASES

	Differences identified	Explanation
Case A:	Various approaches must be contemplated, and then one must justify selecting the one that shall be used for valuing the business target.	Specific reference in Case B: "Both parties agreed that the purchase price would be equal to three times the average normalized income for the past two years."
Case B:	It is not necessary to justify other approaches, and that based on the past normalized earnings is the one to be selected.	
Case C:	It is not necessary to discuss accounting for development costs.	Specific reference in Case C: "The development costs have not yet been expensed. They relate to a project that will take shape in a few months."
Case DFT:	One must discuss accounting for development costs. (A14)	
Case E:	One must discuss the terms to be renegotiated as part of the renewal of the lease.	Specific reference in Case F: "The signing of the lease renewal is imminent, since the Executive Vice-President has already settled all the relevant issues with the lessor."
Case F:	No discussion of the renewal of the lease should take place, even if the deadline is approaching.	

POINT OF VIEW

You will note that I am greatly in favor of preparing tables as part of the comparative analysis of simulated cases.

This approach energizes the learning activity.

The need to structure one's observations in a table yields concise information.

It will be easier later to review the work done.

Part 10
Putting The Means For Success On Your Side

Flesh Out The Analytical Structures
Building Info-Cards
Fleshing Out Theoretical Concepts

"The challenge is to differentiate between looking alike and being alike."

Part 10

Putting The Means For Success On Your Side

Part 9 highlighted the usefulness of fleshing out the fundamentals of each of the simulated cases in order to then compare them using a comparative analysis. Such a planned reflection allows one to go beyond the solution to the case as such. Let us say that it is insufficient to understand the ideas put forth regarding the decision between either of the financing options available to the entity, for example. One must also grasp where the need to tackle this issue originates, establish how it is positioned in relation to the rest of the solution, and then uncover the approach used for its resolution. The analysis of simulated cases can definitely lead you to make a great number of insightful observations. This part sets out several means that can be implemented in order to remember these observations and promote your success.

Flesh Out The Analytical Structures

I suggest that you identify the analytical structures you have encountered throughout the case simulations you have conducted. What lies at the heart of the analysis or of the evaluation of a problem or issue? What are the steps making up the approach to resolution? What are the various facets of a topic?

It is possible to flesh out the gist or large segments

WHICH MAY FORM PART OF AN ANSWER TO A CASE.

Encountering the same problem, issue or topic more than once often highlights manners of proceeding that are similar from one case to the next. You will easily observe, for example, that the analytical structure of the planning of an audit is usually the following: Risk assessment – Materiality – Approach – Risk areas and procedures. (A25 to A30)

Incidentally, in the course of this activity, one can initially use the following basic approach, which adapts to the situations encountered.

Identification: Problem / Issue / Topic	"ID/P"	"P"
Analyse/Evaluation (qualitative and/or quantitative)	"ANAL/EVAL"	"A"
Conclusion or Recommendation	"CONC/REC"	"R"

EXAMPLE OF ANALYTICAL STRUCTURE[1]

Issue: Appropriateness of the going concern assumption

Analytical structure:

→ Identification of the issue – usually less explicit or non-explicit – using the case facts

→ Conclusion as to the entity's ability to continue as a going concern

→ Future cash flows (where financial data is available)

→ Qualitative aspects – in light of the role to be played
E.g.: Impact on the audit work or the audit reporting
E.g.: Means of financing contemplated or reorganization contemplated

→ Conclusion justified by the analysis

1 Other examples of situations that can be subjected to an analytical structure: Acquisition of a business (point of view of the purchaser, point of view of the vendor), Startup of an entity, Planning a due diligence, Preparing a financing proposal or Analysis of a capital project.

The example below highlights the manner in which the issue "Analysis of internal control procedures" is usually resolved. The number of observations and the scope of explanations can, of course, vary from one candidate to the next. Some will only flesh out critical aspects whereas others will add concrete examples in support of their observations. Situations where a similar analytical structure can be used have been identified (e.g.: analysis of financial risks). One also observes a different manner of submitting the answer when issues of lesser importance are involved or where there is not much to say.

EXAMPLE OF ANALYTICAL STRUCTURE

Issue: Analysis of internal control procedures

Analytical structure:	Weakness (or deficiency, problem)	"W" or "D"
	Implications of the deficiency (or Impact)	"I"
	Recommendation / suggestions / ways to improve	"R"

Observations:

→ There is generally no option to consider prior to making a recommendation. One notes the deficiency (and its implications), then one remedies the situation, taking into account, as often as possible, case facts: names of persons, supporting documents, amount involved, etc.

→ One must explain the nature of the deficiency or justify its existence using case facts.

E.g.: Since there are no restrictions as to the amounts that he can commit (W), the Secretary made significant purchases without the authorization of the owners (I).

→ One must always recommend concretely (WHAT TO DO) and precisely (HOW TO DO IT) the improvement that needs to be implemented. Who? What? When?

E.g.: I recommend that all purchases in excess of a pre-established limit, say $1,000, be approved by one of the owners (R).

→ ...

The structure MAY also be used when called upon to:

- analyze the financial risks or the terms of a shareholder agreement
- comment the IT-related internal controls
- evaluate the entity's governance structure or its decision-making process

Note: One can adopt the following answer structure for issues of lesser importance. Each of the parts of the analysis appears, however the final text is shorter.

Title (Identification of the deficiency (W))

Recommendation justified (R) by one or two arguments. The justification ("because") then corresponds to the consequence of the deficiency (I) that has now been eliminated.

Warning: The W-I-R structure cannot be followed for any issue whatsoever.

So as not to forget any parts of the analysis, it is possible to refer to a drafting code, such as the letters W-I-R. During the case resolution, such a code is a useful prompt, since it constantly reminds the candidate to refer to the implication (I) of each of the deficiencies (W) identified. THIS TYPE OF CODE MUST ALWAYS BE APPLIED WITH DISCERNMENT. It must not, for instance, lead to the useless repetition of the same ideas. Stating the impact of a deficiency so as to then repeat the same idea as a justification for the recommendation is a waste of time. In addition, as you already know, one must constantly remain within the bounds of the case parameters.

POINT OF VIEW

The various analytical structures that you establish throughout your learning process enable you to determine faster what steps to follow in a given situation. Incidentally, I suggest, as stated in Part 2 (p. 28), that you take the time to do so at the answer planning stage. Since cases must be resolved within a restricted time frame, this advantage is not insignificant.

ANALYTICAL STRUCTURES ARE GUIDES.

Note, for example, that knowing one must usually discuss financing following the analysis of a capital project can remind you to consider this aspect.

This observation is a starting point, to be used with discernment.

It may happen that the next case will state that "The business has decided to use its surplus invested in short-term investments to finance the project.". This information must change the outline of your answer, since the Financing issue is now settled.

ANY ANALYTICAL STRUCTURE
MUST BE ADAPTED TO THE PARTICULARS OF THE CASE.

EXAMPLE – ACCOUNTING ADJUSTMENTS

Understanding what has been done
↓
Determining what needs to be done
↓
ACCOUNTING ADJUSTMENTS
(A10 to A18)

PROFESSIONAL JUDGMENT

EXAMPLE – STEPS TO CONSIDER IN THE ANALYSIS

Topic: Breach of ethics by a colleague

1- Try to speak to him or to her
2- Notify the professional association
3- Consult legal counsel, if need be

N.B.: Refer to the Code of conduct/of ethics

Think about it? YES
Force a discussion? NO
Be wary of automatic reactions!

Building Info-Cards

As early as the first simulations, one must adopt a classification system that will collect in the same place all the observations made as you progress along through the learning process. In order to create a register of information of a reasonable size, that is easy to consult, I suggest that you create info-cards. Their content, which is frequently updated and re-read, is adapted to the circumstances as well as to your needs. For example, you can prepare cards on any of the particulars of the context found in simulated cases.

EXAMPLE – EXCERPT OF AN INFO-CARD[1]

Context: Non-profit organizations

Features:

→ The primary objective is not to make a profit → budgetary balance

→ Registered charitable organization? → NO income taxes

→ No corporate securities that can be transferred

- no shareholders (only members)
- outside financing through grants/contributions/loans

→ Financial statements must necessarily be audited

- "usual" restriction on completeness of contributions received in cash
- possibility of audit reports on compliance with agreements, statutes and regulations

→ Governance: management team and Board of Directors

→ Importance of internal controls → bookkeeping, revenues from donations

→ Distinguish between restricted contributions and unrestricted contributions

→ Use the Accounting Standards for Not-for-Profit Organizations

→ ...

This example of an info-card lists succinctly the basics of what characterizes "non-profit organizations". The ideas are added as the candidate simulates cases in this context. The order in which these ideas appear, incidentally, is not necessarily important. When the candidate will be called upon to resolve a case dealing with a non-profit organization, he or she will be able to consider the features he or she has gleaned in order to assist in submitting a complete and integrated answer.

Naturally, info-cards can go into more detail than in the above example. Some contexts are more recurrent than others, which allows for the creation of a more extensive list of observations. In addition, a candidate might decide to dig deeper into a situation with which he or she is experiencing difficulty, or which is unusual or complex.

FEATURES
OBSERVATIONS
↓
INFO-CARDS

1 Other examples of a context that could be contained in an info-card: Partnership, First share offering, Public utility, Franchises or Public company/Private business.

An info-card can contain, among others:

- The list of simulated cases using the same context as a backdrop;
- A reference to the standards, rules, laws, principles, etc. involved;
- A report of similarities and differences between simulated cases;
- The analytical structure(s) identified;
- A brief reminder of the ideas or interrelations often encountered, which can be expressed as follows: "Where there is (are)..., one must think of...";
- Concrete examples originating from simulated cases;
- A reminder of the most difficult aspects to analyze, including those that are less explicit;
- Any trick liable to improve efficiency in drafting.

On the following page, you will find a more comprehensive example of an info-card: "Planning an audit of financial statements".[1] This card contains a great many observations that a candidate may make on the topic of the situation or context in question; they are certainly not exhaustive. On the one hand, one must appreciate that the content of these cards depends on the simulated cases. On the other hand, it also depends on what the candidate has been able to observe through his or her various analyses. Naturally, serious and disciplined work translates its full usefulness in the relevance of the observations that are included on these cards.

Plan meetings with other candidates

It is very beneficial to plan meetings with other candidates who have followed a similar path as you, in order to share your knowledge and experience. It is motivating, and reassuring, especially where the learning process is stretched out. In my opinion, ideally one should form a team of two to five people where each one can improve and supplement his or her own analyses by exchanging with the others.

A team can meet, for example, to analyze the proposed solution and the evaluation guide for a more difficult or complex case. Taking stock of a different way of seeing things allows for the confirmation and enhancement of your personal observations. One of your colleagues could explain to you why a particular topic is of lesser importance, for example, or answer any "outstanding question". In addition, as indicated previously (Part 8, p. 112), an annotated assessment of your answer by another candidate enables you to draw up a more objective report on your performance.

POINT OF VIEW

It is no doubt tempting to simplify one's life by just taking the info-cards prepared by another candidate. I do not endorse this manner of acquiring information. Building the cards up is the result of an individual reflection that, to me, appears to be crucial to the learning process. When done in a timely fashion, it is very useful to compare one's notes and observations with one's colleagues. However, in order to fully reap the benefits, individual work must be performed beforehand.

Share in order to enhance? Absolutely!

Take without becoming involved? NO!

1 Other examples of situations that could be included in an info-card: Arbitration between two parties, Transition from a review engagement to an audit engagement (or *vice-versa*), Transfer of the family business to the next generation, Fraud situation or Assessment of the work of another auditor.

EXAMPLE OF AN INFO-CARD PER CONTEXT

Context: Planning an audit of financial statements

Analytical structure: Risk Assessment
Materiality
Approach
Risk areas and Procedures

Observations:

→ The factors considered in the appreciation of the risks involved derive directly from the case facts.

Most of the time, these factors relate to NEW events, that is to say that surfaced during the current period or that are specific to the entity.

Example: Since cash transactions are much more frequent, it may be that the audit trail is minimal, maybe even non-existent. The risk that the revenues may be undervalued is therefore higher.

Where the audit has already been planned, this planning must be UPDATED in order to take into consideration NEW events that took place since this planning was done. (A23 to A30)

→ One must always end the risk assessment with a clear and precise conclusion as to the level of risk of the audit engagement.

Note: Most of the time, this level is high. REMAIN VIGILANT!

→ The determination of the materiality takes into account the users (actual and potential) involved and the influence of financial statements on their decisions.

MATERIALITY → USERS

Example: The possibility that the financial statements will now be used by foreign authorities leads us to set the materiality at a lower level than last year.

Example: It is well advised to set the materiality at a lesser amount for items having an impact on the EBITDA, due to the increased user reliance from management for purposes of the bonus calculation. (A23)

→ The discussion as to the approach doesn't usually take very long. In any event, it takes into account the control environment of the entity. In fact, one must seek to tie the discussion of the approach to the case facts.

Example: (A25)

GST/HST reassessment → quality of the record-keeping → approach

→ The relevant audit procedures are directly related to specific risk identified. They must be clear, concrete, and take into account the case facts.

"In order to ensure..., one must..."

Examples: see the MAX case, the DFT case (A25 to A30), etc.

→ ...

Exchanging ideas amongst colleagues gives impetus to the learning process.

Personally, I consider that team meetings are especially useful when conducting a comparative analysis of simulated cases. Fleshing out the particulars, the similarities and differences becomes easier. Considering different points of view allows you to enrich and consolidate your personal achievements, which is particularly helpful when an official exam is looming on the horizon. Incidentally, I suggest that you have exchanges on contexts, roles or requirements for which little information is available to you. The creation of info-cards per context arises from past experience. The trend is then to naturally focus on recurring situations.

A situation you have never encountered before may lie at the heart of the next case.

It is constructive, to my mind, to imagine unusual situations or unprecedented scenarios, and to ask oneself what that implies.

"WHAT IF ... " or **"ASSUME THAT ... "**

EXAMPLES OF UNUSUAL SITUATIONS OR UNPRECEDENTED SCENARIOS

- In most cases, the audit risk is higher for the current fiscal year. How should one react in the reverse situation where the audit risk is lower than the previous fiscal year?
- Your role is to represent the government. How should you plan and carry out an audit engagement in which you are asked to verify the legitimacy of expenses claimed as part of a government grant (government assistance) program?
- The creditors of a financially troubled entity have just accepted a proposal. What is the impact on the accounting, the auditing, the taxation and the governance of the entity?

The purpose of the exercise is to contemplate the existence of other possibilities. Of course, it is impossible to anticipate everything, but one can at least learn how to confront a case requiring a different approach. In other words, one can **develop one's adaptability**. When you take the time to think about it, the fact that the audit risk is lower than in the previous fiscal year isn't that complicated a situation. Most of the ideas will be expressed as the reverse of what is "usual". However, in the restricted time frame allotted for case resolution, being faced with an unusual situation can be destabilizing.

Knowing how to summon one's previous knowledge and experiences is an asset.

NEW SITUATION

↓

ADAPTED REACTION

Fleshing Out Theoretical Concepts

Knowing how to apply one's acquired knowledge is one of the many reasons justifying the use of cases in the teaching of accounting. A case is a teaching tool setting out a unique scenario (context, role, requirement) intended to assess your competence. It goes without saying that this includes a full grasp of the various concepts studied throughout your education. You will no doubt agree with me that the quantity and diversity of topics tackled as part of the program is not insignificant. In my opinion, one must devise methods to remember the basics of the notions and concepts studied in order to be in a better position to determine "when" and "how" to use them.

You are sometimes authorized to consult certain reference materials (accounting standards, tax rules or other materials) during a case resolution. However, given the restricted – if not tight – time frame, one must be aware that such consultation must be occasional, especially when asked to resolve short cases. It is definitely not the time to be "learning" new things.

It is crucial to grasp basic knowledge in our field.

Incidentally, it is often said that it is preferable to know the basic concepts of all the important topics on the program than to grasp only half of them in-depth.

DFT CASE

Let us take up the example of the agreement entered into with Indo-Tech (A5).

The problem arises at the level of the "revenue recognition of the ordinary activities – sale of goods" (A11, A12). Once that has been established, the candidate must determine what the critical aspect to analyze is, in light of the case facts. He or she must then decide which theoretical concept(s) to refer to. A candidate who previously drew up a list of key concepts relating to the topic in question, will be able, in his or her own mind, to review them quickly and select the appropriate one. As you gain experience, this process is nearly instantaneous.

In the DFT case, you are required to discuss the "transfer of significant risks and rewards of ownership". A discussion bearing on "the need for the amount of revenue to be measured reliably", for example, would be inappropriate under the circumstances.

A candidate must, therefore, first of all, recall the various concepts underlying revenue recognition in order to make an informed choice as to what is relevant. Since basic concepts are at play, he or she should not have to re-read IAS 18 along the way. In addition, a candidate must be sure to know the terms precisely, since stating, for example, that "the inventory has not changed hands" does not necessarily mean the same thing as "the risks of ownership have not been transferred".

The understanding and assimilation of knowledge is fundamental to successfully completing a case. As indicated in Part 7 (p. 91), developing a good technique in case resolution is a good thing, but it does not make up for a lack of knowledge. Consequently, one must know:

- the **various aspects of a topic** in order to be able to precisely identify what the critical aspect at play is.
- the **methods of application** in order to be in a position to use the knowledge properly.

POINT OF VIEW

Knowing the material placed at your disposal well is a definite asset during case resolution. A candidate who needs to clarify his or her thought or who needs to confirm what the exceptions to the rule are must be able to do so quickly. Therefore, he or she must know the nomenclature or the Table of contents of the reference material at his or her disposal in order to get straight to the point. One must be able to remember, for example, that a single transaction may occasionally include separable identifiable items (A10, IAS 18 para. 13).

It is understandable that one cannot remember everything,

but it is necessary to determine, and then to find, what one is looking for.

A candidate who does not see, for example, that the new building could be considered to be a replacement property for tax purposes will certainly not be able to conduct an appropriate analysis of this topic. He or she will then discuss general tax rules regarding the disposition of property without bothering with the rest. His or her incomplete answer will probably not achieve the passing standard.

Preparing summaries of topics studied is an activity that varies widely from one candidate to the next, based on their needs and their personality. Some write very detailed summaries whereas others only write a few sentences. Some candidates systematically summarize all the topics forming part of the program while others do so sporadically. Regardless of the way you go about it, I suggest and strongly recommend that you:

TAKE THE TIME TO FLESH OUT, IN A FEW BULLET POINTS, THE THEORETICAL CONCEPTS OF THE IMPORTANT TOPICS INCLUDED IN THE PROGRAM.

These concepts must be stated in a succinct and precise manner, using a few key words, in order to highlight the various aspects of a topic. From experience, I can tell you that **it is one of the most effective means of remembering information.**

EXCERPT FROM AN INFO-CARD

Topic: Internal Control

→ OBJECTIVES:

reliable financial reporting
prevention and detection of error and fraud
safeguard of assets

→ authorization of transactions

→ segregation of duties
3 aspects: authorization, asset control, recording

→ physical controls

→ information processing

→ documentation and reports

→ cost-benefit analysis to implement a control

→ compliance with instructions, business practices, laws

→ ...

EXCERPT FROM AN INFO-CARD

Topic: Inventories (IAS 2)

→ DEFINITION: held for sale – ordinary course
(+ in the process of production + materials or supplies to be consumed)

→ MEASUREMENT: at the lower of cost and net realizable value (NRV)

→ COSTS: incurred in bringing the inventories to their present location and condition

costs of purchase	costs of conversion	costs excluded
– purchase price – import duties – taxes (not recoverable) – transport – handling – other direct costs LESS: discounts, rebates	direct costs (material, labour) + indirect costs (production overheads) FIXED and VARIABLE ↓ systematic allocation fixed: based on normal capacity * variable: actual use * actual level OK if approximation	– abnormal waste (material, labour) – storage costs – administrative overheads – selling costs – unallocated overheads (up/down in production) ↓ EXPENSES

→ COST FORMULAS:
Interchangeable items: first-in, first-out (FIFO) OR weighted average cost
same cost formula for inventories having similar nature and use
Specific projects, NOT interchangeable: specific identification of costs
N.B. retail method/standard cost method: if results approximate costs

→ NET REALIZABLE VALUE = selling price - completion costs - selling costs
– based on the most reliable evidence available at the time the estimates are made
→ consider events occurring AFTER Y/E – confirming conditions existing at Y/E
→ usual: item by item OR group similar or related items
– clear evidence of an increase in NRV → writedown is reversed (max original writedown)

→ EXPENSE: – inventories sold → cost of sales → same period than revenue
– writedown → in the period it occurs
– reversal → reduce cost of sales → in the period it occurs

→ OTHER: construction (IAS 11), agriculture (IAS 41), borrowing costs (IAS 23)

This example makes the main theoretical concepts clearly stand out by using a different color. The explanations are clear and brief; large segments of the standards are identified. Certain words or expressions could still warrant further abbreviation.

A table summarizes in a structured manner the components of the cost of inventory. A candidate who creates such a table can, therefore, better understand the concept: "incurred in bringing the inventories to their present location and condition". Another candidate might completely skip over this aspect, and focus instead on the overhead allocation to inventory, for example. As stated regularly throughout this volume, any learning activity whatsoever must be PERSONALLY USEFUL to you.

The previous examples of info-cards per topic both contain a concise reminder of the applicable theoretical concepts. This is the objective to aim for. Naturally, some candidates expatiate somewhat more by adding explanations, examples or additional references. Regardless, **make sure to clearly identify what the key concepts are, in order to be able to quickly consult them.**

From experience, I can tell you that info-cards per topic can be especially enhanced throughout your learning process:

- *by adding examples taken from simulated cases.* Analyzing cases enables you to identify or confirm the validity of the theoretical concepts noted. You can jot down the concepts that keep coming back more often than others, such as the "future economic benefits" in relation to intangible assets (A14). This also allows you to examine the manner in which the various concepts are applied in the case resolution. For those topics that cause you more difficulty, I suggest that you note the examples encountered throughout your learning process. A candidate who finds it hard to analyze situations involving the presence of related parties, for example, could examine in one shot all that was written on this topic in previous cases.

EXCERPT FROM AN INFO-CARD – AUDIT PROCEDURES ON INVENTORY

Audit Assertion (account balances at the period end)	**Examples of audit procedures on inventory (CASE)**
existence	– examine the reports created by the consignees to determine if the balance of goods on consignment is plausible. (NIP) – obtain the quantities purchased as well as the quantities used to calculate the missing inventory. (CP)
rights and obligations (hold or control)	– identify, during the physical count, the items sold on layaway against deposit in order to... (NIP) – examine the documents relating to inventory in transit for...
completeness (what should have been recorded have been recorded)	– communicate with Safe Storage as soon as possible to ensure the amount can be confirmed at Sept. 30. (DFT, A27) – review the sales reports created by the consignees to ensure that the inventory sold has been excluded from the physical count. (NIP)
valuation and allocation (appropriate amounts, appropriately recorded)	– examine the recent sales agreements to determine the net realizable value. (MAX) – ask management and installers about the technical obsolescence of these parts to... (PS) – compare to the recorded cost in inventory of these units to ensure they are recorded at the lower of cost or net realizable value. (DFT, A29) – compare the invoices to later selling prices, because... – identify items that are obsolescent or have a slow turnover during the physical count in order to... (MAX)

N.B.: In the simulated cases, it can be observed that the "valuation" assertion is the most often analyzed.

POINT OF VIEW

When is the best time to create info-cards?

Ideally, you should flesh out key concepts from fundamental topics all throughout your accounting studies. However, most candidates recognize the need to review previously-studied knowledge when they start simulating multi-subjects cases.

I suggest you prepare info-cards on those topics that recur regularly in cases, that are complex, that are "the flavor of the day", that appear to you to be more difficult or in respect of which little has been written so far.

The selection of topics also depends on your strengths and weaknesses. A candidate who, for instance, experiences a great deal of difficulty resolving taxation issues will create more info-cards on this subject.

The creation of info-cards per topic is an integral part of the knowledge review process.

- *by preparing diagrams or tables.* When it is possible to present the information in a more visual manner, do not hesitate to do so. On the one hand, summarizing concepts in a few strokes or a few lines requires a sound understanding of the topics. On the other hand, **it is easier to study or to commit to memory a diagram or a table**. Incidentally, it is faster – and often more effective – during a case resolution to rely on the image created.

EXAMPLE OF A TABLE

Long-term financing / Particulars	Bonds	Redeemable shares	Common shares
Usual features (maturity, guarantee, duration, etc.)			
Accounting treatment and presentation in the financial statements			
Tax implications – scheduled payments (interest, dividend, etc.)			
Tax treatment – repayment			

ANALYSIS OF SIMULATED CASES

↓

ENHANCEMENT OF INFO-CARDS

EXAMPLES OF TABLES

International Financial Reporting Standards (publicly accountable)	Accounting Standards for Private Enterprises

One could, for example, resolve the DFT case (A9 to A17) by relying instead on the Accounting Standards for Private Enterprises so as to bring out the differences.

Accounting treatment – Type of revenue – Expense category	Tax consequences – When taxable? – When deductible?

Audit engagement	Review engagement

**Relying on appropriate concepts,
at the right time,
is critical to success.**

POINT OF VIEW

The cards, sheets and tables you prepare are excellent sources of information, that is regularly updated, read and re-read. The collated information contains the fruit of your analyses, conducted as you gained experience in case simulations. I insist that this file is very important.

It contains the last documents you will read right before an official exam.

It is your most precious asset!

I frequently observe candidates preparing info-cards that they do not re-read. One could admittedly say that part of the learning process takes place as the cards are being created. However, regularly re-reading one's info-cards is an excellent means of committing them to memory so as to be able to retrieve them at the right time. For example, I recommend setting aside three periods of twenty minutes per week for this purpose.

Do not wait forever

for the "right time" to read your info-cards!

Conclusion

Here are my answers to various questions that candidates have asked me throughout their learning process through case resolution:

Q1: *I regularly write four-hour exams containing three cases. In which order should I do them?*

A1: Where an exam includes more than one case, they are usually independent from each other. Under these circumstances, whether you do them in the order they appear or not makes no difference.

EACH CASE MUST BE RESOLVED,

IN KEEPING WITH THE TIME ALLOTTED.

Personally, upon receipt of an exam, I look very quickly at two things: the contents and the duration of each case included. I prefer to start with the case with which I am most comfortable so as to build up a climate of confidence.

I usually do not resolve the shortest case last. Indeed, time is often tighter towards the end of an exam or simulation. However, this should not happen, since the time allotted to each case ought to be observed. Let us say that being only 3 minutes late in each of the first two cases means 6 minutes less for the last. The damage is greater when it is a 70-minute, as opposed to a 90-minute, case.

Q2: *When I structure my answer, I write next to each topic the time expected to be spent on its resolution (e.g.: "11:20-11:25 a.m." or "5 minutes"). Does this bother the person grading the answer?*

A2: I most certainly encourage you to take the time to establish an outline to the answer, at least mentally. You must determine what is essential and plan how to resolve the problems or issues in the time allotted.

I understand that writing down in detail the allocation of minutes between each of the topics may be useful but it takes time. You must ensure that it is worthwhile under the circumstances. The determination of time per problem or issue, which involves the resolution of several topics, can be sufficient.

As for the person grading the answer, it is not really bothersome. Where an idea "has no value" as such for the purpose of the assessment of an answer, it is simply not considered. Although it somewhat takes away from the professionalism of the report, the performance of a candidate is not penalized.

Q3: *I write down many ideas in my answers that I do not find in the official solutions. Since they are good, I take them into consideration in my assessment. Do you agree?*

A3: Not really.

One must determine the value to ascribe to these "good" ideas. It is easy to write ideas that are valid per se, but that do not count. The case may ask for a list of internal controls, for example. If, instead, the answer contains list of management controls, it is not the same thing. Even if the management controls set out in the answer are "good" ideas, they do not answer the question. By way of conclusion, the person grading an answer does not consider all the ideas put forth, only those that are **relevant and new**.

DOES THE IDEA FIT WITHIN THE CASE PARAMETERS?

Q4: *I have trouble structuring my answer. I start with topics that I consider important, only to discover along the way that they are not. In addition, it often happens that I deal with the less important topics at the beginning. Does that adversely influence the assessment of my answer?*

A4: Generally speaking, in the resolution of a case, the important topics are analyzed first, followed by those of lesser importance. In a time-restricted context, topics of little importance are simply discarded. As a result, the most important topics, set out at the beginning of each problem or issue, are analyzed more in depth.

CREATING AN OUTLINE FOR YOUR ANSWER,
IN WRITING OR IN YOUR MIND,
IS A USEFUL GUIDE TO DRAFTING.

When a candidate realizes that he or she has misjudged the importance of a topic during the drafting of the answer, he or she must adjust as soon as he or she makes that realization. If he or she is spending too much time analyzing a topic of lesser importance, he or she must curtail the discussion. Some candidates stubbornly insist on duly finishing their discussion anyway. This is not a good idea.

The person grading an answer takes into account the depth of the analysis conducted, regardless of where it is found in the answer. In other words, it is not so much the location where a topic has been placed that matters, but the importance it has been given in the answer. You will appreciate that realizing late, for example, that the survival of the entity is at stake does not invalidate the ideas put forth as to this aspect.

N.B.: The "cut/paste" function makes moving text a lot easier.

Q5: *My sentences are too long. I take too much time writing what I want to say.*

A5: You are going to have to expend efforts in order to find a way of expressing ideas that are both complete and concise. The objective to strive for is writing more relevant and new ideas. Taking an answer and removing everything that is useless is an exercise that could help you. You can also practice rewriting one or two sections of a case that were especially poorly done.

It is often possible to reduce the length of the text without altering its content, for instance:

- "The $4,000 ..." *is to be preferred to* "The amount of $4,000 ...".
- "One can ..." *is to be preferred to* "It might be conceivable to ...".
- <u>Retirement allowance:</u> (sub-title)

  is to be preferred to "First of all, I will discuss the possibility of paying a retirement allowance."

Q6: *I must rethink my way of approaching calculations. When I do any, they are always too long!*

A6: Especially in a short case, one must, from the outset, plan one's calculations by going straight to what is essential. What is the usefulness of the calculation? What are its important components? A perfect calculation is not called for, just one that enables you to support the analysis or to justify the conclusion. I suggest that you set your sights on **what can make a difference**. Where an adjustment or a component makes a difference to the interpretation of the result arrived at, it must be considered. As for the other adjustments, their lack of influence makes them less important.

AN INCOMPLETE, BUT SUFFICIENT, CALCULATION
MAY BE ENOUGH TO MEET THE OBJECTIVE SOUGHT TO BE ACHIEVED.

Q7: *Some cases provide a sample answer by a candidate following the proposed solution. How should one analyze such an actual sample answer?*

A7: Such examples provided are usually answers by candidates who achieved the passing standard in all the main assessment opportunities. It demonstrates what a candidate can "reasonably" do in the allotted time. These answers, however, do not contain all the valid ideas that can be put forth in the resolution of the problems or issues.

THERE IS MORE THAN ONE WAY TO ACHIEVE THE PASSING STANDARD.

What should one look at?

- ***The depth of analysis.*** How many topics were tackled? How many ideas were put forth? How was time allocated between the qualitative analysis and the quantitative analysis?
- ***The quality of the ideas.*** What theoretical concepts were used? What is the nature of the conclusions or recommendations? What are the integration links?
- ***The submission of ideas.*** What is the sequencing of the problems or issues? How were the analyses structured?

Q8: *When I simulate a case, I often exceed the time allotted for its resolution, because I want to know if I am able to answer all the questions asked. I often run out of time to complete a case.*

A8: From the outset, one must appreciate that there is nearly always insufficient time to complete a case as we wish. This is especially true of short cases.

It is more difficult for some candidates, but one must absolutely learn to follow the instructions of the simulated case. Incidentally, an assessment of the performance under more "favorable" conditions than what is provided is biased. No time extension will be granted during an official examination.

IT IS CRUCIAL TO DEVELOP ONE'S ABILITY
TO ANSWER A CASE IN THE TIME ALLOTTED.

On the other hand, especially during the first simulations, it sometimes happens that candidates finish the drafting of their answer to a case before time is up. In this situation, stopping the exercise before the end is not a good idea. Some candidates then try to justify a poor performance by saying: "I did not achieve the passing standard, but I finished twenty minutes ahead of time."

ONE MUST USE AS WISELY AS POSSIBLE
THE TIME ALLOTTED FOR THE RESOLUTION OF A CASE.

Each idea matters and, as discussed in this volume, drafting a greater number of ideas promotes success. Where a candidate has extra time during the resolution of a case, he or she ought to try to enhance his or her answer by:

- ***Taking a step back*** in order to detect the existence of a less explicit or a non-explicit issue. Take into consideration the profiles, trends, inconsistencies, biases, similarities, improprieties or irregularities, unusual conduct, etc.
- ***Returning to the list of important topics*** in order to ensure that they have all been analyzed in sufficient depth. It is often possible to slip in one or two ideas that do not alter the recommendation or conclusion. Thereafter, time permitting, one can briefly analyze topics of lesser importance.
- ***Reviewing the calculations*** in order to make sure they contain the important components. Time permitting, components of lesser importance can be added without altering the final result.

Q9: *Is it a good idea to simulate once more a case I previously did?*

A9: Rarely.

The "novelty" aspect inherent in each case has worn off. The identification of a less explicit or non-explicit issue or the determination of the importance of the topics, for example, are already known. The performance achieved in such a case simulation is quite simply not representative of your ability to resolve problems or issues in a given scenario.

THE ABILITY TO ADAPT TO THE PARTICULARS OF A CASE

IS A SKILL TO BE HONED.

A candidate who wishes to simulate a case that he or she already knows should first ask himself or herself what goal he or she is seeking to achieve. Where the objective is to improve the efficiency in the drafting of ideas, it may be justifiable. A candidate might thus want to practice drafting an "appropriate" solution in the allotted time frame. He or she might also wish to draft a new section that he or she missed abysmally the first time or practice quickly generating a required calculation. In these situations, the candidate should redo one or more segments of the simulation, not all of it.

Where the case was not analyzed or where several months have elapsed between the two simulations, of course, this mitigates the disadvantages of re-simulating the same case.

Q10: *In order not to run out of ideas and to better structure my answer, I systematically use the W-I-R (Weakness/Problem-Impact-Recommendation) approach for all topics.*

A10: I disagree.

The use of such a structure implies that the "analysis" portion of each topic discussed involves looking for the impact of the problem identified. This can surely not be appropriate in all instances.

ANY ANALYTICAL STRUCTURE WHATSOEVER

MUST BE USED WITH DISCERNMENT.

In the analysis of an accounting issue, for example, one must usually 1- identify the critical aspect involved (ID), 2- discuss the possible accounting treatment (ANAL) and 3- recommend the appropriate accounting treatment (REC). Under certain circumstances, the impact on the financial data, such as the EBITDA in the DFT case (A10 to A22), is part of the solution. A candidate who, however, considers that the impact of a transaction lies at the heart of the analysis will submit an incomplete or inappropriate answer.

The experience gained through the resolution and analysis of past cases must promote success in future cases, not stand in its way.

APPENDIX A

Digital Future Technologies (DFT)

Author's Note:
Aside from several words changed in order to reflect the new terminology, no alterations were made to the documents published by the Chartered Professional Accountants of Canada.

DFT CASE

(70 minutes)

SEPTEMBER 12, 2012

Digital Future Technologies (70 minutes) a

IFRS

Digital Future Technologies (DFT) is a public technology company. It has a September 30th year-end, and last year it adopted International Financial Reporting Standards (IFRS). Kin Lo is a partner with Hi & Lo, the accounting firm that was newly appointed as DFT's auditor in July for the year ending September 30, 2012. DFT's previous auditor retired. Kin met with the CFO, Anne Rather, to gather information on the business, and has completed the client acceptance procedures and initial audit planning. DONE!

It is now September 12, 2012. You, CPA, work for Hi & Lo. Last week, Kin provided you with the notes that he took in his initial meeting with Anne (Exhibit I). You met with Anne a couple of days ago to find out what has happened at DFT since Kin's meeting, and have summarized your discussion in Exhibit II. Anne gave you updated projected results for September 30, 2012 (Exhibit III).

ACCT ↓ EARNINGS ↓ EBITDA ↓ BONUS

Kin asks you to prepare a memo summarizing the accounting issues of significance, and to discuss their impact on the year-end audit planning and the procedures to be performed. He is particularly concerned about issues that affect earnings because management is anticipating a more profitable year than previous years. Management is now part of a new bonus program that is based on earnings before interest, income taxes, depreciation, and amortization (EBITDA). The bonus begins to accumulate once EBITDA exceeds $14 million. AUDIT BIAS?

FOCUS 14M

b

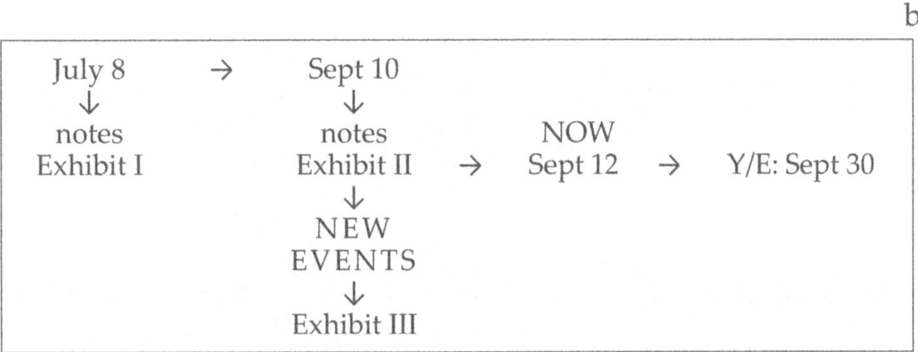

---

a Throughout the reading process, the relevant case facts were highlighted in yellow whereas anything relating to the requirement was highlighted in green. The comments that a candidate may write down regarding the text of the case appear in blue highlighter.
N.B.: Since the annotations are only useful to the candidate, the words and expressions are abbreviated. One can therefore observe: "Y/E" (year-end), "ACCT" (accounting), "M" (millions), "k" (thousand), "MEET" (meeting), "OBJ" (objective), "R&D" or "R+D" (research and development), "EQUIP" (production equipment), "REV" (revenue), "amort" (amortization), etc.

b A brief timeline allows for a quick visualization of the progression of events. This is especially useful in this situation, since the DFT case contains a great many references to any one of these dates.

EXHIBIT I

MEET #1

NOTES FROM KIN'S INITIAL MEETING WITH ANNE — JULY 2012

Knowledge of the Business

DFT manufactures electronic components for telephone and cable in both the wired and wireless markets. While quarterly sales can be quite variable due to inconsistent demand, the company has grown significantly over the past few years. It must constantly reinvest in research and development to ensure that its products remain relevant and can integrate with the latest technology. ***

ZEUS

A new growth market in the industry is the development of equipment that can convert transmissions from analog to digital signals. The equipment allows companies to maximize their transmissions through the bandwidth of existing infrastructure. DFT is anticipating completion of Zeus, a new product that is targeted to this growth market and is expected to be the first of its kind on the market, by mid-August. sept 30

A new bonus program was instituted at the beginning of fiscal 2012 with the objective of motivating management to contribute to profitability by being innovative and developing new products. OBJ

Planning

Materiality is currently estimated to be $434,000, based on 5% of preliminary net income before tax of $8,681,000. TO REVIEW!

Revenue Recognition [a]

Product: Most revenue relates to product sales. Revenue is recognized once the products are shipped, assuming collection is reasonably assured. DFT targets an average margin of 40%. [b]

Service: DFT also has non-recurring engineering (NRE) revenue, which it expects to be $1.5 million by year-end. Customers pay DFT to research and develop add-on components for existing DFT products. In most cases, DFT is not required to do anything beyond the initial engineering phase, NRE revenue is therefore recognized as soon as the work for the specific component is complete. DFT targets a margin of 60%. [b]

---

a The information appearing on this page is factual in nature, since it describes DFT's activities as well as the type of products it manufactures. It is not possible, for the time being, to determine the topics to be discussed. As one reads, it is useful to note the revenue category: Product or Service.

b The margin for these two types of DFT revenues is information worth gleaning, since any potential "adjustment" to the Revenue item will also result in an adjustment to Cost of sales.

EXHIBIT II

MEET #2

AUDIT RISK

NOTES FROM CPA'S MEETING WITH ANNE — SEPTEMBER 10, 2012

A number of events have occurred since July that gave rise to revisions to the projected results for the year ending September 30, 2012. ***

REVENUE ↙ ↘ ACCT AUDIT IMP

Indo-Tech Product

DFT had been negotiating since early in 2012 with Indo-Tech (Indo), a major customer based in India. The deal described below was signed. a

DFT and Indo have contracted with Safe Storage, an unrelated third-party warehouse in India. Indo provided DFT with its forecasted production needs by component and the dates the components are required to be at the warehouse. DFT must ensure that the components arrive at the warehouse in time. Inventory stored at the warehouse is owned by DFT. Safe Storage must notify DFT when Indo takes components from the warehouse, and ownership of the inventory transfers to Indo once it is taken. At no time shall inventory remain in the warehouse for more than 60 days. Any inventory not taken within 60 days of arrival is considered sold to Indo and shall be segregated for removal by Indo as soon as possible.

REV 1.5M A minimum of $1.5 million in components inventory had to be at the warehouse by June 30, but nothing was taken by Indo from the warehouse until August 2. DFT could only recognize the $1.5 million in revenue at that time. Because DFT had not included the sale in the projection done on July 8, the sale was picked up in the revised projection. OK REV 1.85M Since August 2, DFT has sold another $1.85 million in components and shipped them to the warehouse. Based on Indo's forecasted needs, DFT will not be shipping any more components prior to year-end. Indo has not taken out any of the $1.85 million in inventory that is in the warehouse, ? sold but DFT is confident it will do so and has recorded the revenue. b $

REVENUE ↙ ↘ ACCT AUDIT

Non-Recurring Engineering (NRE) Contract Service

DFT has booked a total of $2.5 million in NRE revenue. The amount exceeds expectations because DFT had additional NRE revenue in July that was worth $1 million.

The customer only accepted our normal price on the NRE portion because DFT agreed to provide a discount in fiscal 2013 of $225,000 on product sales with a usual selling price of $750,000. Of the total contract, the $1 million NRE revenue portion was recorded in the current year's projection as the work was completed before the September 15, 2012 deadline. 225,000 / 1M $

---

a Since the deal "was signed", it would be pointless to indicate the weaknesses of this agreement, and then to suggest improvements. It is too late to change anything. When playing the role of external auditor, it is not a good idea anyway.

b The amounts of $1.5M and $1.85M represent the "value" of inventory, that is to say the selling price or the amount of revenues. Generally speaking, when inventory is involved, one refers to its cost instead (purchase or conversion). Hence, one must pay attention to the terms used in order to properly carry out the requisite adjustment. Incidentally, one can consider that this is a hint in and of itself in the identification of the topic to be analyzed.

EXHIBIT (suite)

AUDIT RISK

NOTES FROM CPA'S MEETING WITH ANNE — SEPTEMBER 10, 2012

IMP

Zeus (A4-2) Product

R&D – ZEUS ↙ ↘ ACCT AUDIT

Due in part to the focus on the above NRE project, as well as unanticipated technical difficulties, development of the new product, Zeus, was delayed. DFT will likely only realize total sales of $200,000 for Zeus by year-end. It will also likely have $400,000 of units in inventory at year-end. However, production has just begun. Also, due to the delay, a competitor was able to place a similar product on the market first. As a result, DFT isn't sure it can sell Zeus at the planned price. $

IMP

Research and Development [a]

GRANTS ↙ ↘ ACCT AUDIT

DFT defers and amortizes eligible development costs. Deferral ceases once a product is ready for market, and the costs are amortized over the estimated life of the product, generally three years or less. DFT successfully pursued government funding for research and development. The funds received from the grants, totalling $800,000, were not anticipated in the July projection, and have now been included in revenue. Approximately 75% of the related development costs remain in deferred development costs. $

R&D – ARES ↙ ↘ ACCT AUDIT ↓ HADES

DFT has now abandoned development of one of its products, Ares, which still had approximately $450,000 in deferred development costs. However, DFT's R&D manager believes that the development can be leveraged for a new product, Hades, so it continues to defer the development costs. $

Other [b]

A GST/HST audit was finally completed in late August 2012. It resulted in a reassessment of $125,000. DFT paid the amount immediately to prevent incurring any penalties, but has recorded it as a prepaid expense. It is appealing the reassessment, based on the belief that it is incorrect. $

prepaid "+/–"

DFT has incurred an impairment loss of $100,000 on production equipment that is becoming obsolete. The impairment loss has been included in amortization of capital assets. $

ACCT: equip "minor"

Based on the revised projection for September, Anne believes that everyone in the program will receive a bonus. Therefore, she will accrue an estimate of $300,000 before year-end and needs to adjust the projection. $

BONUS

TO BE SEEN!

---

a One must be careful here. The case does not state which project(s) received the government funding of $800,000. The information regarding the Zeus product may appear in the previous paragraph, but this does not warrant making any connection whatsoever. This would have to be clearly spelled out.

b The title "Other" insinuates that the items that follow are of lesser or little importance. Nevertheless, one must take the time to read a case until the very last line! In the very last paragraph, the fact that Anne – and, therefore, management indirectly – "believes" that everyone in the program will receive a bonus is a case fact that should not be ignored.

EXHIBIT III

BONUS

PROJECTED NET INCOME FOR THE YEAR ENDING SEPTEMBER 30, 2012
(in thousands of Canadian dollars)

PROJECTION
↓
"HUNT MISTAKES"

	Sept. 30, 2012 Original Projection (prepared on July 8, 2012)	Note	DFT Adjustments	Note	Sept. 30, 2012 Adjusted Projection (prepared on Sept. 10, 2012)
Revenue	$ 55,374	1	$ 3,850	5	$ 59,224
Cost of sales	31,942	2	1,930	5	33,872
Gross margin	23,432		1,920		25,352

REV 55,374 + 1,500 + 1,850 + 1,000 + 800 - 1,300 = 59,224
COST 31,942 + 900 + 1,110 + 400 - 480 = 33,872

	Original Projection	Note	DFT Adjustments	Note	Adjusted Projection
Operating expenses:					
Research & development	3,991	3	–		3,991
Sales and marketing	2,622		–		2,622
General & administrative	7,824	4	100	6	7,924
Interest	314		–		314
Total operating expenses	14,751		100		14,851
Income before taxes	8,681		1,820		10,501
Income taxes (30%)	2,604		546	7	3,150
Net income	$ 6,077		$ 1,274		$ 7,351
EBITDA (for bonus calculation)			to be determined		

10,501 + 314 + amort? VS 14M

Notes *(also in thousands of Canadian dollars)*

Initial projection notes (as of July 8**):** EXH I

1) Revenue includes anticipated sales of $1,500 for the new Zeus product. The related costs are reflected in cost of sales.
2) Cost of sales includes cost of Zeus product and projected amortization of $430 for production-related assets.
3) Research and development expenses include projected amortization of $1,620 related to deferred development costs.
4) General and administrative expenses include projected amortization of $2,995 related to capital assets.

5,045

IMP **Revisions to projection (as of** September 10**):** EXH II

5) Revenue and cost of sales
   - INDO For Indo, sales have been increased by $3,350 ($1,500 + $1,850), and cost of sales has been increased by $2,010 ($900 + $1,110) (based on 40% gross margin). For new NRE revenue, sales have been increased by $1,000, and cost of sales has been increased by $400 (based on 60% gross margin). Nothing was booked for the product sales since they only occur in 2013.
   - GRANT Government grants of $800 were recorded in revenue. !
   - ZEUS For Zeus, sales have been decreased by $1,300 and cost of sales has been decreased by $480 (based on 40% gross margin) due to lower than projected sales.
6) Impairment loss related to production equipment is $100. "minor"
7) Tax provision has been adjusted by $546.

EXAMPLE OF READING NOTES

CONTEXT

public company → IFRS NOW: Sept 12, 12 – Y/E: Sept 30

technology → variable sales / significant growth (4-1)
→ constant R&D reinvest
→ life of prod 3 years or less (6-2)
quick obsolescence

NEW bonus program
→ EBITDA > 14M BIAS?
obj: innov / develop new prod (4-3)
acct $300k bonus? (6-6)

margin: product 40%
service 60%

COMMENTS:

– If one steps back a little and looks at pages A5 and A6 together, one observes the regular presence of the "$" sign. It is an indication in itself to the effect that it is possible to rectify the adjusted financial data appearing in Exhibit III (prepared on September 10, 2012).

– One must take the time to analyze the contents of Exhibit III prior to planning the resolution of the case. Since this Exhibit contains several explanatory notes, one needs to focus on what is essential. As can be seen, the notes are split into two parts: the first is dated July 8 (Exhibit I) and the second September 10 (Exhibit II). These two dates coincide with the two meetings with Anne. Since the latter meeting dealt with NEW EVENTS occurring during the period, its contents are more important.

– In Exhibit III, the reconciliation of the revenue figure, as well as that of cost of sales, was conducted as the case was being read (Exhibit II). A better understanding of "what was done" will make the discussion of "what needs to be done" easier. This also allows for a quick visualization of the net effect of each of the adjustments.

One also realizes that most of the adjustments are occurring at the revenues level. The adjustment of the cost of sales, at 40% or 60%, is a mere formality.

Finally, writing the figures one after the other underscores in a clearer fashion that they nearly all lead to an increase in net income.

– In Exhibit III, it is possible to make a brief calculation – in one's mind or in writing – in order to determine if the $14M target has been met. Since Anne "believes" management will receive a bonus (A6), you will not be surprised to see that the projected EBITDA exceeds $14M.

You already know, in light of the significance of the amounts involved, that an accounting treatment that is different from any of the important accounting issues will make a difference in the payment (or non-payment) of bonuses.

After all, you are doing a case!

EVALUATION GUIDE a
DIGITAL FUTURE TECHNOLOGIES
ASSESSMENT OF OPPORTUNITIES
(INDICATORS OF COMPETENCE)

One must flesh out relevant concepts, and not necessarily repeat the standards.

case simulation ↓ learning purpose

The reader is reminded that the solutions are developed for the UFE candidate; therefore, all the complexities of a real-life situation may not be fully reflected in the following solution. The UFE Report is not an authoritative source of GAAP.

OBJECTIVE ↓ application of the standards

In addition, the Handbook sections referenced in this suggested solution are intended for learning purposes only. While candidates are expected to apply the guidance in the Handbook when analyzing financial reporting and assurance issues, they are not expected to directly quote from the Handbook. Candidates who choose to quote Handbook sections are reminded that no credit is given unless the quotation is integrated into a meaningful analysis and applied to the relevant case facts.

QUOTATIONS FROM HANDBOOK ≠ ANALYSIS OF THE ISSUES

To: Kin Lo, Partner
From: CPA
Subject: Memo regarding DFT b

Attached is my memo describing the accounting issues relevant to Digital Future Technologies (DFT). I have also identified the impact of these issues on our audit and our planned procedures. You indicated that you were concerned about the impact of any accounting issues on income due to the new management compensation plan that is based on EBITDA. A number of the issues I have discussed have an impact on interest, taxes, depreciation and amortization, or elements included in earnings before tax. As a result, I have explained the impact of these issues on EBITDA as applied in the bonus calculation.

This first paragraph is an introduction that contains no relevant or new idea.

The tone used in the second paragraph clearly shows that one is speaking to the partner, namely the immediate supervisor, and not to the client.

I believe you will need to speak with Anne as soon as she is available with respect to the bonus. In my conversation with her, she explained that she was confident management would be getting its bonus and planned to accrue an estimated amount. Based on my revised projected income, management may not meet the threshold amount, and therefore would not obtain a bonus. I have also provided some additional comments and considerations with respect to the new bonus plan. c

KEY ASPECT highlighted from the outset ↓ NEW bonus program

---

a In this evaluation guide, the case facts are highlighted in yellow, whereas theoretical concepts appear in orange highlighter. The comments that a candidate or a professor could make throughout the analysis of this proposed solution are in blue. The comments made by the persons grading the answer, incorporated in the evaluation guide, appear in boldface/italics. Several abbreviations are used to cut down on the annotations: "ID" (Identification of problem/issue), "ANAL" (analysis), "REC" (recommendation), "F/S" (financial statement), "CONC" (conclusion), "NRV" (net realizable value), "G+A" (general and administrative), etc.

b The "To, From, Subject" sections act as an introduction to the requested memo. Personally, as explained in Part 2 (p. 26), I briefly recall the thrust of the Required/ Requirements in the Subject section of the report. This replaces the contents of the first paragraph above. I also write "Date: September 12, 2012". As part of the year-end audit at September 30, it seems to me that it is important to indicate one's place in time. For example, this enables an adequate planning of the gathering of evidence as to the existence of the assets.

c Although this paragraph appears at the beginning of the solution, the link to the schedule containing the calculation could nevertheless be included in order to support the statements made.

REQUIREMENT: analyse the accounting issues of significance

Assessment Opportunity (Indicator) #1
Financial Reporting

REMINDER: materiality of $430,000

Assessment opportunity/Primary Indicator #1	*(V-2.2, V-2.3)*
The candidate provides appropriate analysis of the accounting issues.	
The candidate demonstrates competence in Financial Reporting.	

As a Canadian public company, DFT is subject to reporting under IFRS, which it adopted previously. I have identified a number of accounting issues, many of which will significantly affect the projected results for the year, which in turn will directly affect the bonus amount, and could also lead to material misstatement of the financial statements.

accounting issues
↓
projected results
↓
bonus amount
↓ ↓ ↓
material misstatement

1- NRE discount
2- Indo inventory
3- grants

Revenue Recognition

1- of lesser importance

Non-recurring engineering (NRE)

NRE represents a significant revenue stream. DFT has booked a total of $2.5 million in NRE revenue. The first $1.5 million in NRE revenue, which appeared to have no further obligations beyond the initial engineering work, was appropriate to recognize under IAS 18, *Revenue*, as it had been fully earned. a

CONC

2 aspects:
– 1.5 M
– 1 M add'l

However, the latest arrangement differs from previous NRE revenue. DFT obtained NRE work in July for $1 million. The difference is that the customer only agreed to the normal price on the NRE portion because DFT agreed to provide a $225,000 discount, on product that usually sells for $750,000, on sales in the 2013 fiscal year. The NRE revenue would not have occurred without this concession by DFT. Therefore, the NRE revenue is linked to the future sales of product. Under IAS 18, Paragraph 13, the transactions are considered linked and should be looked at as a whole:

THEREFORE

CRITICAL ASPECT: TWO LINKED TRANSACTIONS

[I]n certain circumstances, it is necessary to apply the recognition criteria to the separately identifiable components of a single transaction in order to reflect the substance of the transaction. For example, when the selling price of a product includes an identifiable amount for subsequent servicing, that amount is deferred and recognised as revenue over the period during which the service is performed. ***Conversely, the recognition criteria are applied to two or more transactions together when they are linked in such a way that the commercial effect cannot be understood without reference to the series of transactions as a whole.*** *For example, an entity may sell goods and, at the same time, enter into a separate agreement to repurchase the goods at a later date, thus negating the substantive effect of the transaction; in such a case, the two transactions are dealt with together.*

A candidate who does not remember this specific aspect of the accounting standard can, however, rely on his or her general knowledge and "common sense". It is logical to consider that the discount applies both to the current period and to the subsequent period.

a The recognition of the first part of the NRE revenues, in the amount of $1.5M, is not especially problematic. Since the accounting treatment to apply is clear, a conclusion justified using theory and case facts is sufficient.

clear and precise REC

The NRE revenue should have a portion of the discount applied to it, since the amount being charged is determined in conjunction with the pricing of other elements (the product sales) of the transaction. The total gross sales value is $1.75 million ($1 million NRE plus $750,000 product). a Since DFT provided a discount of $225,000 on the product sale in order to get the entire contract, a portion of the discount should be attributed to the NRE revenue. As a result, a portion of the $1 million NRE revenue that would otherwise be recognized must be deferred.

CONCEPT: CUT-OFF

SO? F/S IMPACT

easy assumption: proportion

The percentage of the contract performed before year-end, based on revenues $1 million divided by $1.75 million, is 57%. DFT should therefore allocate 57% of the discount to the NRE part of the contract by deferring 57% of the discount amount of $225,000 ($128,571). b

1 / 1.75 M = 57%

A simple and short calculation should be incorporated into the body of the text itself.

Integration link ACCT – AUDIT

The reduction in revenue is significant, although not material on its own, in terms of the financial statements audit (see recalculation of materiality). The net reduction will have a direct impact on the bonus calculation.

ACCT: significant, 250 / 1 000
AUDIT: not material, 129 < 434

focus of attention ↓ 2012

(Most candidates did not recognize that the discount was linked to future product sales and should have been considered as part of the transaction that included the NRE $1 million revenue. Instead, they focused on the fact that the discount had not been recorded and that it should be reflected in the financial statements of the current year. Strong candidates recognized the underlying substance of the arrangement and understood that the two sales transactions should be looked at as a whole, and applied case facts to support their technical understanding. Those candidates properly allocated the discount over a rational basis between 2012 and 2013.)

CONCEPT: substance over form ↓ 2 transactions as a whole

allocation? ↓ rational basis

2- Indo-Tech (Indo)

deal in force → compliance with its terms

IMP

The arrangement with Indo is structured in such a way that revenue is earned either when Indo takes possession of the inventory or when 60 days have elapsed from receipt at the third-party warehouse. As a result of the agreement in place, all of the $1.50 million related to inventory shipped by June 30 could be recognized by September 30, even if Indo had not taken the inventory on August 2. It is appropriate to recognize the revenue under IAS 18. c

2 aspects:
– 1.5 M
– 1.85 M

CONC

---

a One must have properly understood that DFT has two types of revenues: Products and Services (A4) and that the non-recurring engineering (NRE) contract falls under Services. $1.5M of these services was anticipated at the reporting date; the balance of the item Revenue amounting to approximately $50-55M (A7) relates to Products. However, there has been $1M in additional NRE revenues (Services) at the usual price IN 2012 due to a discount that will be granted IN 2013 on the sale of Products. One must therefore allocate to each of the fiscal years its appropriate share of the $225,000 discount.

b **what DFT intends to do**

revenues	2012	2013
services	1,000,000	–
products	–	750,000

what ought to be done

revenues	2012	2013
services	871,429 *	–
products	–	878,571

* 1,000,000 - 128,571

N.B.: It is the allocation of the amount between the two fiscal years that changes; the total revenue is still $1.75M.

c The accounting for an inventory valued at $1.5M is not particularly problematic. Since the accounting treatment to recommend is clear, a conclusion justified using theory and case facts is sufficient.

ISSUE TO ANALYZE: REVENUE RECOGNITION

However, the remaining $1.85 million of revenue related to the inventory shipped to the third-party warehouse cannot be recognized as revenue unless Indo takes the inventory by September 30, since 60 days will not have passed since its arrival at the warehouse (we don't know the exact shipping and arrival dates, but if we assume it was shipped on August 3, it is about 57 days at September 30). The only revenue that should be recognized by September 30 is the sales value of the items taken by Indo by September 30. a The remainder of the items should be recorded in inventory at cost until the 60 days in the warehouse have passed. b

CONCEPT: cut-off

REC

IMPACT ON F/S

The agreement with Indo is an unusual one in that it passes title to Indo after 60 days for goods sitting in a warehouse. It seems unlikely that Indo would pay for goods it hasn't taken from the warehouse. If the goods sit in the warehouse and are not paid for, there may be issues of collectability (see IAS 18.14(d)).

CRITICAL ASPECT: TRANSFER OF RISKS AND REWARDS

(Many candidates addressed this issue, and most were able to apply simulation facts to their discussions. However, some candidates failed to recognize the significance of the 60 days in inventory at Safe Storage, and considered only the transfer of risks and rewards in their discussions. As a result, they concluded that since Indo had not taken the inventory, the sale should not have been recorded.)

particular detail from the case: 60-day delay
One must use this information!

3- Grant

"funds received" → cash basis of accounting ≠ accrual basis of accounting

IMP 800 > 434

The government grant revenue has been inappropriately recognized in full upon receipt. Paragraph 17 of IAS 20, *Accounting for Government Grants and Disclosure of Government Assistance*, states: ID

In most cases the periods over which an entity recognises the costs or expenses related to a government grant are readily ascertainable. Thus grants in recognition of specific expenses are recognised in profit or loss in the same period as the relevant expenses. ***Similarly, grants related to depreciable assets are usually recognised in profit or loss over the periods and in the proportions in which depreciation expense on those assets is recognised.***

problem identified
↓
targeted analysis

CRITICAL ASPECT:
GRANTS ARE RECOGNIZED IN THE SAME PERIOD AS THE RELEVANT EXPENSES

---

a

August 2		Y/E September 30
↓		↓
Indo takes up $1.5M in inventory at the warehouse.	DFT ships $1.85M of inventory to the warehouse.	The $1.85M in inventory is still at the warehouse.
↓		↓
DFT records the revenue of $1.5M.		DFT must not record the revenue of $1.85M.

b Fundamentally, the accounting issue to be analyzed relates to revenue recognition. Of course, the case facts follow the shipment of the inventory all the way to India, and then onto Indo. However, the core issue is the following: WHEN SHOULD ONE RECOGNIZE THE REVENUES? IN 2012 OR IN 2013? Once this issue has been settled, it will be easy to determine the corresponding cost of sales as well as the inventory on hand, pursuant to the matching principle.

estimated life of the product: 3 years or less (A6)

REC

Therefore, DFT's government grant of $800,000 would be related to depreciable assets, and therefore should be recognized in income over the period, and in the same proportion in which the depreciation expense on those assets is recognized (or it could be used to reduce expenses). Since 75%, or $600,000, of the related costs remain in deferred development costs (in the information from Anne), only $200,000 of the grant revenue should be recognized in income. The remaining $600,000 should be deferred and recognized in income as the related costs are amortized. Currently, DFT has recorded all the grant monies in revenue (note, therefore, that there is a classification error).

800:
– 600 B/S
– 200 I/S

DFT: 800 in revenue
TO DO: 200 in income; 600 to defer / to amortize on 3 years

REC
F/S IMPACT

Therefore, revenue needs to be reduced by the full $800,000. Since $600,000 should be deferred, the remaining $200,000 is reallocated to research and development. Amortization expense will also be adjusted. DFT's policy is to amortize over a period of up to three years; therefore, the adjustment would be to amortize the grant over the same period of three years, resulting in an estimated amortization of $200,000 per year (note that the yearly amount then needs to be pro-rated for the portion of the year that applies).

N.B.: This adjustment of the amortization of the deferred development costs has not been included in the adjusted net income.

asset
↓
amortization

Note: Some of the grant received is likely for research rather than development. There would be immediate recognition of the grant income when the research costs were recognized, and the amortization amount would be adjusted accordingly. a

hypothetical
↓
minor

(Most candidates addressed this issue. When addressed, it was generally well done. Candidates applied case facts to their technical knowledge and concluded on an appropriate treatment that was consistent with their analysis.)

Zeus — Inventory CRITICAL ASPECT: NRV OF INVENTORY

Even if it would be preferable to have more extensive information on the net realizable value of this inventory, one must nevertheless submit a conclusion.

Zeus was expected to be developed by mid-August. The delayed development, and the subsequent entry into the market of a competing product before Zeus, may raise concerns about the valuation of the Zeus inventory (just beginning to be produced). Under IAS 2, *Inventories*, a writedown would be required if the net realizable value of inventory is below the recorded cost. Given that DFT's products generally have a 40% gross margin, a decrease in the planned selling price, while reducing DFT's margins, would likely not result in a net realizable value that is below cost, and therefore, no writedown would likely be required as of September 30. A4

Be wary of making drastic conclusions! The inventory is not valued at $0.

↓ sales price up to 40% → positive margin
THUS highly likely that NRV ≥ cost

Since production just began, there is the risk of there being potential quality assurance issues, which could lead to the need to set up a warranty provision for potential claims. This risk is increased when considering management's bias to increase sales in order to achieve a higher bonus.

few case facts
↓
hypothetical
↓
minor

LINK
BONUS

---

a It is actually unknown which portion of the grants applies to research costs, since the case only states that it is government funding for R&D (A6). In the absence of information, one cannot assume...
I draw your attention to the fact that the ideas put forth in this paragraph are general and hypothetical in nature, due to a lack of concrete support that can be found in the case. The contents of this Note, therefore, do not appear to me to be necessary to achieve success in respect of this topic.

case + knowledge ↓ ↓ analysis

(Candidates sometimes considered whether the valuation of the Zeus inventory was still appropriate, and used case facts to support their concern (for example, the fact that the competitor's product was out to market before Zeus). Those candidates recognized that net realizable value needed to be compared to cost and frequently linked their discussions to the audit work that would be required in this area before a decision could be made as to whether a writedown was required.)

link ACCT – AUDIT

1- Zeus
2- Ares

Research and Development

Although the critical aspect is the same – whether to writedown the deferred R&D costs – the analysis of the Zeus product and the analysis of the Ares product are to be conducted separately. Indeed, the case facts, as well as the theoretical concepts involved, are not the same.

of lesser importance

Zeus a CRITICAL ASPECT: CRITERIA FOR DEFERMENT – WRITEDOWN

Unanticipated technical difficulties b have caused delays in the development of Zeus. DFT plans on having sales and producing inventory by the end of the year, but it has just begun production (it is now two weeks before year-end). Based on the nature of DFT's business, in which it is important to stay ahead of the competition and produce new technology, and considering that the plan for Zeus was to tap into a growth market, the value of the Zeus product may be questionable, now that a competitor has beaten it to the market. DFT thinks it will need to sell at a lower price. We may need to assess the likelihood of bringing Zeus to market (in other words, assess whether the terms for deferment are still being met). c

Link to the specific features of DFT's industry (A3-A4)

practical sense

ID

no figures in the case → no adjustment to net income

(Few candidates addressed this issue, perhaps due to the fact it was not clearly directed in the simulation. Some mention was made as to the development of the new product (Zeus) but little additional information was provided. Most candidates who did question whether the development costs would continue to satisfy the criteria for deferment were able to apply the relevant case facts in their discussions of the technical considerations for deferral.)

IMP
450 > 434

Ares CRITICAL ASPECT: CRITERIA FOR DEFERMENT – WRITEDOWN

The abandoned development of the Ares product would normally indicate the need for a writedown. Under IAS 38, *Intangible Assets*, the conditions for recognizing an intangible asset include the technical feasibility of and intention to complete the intangible asset so that it will be available for use or sale, and the probability it will generate future economic benefits. These conditions must be met at a point in time, such as when evaluating the project.

2 separate products: ARES + HADES

1- consider the Ares product from an individual point of view (paragraph above)
2- consider a transfer of costs to the Hades product (1st paragraph of page A15)

---

a The discussion of the issue of writing down of part or all of the deferred development costs for the Zeus product is an "indirect issue". However, it forms part of the "direct requirement" to discuss the accounting issues of the period.

b Upon reading the case (A6), the term "technical" might evoke the criterion of "technical feasibility" inherent in development costs (IAS 38, para. 57*(a)*). In addition, the fact that "a competitor was able to place a similar product on the market FIRST" alters the capacity to generate "probable future economic benefits" (IAS 38, para. 57 *(d)*). These case facts lead us to look beyond the issue of the inventory to also inquire about the deferred development costs.

c The analysis of this topic could be drafted in another manner. One could start by saying that a writedown of Zeus' R&D costs is probably necessary by supporting this conclusion with the many case facts available.

Although the related development may be at least partially transferable to the new product, Hades, DFT clearly has no intention of continuing with Ares. At some point in time there would need to be an assessment of Hades to determine whether the conditions of IAS 38 are met. It would not be possible to link the Ares costs to the Hades project, unless some of the costs had been identified as applying to both projects when first initiated. As a result, the related development costs of $450,000 should be written off.

SO?
F/S IMPACT
↓
net income

clear and precise
REC

The write-off results in an increase in expenses of $450,000.

(Most candidates who addressed this issue did so briefly, concluding that the costs should be written off because the development of Ares had been abandoned. Their discussions did not consider management's position that the costs may be transferrable to Hades, which made it difficult for them to demonstrate depth in their responses.)

Whether one agrees with it or not, the point of view of management must be analyzed.

MINOR
125 < 434

Contingency

CRITICAL ASPECT: CONTINGENT ASSET? DEBIT?

what has been done:
Prepaid 125
Cash 125

The reassessment of $125,000 related to GST/HST has already been paid, and there is no guarantee that the courts will allow the money to be returned, even though DFT believes there has been an error. As a result, it is a contingent asset, which IAS 37, *Provisions, Contingent Liabilities and Contingent Assets*, defines as "*a possible asset that arises from past events and whose existence will only be confirmed by the occurrence or non-occurrence of one or more uncertain future events not wholly within the control of the entity.*" IAS 37, Paragraph 33, states: "*Contingent assets are not recognised in financial statements since this may result in the recognition of income that may never be realised. However, when the realisation of income is virtually certain, then the related asset is not a contingent asset and its recognition is appropriate.*" Because DFT cannot be certain that the courts will allow the money to be returned, virtual certainty does not exist, and therefore no asset should be recorded.

CONCEPT:
VIRTUAL
CERTAINTY

THEREFORE

Contingent assets are not recognized under IAS 37, but can be disclosed in the notes to the financial statements when an inflow of economic benefits is probable. It appears to be too early to determine whether the amount will be realized or not. As a result, the amount should not be recorded as a prepaid asset, nor should it be disclosed in the financial statements. Rather, DFT should examine the source of the reassessment — was it due to not charging GST/HST when it should have, or to claiming an ITC when it was not eligible? Instead of booking as a prepaid, the amount should be posted where the reassessment indicated the errors were. Either way, expenses will be increased.

few info
↓
arbitrary

THEREFORE

The $125,000 is treated as an increase in general and administrative expenses for now.

SO?
F/S IMPACT
↓
net income

(Few candidates recognized that the $125,000 represented a contingent asset. Candidates' discussions of this issue were very brief, and most concluded that the prepaid item had been erroneously recorded and should have been expensed instead.) a

not important
↓
be brief
↓
justify
the conclusion
directly

The item G+A is the best choice under the circumstances.

---

a Since it is not a very important topic, it is normal to conduct a more succinct analysis. At the very least, one must make sure to justify the recommendation.

It is clear that the impairment loss must be included in net income. The issue is rather to determine WHERE?

MINOR
100 < 434

Impairment Loss

ID

The impairment loss of $100,000, related to obsolete production equipment, should not be included in amortization of capital assets (adjusted general and administrative), but in cost of sales.

CRITICAL ASPECT: CLASSIFICATION OF THE LOSS

IAS 16, *Property, Plant and Equipment*, defines depreciation as the systematic allocation of the depreciable amount of an asset over its useful life, whereas impairment is a valuation assessment not part of the normal allocation process. It could be included as a separate charge.

It is not, however, a significant amount.

Practically speaking, since amortization of production-related assets is included in cost of sales, it could be argued that the impairment charge should also be included in cost of sales since it is related to the production equipment. In addition, it should be disclosed separately from amortization in the notes to the financial statements, rather than grouped into one amount to ensure full disclosure, depending on how material the amount is (see IAS 1.85 and 1.86 regarding separate line items). a

CONCEPT: MATERIALITY

As a result of this writedown, management may also need to question the amortization periods.

"MAY ALSO" ↓ hypothetical

IMPACT

Consideration should be given to the impact on the bonus calculation. Since the bonus is based on EBITDA, including the impairment loss in amortization means it is excluded as an expense in the calculation. If, however, it is separately disclosed, it could be argued that it is part of cost of sales and should be included in EBITDA.

LINK BONUS

Relevant issue: impairment loss INCLUDED or EXCLUDED from EBITDA?

The $100,000 impairment adjustment should be moved from general and administrative expenses to cost of sales, and should not be considered amortization.

SO? F/S IMPACT ↓ net income

CONC

(Only about a third of the candidates discussed the impairment issue. Most candidates who addressed it were able to provide appropriate discussions, noting that the impairment loss should not be included with amortization and should be presented elsewhere in the financial statements.)

MINOR
100 < 434

The amount of $100,000 is not very significant, but it nevertheless enables you to show your understanding of the impact on the calculation of the bonus.

---

a

DEPRECIATION production equipment ↓ systematic allocation of the depreciable amount of an asset over its useful life ↓ PART OF the normal allocation process ↓ Cost of sales	IMPAIRMENT production equipment ↓ excess of carrying amount over its recoverable amount ↓ NOT PART OF the normal allocation process ↓ separate charge OR Cost of sales

Management Bonus a

DFT has a new bonus plan this year. The $300,000 about to be accrued by Anne for the management bonuses cannot be booked until certain requirements are satisfied. It is contingent on achieving the set amount of EBITDA. b

ID

Condition to be met EBITDA > 14 M

CRITICAL ASPECT: EXISTENCE OF AN OBLIGATION

In this case, the issue is whether the entity has a present legal obligation or a constructive obligation. Based on IAS 19.17 to 20 and IAS 37, there does not appear to be a legal obligation yet because the terms of the bonus have not been met. The question is whether the bonus might be considered a constructive obligation. Because this bonus plan was not in place in the past, it does not look like there is a constructive obligation either. The bonus might be considered a provision. However, there is no guarantee that the minimum EBITDA will be met; therefore, no accrual should be made at this point. If the conditions are met at September 30, then a provision can be booked. c

legal obligation

constructive obligation

CONC wait for the completion of the F/S to account for the provision

MATCHING PRINCIPLE

(Very few candidates considered whether the management bonus represented a legal obligation or a constructive obligation. More candidates concluded on whether the bonus threshold would be met, usually as a result of their recalculation of the adjusted net income and the EBITDA calculation.)

One must refer to the calculation appended hereto.

accounting issues
↓
net income
↓
bonus calculation
↓
provision

1- Does the provision exist?
- past event
- legal or constructive obligation

2- If so, for what amount?
- reliable estimation

---

a It is easy to forget the analysis of the provision for bonuses. On the one hand, it is not yet recorded in the books and, on the other hand, it is the last item on the "Other" list in the case (A6). However, do not lose sight of the fact that the implementation of a new bonus program at the beginning of fiscal 2012 represents one of the significant features of the case (A8). From this perspective, one must assess its impact on BOTH of the case requirements: accounting AND audit.
In my opinion, the determination of the importance of the issue of the accounting for the bonuses must take into account the revised EBITDA, which income is likely below the $14M target. Since the awarding of the bonuses depends on the precise nature of this amount, it is normal that his issue should appear last.

b At the time of resolution of the case, the estimated amount of $300,000 in bonuses to be paid has not yet been recorded in the books. The manner in which the ideas are expressed takes this fact into consideration.

c It will be possible to determine more precisely, on September 30, whether bonuses are to be paid to DFT's management. At that time, the item Bonus provision will be an estimated liability. The liability exists, but the amount thereof remains uncertain. Such will be the case so long as the financial statements shall not have been "authorized", since various adjusting entries can affect EBITDA. In fact, one must practically wait until the date the financial statements are authorized for issue (IAS 10) in order to determine the precise amount of bonuses to be paid. In other words, one must be ready to reassess the amount of the provision in light of more recent information.

Adjusted Net Income for the Year Ended September 30, 2012
(in thousands)

SIGNIFICANT drop in net income → no bonus → materiality

	DFT adjusted projection	Accounting adjustments	Note	objective of calculation ↓ Revised projection
Revenue	$59,224	(2,779)	A1	$56,445
Cost of sales	33,872	(1,010)	A1, A4	$32,862
Gross margin	25,352	(1,769)		$23,583
Operating expenses				
Research and Development	3,991	250	A2, A1	$4,241
Sales and marketing	2,622	–		$2,622
General and administrative	7,924	25	A3, A4	$7,949
Interest	314	–		$314
Total operating expenses	14,851	275		$15,126
Income before taxes	10,501	(2,044)		$8,457
Income taxes	3 150	(613)	A5	$2,537
Net income	$7,351	(1,431)		**$5,920**

Note A1
Revenue
↓ 129
↓ 800
↓ 1,850
↓ 2,779

Notes A1, A2
R&D
↑ 450
↓ 200
↑ 250

do not only calculate! ↓ interpret!

The reference (30%) placed next to the item Income taxes can replace Note A5, since it is an item of information supplied as is in the case.

Notes:

Note A1 [a]

- Sales have been reduced by $129,000 for 57% of the NRE discount of $225,000.
- Sales have been reduced by $800,000 for government grants since they cannot be accounted for as revenue. Along with the related deferred development costs, $600,000 should be deferred. The remaining balance of $200,000 has been moved to R&D expenses. (Amortization would need to be adjusted too — if amortized over three years, then there would be $200,000 ($600,000 ÷ 3) more in amortization, which would then also be pro-rated for the portion of the year.)
- Sales have been reduced by $1.85 million not yet earned for the Indo shipment. Cost of sales has also been adjusted by $1.11 million based on the 40% product margin (assumed same margin).

impact on amortization: $600/3y = $200 not considered here, but considered on A20

Since the case contains no case facts as to the number of applicable months, it is reasonable to use a whole year in the calculation.

Note A2

- Research and development expenses have been increased by $450,000 for deferred development costs related to the Ares product (write-off of deferred R&D). They have also been decreased by $200,000 for the grants reallocated from revenue.

Note A3 The amortization will ultimately need to be increased by $450/3y = $150.

- General and administrative expenses have been increased by $125,000 for the GST/HST reassessment (reclassified from prepaid expense).

Notes A1, A4
Cost of sales
↓ 1,110
↑ 100
↓ 1,010

Note A4

- DFT recorded $100,000 for impairment of assets. This can be included in cost of sales, not general and administrative expenses, and should not be considered amortization. Therefore, move $100,000 from general and administrative to cost of sales.

Note A5

- Using an estimated tax rate of 30%, there should be a reduction of $613,000 for the accounting adjustments ($2,044,000 × 30%).

---

a The contents of the explanatory notes can appear, in whole or in part, in the body of the text of the answer as such. It would then not be necessary to repeat them here.

COMMENTS:

- When presenting explanatory notes, I personally prefer to create a separate note for each of the adjustments. This allows for a more specific reference, while cutting down on errors.

- IT IS ABSOLUTELY NOT NECESSARY TO PROVIDE JOURNAL ENTRIES IN THE ANSWER TO A CASE.
  However, in the process of analyzing the proposed solution, it helps to understand what is going on, especially where the transactions involved are complex.

Journal entries (JE) [a]

JEs	Item description	Debit	Credit
1	Revenue	↘ $128,571	
1	Deferred revenue		$128,571
	$250,000 $ x 57% = $128,571		
	To defer part of the discount on the NRE contract.		
2	Revenue	↘ $1,850,000	
2	Accounts receivable		$1,850,000
2	Inventory	$1,110,000	
2	Cost of sales		$1,110,000
	$1,850,000 x 60% = $1,110,000		
	To reverse the sale of inventory that Indo-Tech has not taken out from the warehouse.		
3	Revenue	↘ $800,000	
3	Deferred Development Costs		$600,000
3	Research and Development expenses		$200,000
	To accurately record the grants received during the period.		
4	Research and Development expenses	$450,000	
4	Deferred Development Costs		$450,000
	To write-off the development costs for the Ares product.		
5	Cost of sales	$100,000	
5	General & administrative		$100,000
	To reclassify the impairment loss of $100,000 related to production equipment.		

The first three JE bring about a decrease in revenues.

↓ net income (JEs 1 to 4)

- The main adjustments relate to the items Revenue and Cost of sales. In this situation, a simple calculation of the gross margin, therefore, includes the essence of the required adjustments.
  Consequently, indicating the revised gross margin, instead of the statement of income, is sufficient to demonstrate competence.

---

a THINKING DEBIT–CREDIT WHEN CALLED UPON TO ADJUST FINANCIAL STATEMENTS REDUCES THE OCCURRENCE OF ERRORS AND OMISSIONS. IT IS AN EFFECTIVE MANNER OF PROCEEDING, EVEN IF THERE ARE ONLY A FEW ITEMS TO CORRECT.

Earnings before interest, taxes, depreciation and amortization (EBITDA) based on revised projected net income a

	Per DFT July projection	Adjusted DFT projection	After accounting adjustments	COMMENTS
Income before taxes	$18,681	$10,501	$8,457	(as adjusted – see previous worksheet)
Add back:				
Interest	314	314	314	
Amortization of production-related assets	430	430	430	
Amortization of deferred development costs	1,620	1,620	1,620	
Adjustment to amor of def dev costs (note 1)			(200)	related to deferral of government grant portion (600k/3yrs estimated) b
Adjustment to amor of def dev costs (note 1)			150	related to abandonment of Ares project
			150	(450k/3yrs estimated) c
Amortization of capital assets	2,995	3,095	2,995	
EBITDA for bonus calculation	$14,040	$15,960	$13,766	< 14M Min to get bonus is $14 million If Indo takes delivery before Sept 30 bonus could be achieved
Gross margin of 40% on $1,850 Indo shipment (if happens before Sept 30) d			740	
			$14,506	Management would get bonus again
			> 14M	

Note: Need EBITDA of $14 million for management to get bonus
Further adjustments may be required — additional info is necessary in order to

Zeus: Consideration of value of project (i.e., Is there any? Is any writedown of inventory required?). e	Unknown	Need more information to determine

Note 1 – Development costs amortized over estimated life of product, generally 3 years or less.
Assume 3 years are remaining on project for which government grant was received and on Ares

a One must appreciate the fact that preparing this calculation, in addition to the one above (A18), takes up more time than what is actually available for the resolution of this 70-minute case.
First of all, I suggest that you have a good understanding of the entire proposed solution.
Secondly, I suggest that you take a step back in order to determine what can reasonably be done in the time frame allotted.
Personally, as discussed in Part 6, I would have made one single calculation, namely the adjusted EBITDA, which includes the main adjustments (p. 74 OR p. 81). In addition, to me, it does not appear necessary to include the first two columns of the above table, which merely repeat the case facts. Only the third column contains relevant and new ideas, since the purpose of this calculation is to compare a revised EBITDA amount to the $14M target.

b This adjustment of the amortization was not considered in the calculation of the adjusted net income (A18). It could and should – theoretically – have been included. It is not, however, necessary to go that far in preparing the calculation in order to succeed in this part of the solution.
This adjustment arises as a result of a previous adjustment entry made (JE#3). By reducing the deferred development costs by $600,000 as a result of the receipt of the grants, it goes without saying that this also decreases the amortization as of the date of the accounting for the grants. Its significance arises from the fact that this influences, *via* the calculation of EBITDA, the amount of bonuses to be paid to management.
In order to determine the amount of the adjustment, one must make an assumption. It is assumed here that the grants were received on the first day of the fiscal year and that the remaining life is the usual estimated life of the products, namely three years. This is a reasonable assumption, based on the case facts, and which is easy to work with.

c The same comments as appear under "b" apply to this adjustment that arises as a result of a previous adjustment entry made. By writing off $450,000 in deferred development costs (JE#4) as a result of the discontinuance of the Ares product, it goes without saying that this also reduces the amortization expenses as of the date of this write-off.

d I draw your attention to the manner of presenting this latter adjustment of $740. Since we just don't know whether Indo-Tech will take inventory out from the warehouse BEFORE or AFTER September 30, it is a good idea to establish a sub-total of EBITDA without considering this adjustment. Incidentally, it can be observed THAT THIS ADJUSTMENT MAKES A DIFFERENCE, since the corrected EBITDA is flirting with the $14M target.

e For the time being, it is unknown if a writedown of Zeus' inventory is required and, should it be necessary, the case contains no case facts enabling a determination of the amount. Personally, in my presentation of a calculation, I do not indicate anything that cannot be expressed in numbers.

EXPLICIT REQUIREMENT

For Assessment Opportunity/Primary Indicator #1 (Financial Reporting), the candidate must be ranked in one of the following five categories:	Percent Awarded
Not addressed — The candidate does not address this primary indicator.	0.0%
Nominal competence — The candidate does not attain the standard of reaching competence.	1.5%
Reaching competence — The candidate identifies some of the significant accounting issues for DFT when applying IFRS.	36.7%
Competent — The candidate discusses some of the significant accounting issues for DFT when applying IFRS and considers the impact of the issues on the projected financial statements or the bonus calculation.	61.5%
Competent with distinction — The candidate discusses several of the significant accounting issues for DFT when applying IFRS and considers the impact of the issues on the projected financial statements and on the bonus calculation.	0.3%

Nominal competence ↓ lack of depth OR impact not stated

IDENTIFY ↓ DISCUSS

SOME ↓ SEVERAL

←

impact ↓ financial statements OR bonus calculation

some issues ↓ not all ↓ among the most significant ↓ **at least one aspect** of revenue recognition

(Candidates were asked to provide appropriate analysis of the accounting issues. To achieve competence, they were expected to discuss some of the significant issues for DFT when applying IFRS and to consider the impact of the issues on the projected financial statements or the bonus calculation. Candidates were clearly directed to this indicator, since the partner asked for a memo summarizing the accounting issues of significance.)

knowledge case ↓ ↓ discussion ↓ recommendation ↓ impact

(Candidates performed reasonably well on this indicator. Most were able to apply simulation facts to their technical knowledge in their discussions. Most candidates made recommendations regarding appropriate accounting treatments that were consistent with the analysis provided. In terms of the issues addressed, most candidates discussed one aspect of revenue recognition, which was often the early recognition of the Indo sales, as well as the grant and the Zeus inventory. Many candidates also considered the impact on the projected financial statements or the bonus, or both, at the end of their accounting issue discussions.)

TECHNICAL KNOWLEDGE + DATA CONTAINED IN THE SIMULATION → COMPETENT LEVEL

(Strong candidates provided responses that were well organized and that substantially covered the issues. Their responses were also strong from both a technical perspective and an application perspective. Weak candidates did not demonstrate sufficient IFRS knowledge, did not apply case facts in their discussions, or neglected to do either. Many of their discussions of an issue were general in nature and had no specificity to this simulation.)

strong response ↓ technical + application

structured analysis

ESSENTIAL ISSUES → SIGNIFICANT ISSUES

ESSENTIAL ISSUES ≠ ALL THE ISSUES

COMMENTS:

- Achieving the "Reaching competence" level requires a consideration of **some of the significant accounting issues**. It is obvious that more than one must be tackled; I would say approximately three, among the most important. One must also be aware that one must do a bit more than just "identify" the issue to be analyzed. Stating, for example, that "the grants in the amount of $800,000 were improperly accounted for", will not suffice. One must at least "try" to resolve the outstanding issue. At this level of assessment, the analysis of a topic is incomplete, but on the verge of being complete.

Competence: Financial Reporting

Reaching competence	Competent	Competent with distinction
IDENTIFY SOME accounting issues	DISCUSS SOME accounting issues + IMPACT projected F/S OR bonus calculation	DISCUSS SEVERAL accounting issues + IMPACT projected F/S OR bonus calculation

- One can observe, from the outset, that it is not necessary to perform a calculation of the revised net income or of the revised EBITDA to be successful in respect of this competence. One must, however, wonder about the IMPACT on the projected financial statements OR on the bonus calculation. This can be demonstrated though a qualitative analysis OR a quantitative analysis.

  WHAT IS IMPORTANT IS TO GO BEYOND THE EXPLANATION AS TO THE APPROPRIATE ACCOUNTING TREATMENT AND TO ASSESS THE IMPACT.

  The case facts set the scope of the majority of the accounting issues, present an adjusted net income and insist on the EBITDA target of $14M.

  Personally, I would have made a calculation to bolster my ideas. In this type of situation, it is generally quicker to express the impact in numbers than in words. Incidentally, this enables you to take a step back to better assess the overall situation. We will revisit this point when looking at assessment opportunity #3 (A33) with respect to management's bonuses.

- One of the fundamental issues is to determine what to do to achieve the passing standard – Competent level – in Financial reporting. Let us say that a certain amount of topics must be analyzed sufficiently in depth. I would say three or four topics – at least for a majority of them – among the list of important topics (Part 2, p. 21). To me, it appears to be crucial to analyze the issue of Indo-Tech's products.

  The analysis of the selected topics must be complete, that is to say that it explains and justifies the accounting treatment that was determined to be applicable. The integration of theoretical concepts to the particulars of the case must be demonstrated. The critical aspect to be discussed must be well focused. An analysis of the accounting for the inventory shipped to India, for example, cannot replace a "relevant" analysis of revenue recognition.

  In other words, the analysis of a topic of lesser importance – even if it is well done – cannot compensate for the absence of or lack of depth in the analysis of an important topic.

REQUIREMENT: discuss the impact on the year-end audit planning and the procedures to be performed

Assessment Opportunity (Indicator) #2
Audit and Assurance

explicit requirement ↓ explicit answer

Assessment opportunity/Primary Indicator #2 *(VI-2.3, VI-2.4, VI-2.5, VI-2.9)*

The candidate identifies the impact of the accounting issues on the planning of the audit and suggests procedures to be performed.

The candidate demonstrates competence in Audit and Assurance.

We have been newly appointed as auditors (done in July 2012), and we are preparing for the year-end financial statement audit. Based on a review of the accounting, there are a number of issues related to DFT that must be taken into account in the planning and performance of our audit.

This introduction contains no new and relevant idea.

STRUCTURE:
- Materiality
- Risk Assessment
- Approach
- Risk areas and procedures

Materiality

A short calculation is incorporated into the text of the solution.

First, we need to determine [ID] if our preliminary calculation of materiality of $434,000 is still appropriate. Based on the revised forecast that includes the accounting adjustments, I believe an adjustment will be necessary. Materiality was initially estimated in July to be $434,000 based on 5% of preliminary net income before tax of $8,681,000 (using CAS 320 A4 and A7). My revised estimate, calculated on the same basis but taking into account the accounting adjustments noted (5% of $8,457,000) is $422,850. [a] Based on these calculations, overall materiality should be decreased.

LINK ACCT — INTEGRATION — CONC

MATERIALITY – F/S as a whole – Performance

Preliminary materiality for the financial statements as a whole was calculated during our initial audit planning, but it is not clear whether we also calculated a performance materiality.

The case contains no information on the performance materiality.

REC

In addition, it may be well advised to set a separate materiality (at a lesser amount) on those areas affecting EBITDA directly, as well as considering a performance materiality for those areas of concern, due to the increased user reliance from management for purposes of the bonus calculation.

MATERIALITY? ↓ USERS

ID:	determine if the preliminary calculation of materiality is still appropriate
ANAL:	assess the need for revising the materiality (accounting adjustments, new users)
REC:	revise materiality / set separate materiality on some areas / revisit materiality after year-end

decrease in net income ↓ downward revision of the materiality

a With a view to integration, it is important to make a connection with the accounting adjustments made. What matters is taking 5% of the adjusted net income, not arriving at an exact amount, such as $8,457,000. In the assessment of materiality, one must therefore use the amount arrived at, whatever it may be.
As discussed in the previous section (A22), it was not necessary to compute an adjusted net income or an adjusted EBITDA. The absence of such a calculation must not, however, prevent you from assessing the impact of the accounting adjustments on the preliminary materiality of $434,000. Since the resolution of a majority of the accounting issues is heading in the direction of a DECREASE IN NET INCOME, it is at least possible to state that the materiality will have to be revised DOWNWARDS. Incidentally, it is easy to perform a quick calculation including one or two adjustments that support your argument.

today September 12 ↓ year-end September 30

As the results become more definitive after year-end, and as we accumulate audit adjustments, we should revisit materiality to ensure we have done sufficient, appropriate audit work to support our opinion. As we encounter unadjusted errors like those noted earlier, we should request that management adjust them. a

REC

CAS 450: *Evaluation of misstatements identified during the audit*

LINK ACCT – AUDIT

IMP to link to EBITDA ↓ key case fact

(Some candidates were able to integrate their analyses of the accounting issues with the impact of these issues on the initial audit planning that had been done, and recognized that materiality would have to be revised. Strong candidates performed calculations to determine a new materiality level, in light of the accounting changes recommended. Some of those candidates also considered the need for a performance materiality or a materiality for areas affecting EBITDA directly, or for both. Weak responses did not address this aspect of the initial audit planning at all, despite the information in the simulation from the July 2012 meeting stating that materiality was currently estimated to be $434,000.)

STRONG ANALYSIS ↓ CALCULATION NEW MATERIALITY

new user ↓ management → EBITDA → bonus

Risk Assessment

important concept ↓ revisit risk assessment ↓ update

ID

In addition to revisiting materiality, we should revisit our risk assessment. The auditor is required to document an assessment of the risk of material misstatement at the financial statement level (Ref: CAS 315.25, A105 to A108) and at the assertion level (Ref: CAS 315.32).

Financial statement level Regarding the nature of the business and DFT's operating environment, we know that DFT is a technology company whose quarterly sales can be quite variable based on inconsistent demand. We also know that the company relies heavily on research and development to ensure its products remain relevant (product life is generally three years). DFT has had some changes occur over the year that resulted in new types of revenue contracts (Indo and the unique NRE contract), a new arrangement with a third-party warehouse located overseas, new government grants for research and development, and production delays on its new product, Zeus. These issues need to be considered when planning our procedures.

particulars of context A4, A8

NEW events of the period

We do not have much information on DFT's control environment and will need to spend some time documenting systems to gain a full understanding.

little info ↓ little to say ↓ theoretical

CONC

bonus plan → management's bias ↑ risk of error

The following financial statement level risks need to be considered. First, the existence of a bonus plan based on EBITDA increases the risk of error, since management may be biased to make decisions, or override controls, to increase EBITDA. This risk will need to be taken into account when examining the transactions and account balances. Second, the GST/HST reassessment raises a question as to the quality of the accounting and record-keeping.

Although the amount of this assessment is not very important, it nevertheless raises doubt as to the quality of the record-keeping.

Exhibit II of the DFT case is more than 2 pages long!

CONTROL ASPECT ↓ IMP in audit

(Few candidates considered the impact on risk of the new information that was provided subsequent to the July 2012 initial meeting with Anne.)

ID:	revise risk assessment
ANAL:	consider new events occurring during the period
CONC:	tackle the impact of the new risks

a Personally, in order to demonstrate my integration ability, I would have supplied an example of a mistake originating from the previous analysis of the accounting issues. I would have submitted ONE OF THE MOST OBVIOUS, in brackets, in order to justify my statements.

control environment exam → system reliance → audit approach

Approach a

Only once we have examined the control environment will we be able to determine if we can rely on the system and take a control-based approach to the audit. In addition, we may wish to perform additional procedures in areas that have been identified to be of concern in our previous accounting discussion (for example, revenue recognition relating to Indo transactions and NRE revenue).

concrete examples placed in brackets

I presume that the initial audit planning has already contemplated the work that will need to be done to gain assurance over the opening balances, since we did not do the audit of the prior year's financial statements (as per CAS 510).

While it is true, it does not serve much of a purpose to say it. Instead, one must focus on the tasks TO PERFORM.

Procedures and Planning for Key Risk Areas Identified b

The "HOW" and the "WHY" of each procedure is set out.

✓: procedure

CRITICAL ASPECT: determine if the 2 transactions are linked

Item	Assertion	Specific Risks	Procedures
NRE — revenue ($1,000,000 engineering and $750,000 product sales) of lesser importance	Occurrence, accuracy, cut-off, and classification	Risk that conditions for revenue recognition are not met. LINK with accounting analysis	✓Obtain a copy of the latest contract (the unique one) and review the conditions related to earning the revenue to gain an understanding of when and how much revenue can be recognized in 2012. Consider evidence that supports the need to defer any revenue (i.e., a link to product sales). ✓Verify the completion date for the NRE portion (Sept. 15) and the margins achieved by agreeing to the contract, and verify that the financial statements reflect the substance of the transaction (defer a portion of discount of $225,000 on normal sales of $750,000).

OBJECTIVES When? How much?

allocation of the $225,000 discount

Management's bias towards overvaluing EBITDA taints the audit.

engineering (A4): when the work is completed → OBJECTIVE: What is the completion date?

---

a When discussing the audit approach, one must truly attempt to establish a link with any of the case facts. As indicated previously, the $125,000 reassessment leads the auditor to question DFT's control environment. It is not much, but it is enough to demonstrate your capacity for integration.

b Most of the procedures set out in the proposed solution start with a verb in the infinitive. Since it is an action to be undertaken – both concrete and precise –, it is an adequate manner of expressing them.
A good answer to the requirement with respect to "the procedures to be performed" can take the form of a table. Among others, this allows for a structuring of the analysis by specifying right from the outset what the specific item and risk to be checked are. Moreover, the reference to relevant assertions enables a better focus on the procedure to perform.
Finally, let us observe that the series of procedures to be performed (A25 to A30) appears in the same order as the accounting issues of the previous section.

✓: procedure

CONT'D

Item	Assertion	Specific Risks	Procedures
NRE — revenue ($1,000,000 engineering and $750,000 product sales)	Occurrence, accuracy, cut-off, and classification	Risk that conditions for revenue recognition are not met.	✓Review the calculations of the revenue to ensure they have been recorded in the proper period and at the right amount to ensure proper cut-off. OBJECTIVE Adequate calculation? Right period?

CRITICAL ASPECT: determine if there has been transfer of ownership

Item	Assertion	Specific Risks	Procedures
Indo-Tech — revenue IMP	Occurrence, accuracy, cut-off, and classification	Risk that inventory is recorded prematurely as being sold (since goods get shipped to a third-party warehouse) — consider management's bias to inflate earnings; contract has a 60-day clause that could affect recognition/cut-off. Need to track shipment dates from DFT to know when to recognize revenue.	✓Ensure that the proper amount of revenue is recorded related to Indo sales by reviewing compliance with contract terms. ✓Agree the shipments from DFT to the third-party warehouse to shipping documents/proof of shipment to Indo from warehouse. A perusal of the DOCUMENTS (agreement, shipping documents, etc.) enables evidence to be gathered. Right period? How much?

OBJECTIVE How much?

OBJECTIVE Shipped?

Management's bias towards overvaluing EBITDA taints the audit.

specific risk ↓ specific procedure

It is to be noted that the majority of the procedures to be performed can be expressed as follows:
"In order to ensure..., one must..."

"To test..., we will..."
"To ensure that..., we need to..."
"In order to..., I would suggest..."

✓: procedure

CRITICAL ASPECTS: transfer of ownership + existence

Item	Assertion	Specific Risks	Procedures
Indo-Tech — inventory ($1,850,000 or $0 depending on circumstance) IMP $1,850,000 = selling price (A5) ≠ acquisition cost	Occurrence, completeness, accuracy, cut-off, and classification	As stated, risk that goods should be recorded as inventory, not a sale; risk that off-site inventory doesn't actually exist (falsified inventory). The significance of the amounts involved warrants such a transfer to India.	We should attempt to confirm the existing inventory sitting at the third-party warehouse at year-end — we will need to communicate with Safe Storage as soon as possible to ensure the amount can be confirmed at Sept. 30. We should also confirm with Indo-Tech what it believes the amount in the warehouse is, if it has not all been taken by them. quality of the evidence: 1- third-party 2- management We may wish to visit the warehouse site ourselves to determine if there is inventory there (i.e., Indo does not take out any of the $1,850,000 in inventory that was shipped by DFT).

OBJECTIVE What inventory amount?

Storage → unrelated third-party (A5) → completeness

OBJECTIVE Does the inventory exist?

CRITICAL ASPECT: determine WHEN to recognize the grants

recording in the right period

Item	Assertion	Specific Risks	Procedures
Government funding (grant of $800,000 received for encouraging technical research and development) IMP	Occurrence, completeness, accuracy, cut-off, and classification	Risk that terms and conditions of the grant are not met and funds should be returned to government; risk that split between deferred amount is not correct; risk of amount being deferred over an incorrect period of time.	We should check the documentation and agreements related to government funding to ensure the 1- terms and conditions are met and that 2- monies have been received prior to year-end (event occurred after July projection). a Ensure grants are not recognized until the conditions of the grant are met. Verify the portion deferred (and being amortized) as part of development costs — DFT claims 75% of related development costs remain in deferred costs. Ensure any research monies received as part of grant were not deferred. OBJECTIVE Is it recorded in relation with the appropriate items?

OBJECTIVE Can the grants be accounted for?

2 criteria → 2 aspects to examine

R or D → 2 procedures

a IAS 20, para. 7
Government grants, including non-monetary grants at fair value, shall not be recognized until there is reasonable assurance that:
(a) the entity will comply with the conditions attaching to them; and
(b) the grants will be received.

✓: procedure

CONT'D

Item	Assertion	Specific Risks	Procedures
Government funding (grant of $800,000 received for encouraging technical research and development) IMP	Occurrence, completeness, accuracy, cut-off, and classification	Risk that terms and conditions of the grant are not met and funds should be returned to government; risk that split between deferred amount is not correct; risk of amount being deferred over an incorrect period of time.	In addition, ✓obtain an understanding of the products to which the funding relates and ✓trace these to the products in deferred development costs, to ensure the appropriate amount is deferred, and the appropriate classification - either expense or capital. ✓Verify amortization calculations (policy is to defer development costs over a maximum of 3 years); ✓ensure grant is being amortized over same period and is properly adjusted for a partial year.

OBJECTIVES What is the product involved? How has one expensed the related costs?

ASSET? → amortization

OBJECTIVE What is the impact on amortization? → EBITDA

CRITICAL ASPECT: "value" of deferred costs → CONCEPT: "probable future economic benefits"

OBJECTIVE Can one justify the capitalization?

Item	Assertion	Specific Risks	Procedures
R&D — Ares (abandoned R&D project of $450,000; costs continued to be deferred for new product Hades) IMP	Accuracy and classification	Risk that deferred balance cannot be used for Hades and should be written off; risk that some of Ares costs are still being deferred. development phase: compliance with criteria (IAS 38 para. 57)	✓Gain an understanding of the costs related to Ares versus Hades, likely by discussing with engineering staff, to ensure that costs that have been deferred appropriately relate to products still in development. ✓Ensure a "point in time" assessment was done to determine whether the costs can be deferred. Ensure none of the costs that were directly related to Ares are still being deferred; we should ✓obtain evidence from management of the costs that were written off and ✓calculate the amount to be written off/ expensed. Can it be recognized as an asset?

WHO? engineers or any other in-house expert e.g. project manager

OBJECTIVE Was it written down?

separate topic → separate procedure

Upon examination of the procedures set out in the proposed solution, one observes that:

- The objective is stated for each assertion: "What does one wish to audit?". The indication of the assertion or of the specific risk simplifies the development of procedures.
- The procedures are PRECISE and CONCRETE in response to the question "WHAT should one do?" and "WHY?". If applicable, one must state WHEN to do it (or for which period) and TO WHOM one should turn.
  visualization of what is going on → appropriate procedures
- The person reading the report – who is merely there to do a job / a non-management employee – must understand what is written or be able to apply it without needing any additional clarifications.

PRACTICAL SENSE

✓: procedure

CRITICAL ASPECT: "value" of capitalized costs
↓
CONCEPT: "probable future economic benefits"

OBJECTIVE
Can the capitalization be justified?

Item	Assertion	Specific Risks	Procedures
R&D (amount unknown) — Zeus (delays in bringing to market; competitor has entered market) of lesser importance	Accuracy and classification	Risk that unanticipated technical problems cannot be solved and that Zeus cannot be brought to market and that costs can no longer be deferred.	✓Discuss with management the likelihood of bringing Zeus to market. DFT plans on selling $200,000 worth of Zeus by year-end, but has only just begun production. Not likely to sell that much — inventory balance might be higher. Also risk of lower margin since it likely needs to lower the sales price — see inventory discussion. targeted margin: 40% (A4)

unanticipated technical problems
+
development delayed
=
anticipated decrease in demand

OBJECTIVE
Is the NRV below cost?

CRITICAL ASPECT: "value" of inventory

Item	Assertion	Specific Risks	Procedures a
Zeus — inventory (estimated to be $400,000 at year-end) of lesser importance	Valuation	Risk that inventory is overvalued and needs to be written down. There are no direct case facts on this aspect.	We should ✓attempt to obtain information on the revised pricing planned for the product. The lower price DFT might offer should be ✓compared to the recorded cost in inventory of these units to ensure they are recorded at the lower of cost or net realizable value. If cost is actually higher, we should calculate the amount of any required impairment. Consider that the planned sales may not occur and that the inventory balance might be higher than the planned $400,000. ✓Discuss with management issues related to possible warranty claims and the need to set up a provision due to a high rate of product return, since it is a new product.

production has just begun
+
competitor has placed a similar product on the market
=
anticipated decrease in price

OBJECTIVE
Is a warranty provision necessary?

COMMENT:

All throughout the proposed solution, one can observe that there is a clear nexus between the "accounting issue to be resolved" and the "procedure(s) to be performed". Where the accounting aspect to be analyzed is poorly defined or ignored, it then becomes very difficult – if not impossible – to submit appropriate audit procedures. In addition, the importance of an accounting topic has an undeniable influence on the following section on audit.

In the Accounting issue, one must inquire, for example, if the net realizable value of Zeus' inventory is below cost. In the Assurance issue, the procedures to be submitted relate to the VALUE (valuation) of the inventory (see "a" above). Focusing on other audit assertions, such as accuracy, would not be relevant.

✓: procedure

Item	Assertion	Specific Risks	Procedures
GST/ HST audit (recorded $125,000 as a prepaid on basis of reassessment being wrong) MINOR	Occurrence, completeness, accuracy, and classification	Risk that amount is not a prepaid/ DFT will lose reassessment and amount is an expense. Need to know what the reassessment relates to in order to verify classification.	✓Examine all documentation available related to the GST/HST audit, including the reassessment, and ✓ensure that the appropriate, and complete, amount has been recorded. Since it cannot be recorded as prepaid, this will require ✓reviewing what proportion management relates to expenses and the proportion related to items such as capital assets.

examine third-party document ↓ evidence

OBJECTIVE What is the debit?

expense OR capital asset

Item	Assertion	Specific Risks	Procedures
Impairment adjustment of $100,000 (obsolete production equipment) MINOR	Occurrence, completeness, accuracy, and classification	Risk that there is no impairment, or that the amount is greater than the $100,000 booked; risk that other pieces of equipment require a writedown. bonus plan ↓ EBITDA ↓ amortization	✓Discuss with management the basis of the impairment loss on the production equipment, ✓examine the equipment, and ✓discuss its use with production personnel to corroborate the need for recording an impairment loss. ✓Ensure other adjustments are not required for other related pieces of equipment; discuss with management. We should ✓ensure there is adequate disclosure of the impairment amount, separate from amortization expense (if material to the financial statements as a whole).

unknown reason? ↓ discuss with management

WHO? production personnel

clear + valid PROCEDURES ↓ EXPLAIN WHY ↓ conciseness

RISK ↓ PROCEDURE

(Candidates were generally able to provide clear and valid procedures to address the risks. To a lesser extent, some were also able to explain why the procedures were required. While the quantity of procedures addressed amongst candidates was comparable, strong responses included a more thorough discussion of the procedures and a concise explanation as to why they would be required. Many weak responses included vague or incomplete procedures or procedures that failed to address the problem identified (for example, vouching to journal entries, or inquiring of management but with no specifics as to what to inquire about).)

Where a procedure can apply as is to a great many entities, it is VAGUE.

Where the person reading the procedure does not know how to implement it, it is INCOMPLETE.

For Assessment Opportunity/Primary Indicator #2 (Audit and Assurance), the candidate must be ranked in one of the following five categories:	Percent Awarded
Not addressed — The candidate does not address this primary indicator.	0.2%
Nominal competence — The candidate does not attain the standard of reaching competence.	8.4%
Reaching competence — The candidate identifies some of the audit planning issues (materiality, risk, etc.) and attempts to develop audit procedures to address them, OR discusses the audit planning issues, OR discusses some of the audit procedures.	43.0%
Competent — The candidate discusses some of the audit planning issues and some of the audit procedures.	48.3%
Highly competent — The candidate discusses several of the audit planning issues and several audit procedures.	0.1%

3 different ways to achieve the RC level

The two parts of the requirement (A3) must be answered.

←

requirement
↓
accounting issues
↓
AUDIT
↓
planning AND procedures

(Candidates were asked to identify the impact of the accounting issues on the planning of the audit and to suggest procedures to be performed. To demonstrate competence, candidates were expected to discuss some of the audit planning issues as well as some of the audit procedures. The simulation stated that the initial audit planning had been completed. Candidates were directed to this indicator since the partner had requested a memo discussing the impact of the accounting issues of significance on the year-end audit planning and the procedures to be performed.)

initial audit planning completed
↓
UPDATE

(Candidates performed below expectations on this indicator, particularly in the area of year-end audit planning. Many candidates failed to consider the various aspects of the audit plan and instead focused solely on the materiality calculation, since the initial level of materiality had been provided in the simulation. What most candidates were missing was a discussion of how the audit risk might be affected by the events that had occurred since the initial planning was performed. Most candidates were able to provide adequate audit procedures to be performed relating to the accounting issues, but many were not able to explain why those procedures were required (in other words, what risk they were addressing).) [a]

"standard" audit planning:
– risk
– materiality
– approach
– risk areas & procedures

It is crucial to justify the procedure to be performed.
What is the risk area? What is the assertion?

2 meetings
↓
2 exhibits in the case
↓
events occurring between the 2 are more relevant

(Better candidate responses often contained stronger planning discussions, considering both the impact of the accounting issues as well as the impact of new developments within the client situation, subsequent to the July meeting, on the various components of the audit plan. These candidates also provided more thorough audit procedures for the accounting issues, containing strong discussions of what was required and explanations of the reasons. Weak candidates provided vague, generic, or incomplete procedures with no explanations as to why they would be required.)

treatment of events that have occurred since the July 2012 meeting

INTEGRATION!

a The comments from the persons grading the answer explain why the candidates did not achieve the passing standard.

COMMENTS:

- In respect of the Assurance issue, the case required the analysis of the impact on 1- the planning of the year-end audit and 2- the procedures to be performed. One must submit a reasonable analysis of EACH of these parts to achieve the passing standard. To a certain extent, a very good analysis of one could compensate for a "slight" weakness in the other. In other words, ONE MUST ANSWER, IN A REASONABLE MANNER, EACH OF THE REQUIRED ASPECTS.
- The requirements are, of course, not as high at the "Reaching competence" level, which can be achieved in three different ways. As shown in the table below, a candidate may submit an incomplete analysis of the two parts of the requirement regarding audit or submit a reasonable analysis of either.

Competence: Audit and Assurance

Reaching competence

↙ OR ↓ OR ↘

IDENTIFY SOME audit planning issues + ATTEMPT TO DEVELOP audit procedures	DISCUSS SOME audit planning issues --- ---	--- ⤡ DISCUSS SOME audit procedures

- The allocation of results between the "Reaching competence" and "Competent" levels clearly shows that the candidates had difficulty with the Assurance issue. From experience, I can tell you that there are two reasons that can explain this difficulty.

  First, one must essentially focus on the events that transpired since the initial planning of the audit. One must REVIEW this planning and not start from scratch using, among others, the contents of Exhibit II.

  Secondly, in respect of the "procedures to be performed", one must have properly identified the risk to which each procedure must respond. It is not always obvious, especially where the accounting issue to be resolved has been improperly identified. The manner in which the Assurance competence is assessed reflects the fact that the candidates had difficulty with either of these aspects.

- In order to determine what is necessary to satisfy the requirements, one can use the detailed analysis of the proposed solution.

  It is crucial to analyze the impact of the NEW EVENTS that have occurred since July on the planning of the audit that has already been done.

  In this respect, I consider that one must at least analyze the impact on RISK and on the MATERIALITY. In respect of the latter, a review of the preliminary materiality must be contemplated in relation to the adjustments recommended in the accounting section. Here, the omission of a comment on the strategy may be acceptable, simply because the control environment is not really discussed in the case.

  As for the procedures to be performed, they must flow from specific risks, and then be appropriately described. One must analyze SOME of the audit procedures. How many? The answer is not cast in stone. I would say about four in three different risks areas that are among the most important. Part 8 analyzes the assessment of this competence in greater detail (pp. 104 to 106).

Assessment Opportunity (Indicator) #3
Enabling Competencies

Assessment opportunity/Primary Indicator #3	*(III-1.1 to 1.3, III-2.1 to 2.6, III-3.1 to 3.3, III-4.1 to 4.3)*

The candidate discusses the potential for management bias towards a higher EBITDA due to the bonus.

The candidate demonstrates Enabling Competencies — Professional Skills.

IFRS ↓ adjustments + errors ↓ EBITDA ↓ bonus

I had calculated the EBITDA based on an updated forecast from management, adjusted for accounting changes related to the transactions that occurred between July and September.

A brief reference to the calculation schedule setting out the revised income easily replaces this introductory paragraph.

The projected results showed an EBITDA of close to $16 million. As a result management is likely expecting to be well above the threshold of $14 million required for the bonus, and that appears to be why Anne has indicated she will accrue a $300,000 bonus. a

How this $300,000 is calculated has no influence on the solution.

It is important to link the adjusted EBITDA and the awarding of bonuses to management.

However, based on the recommended accounting adjustments, adjusted EBITDA would be approximately $13,766,000, which is under the $14-million threshold. As a result, management will be very sensitive to any adjustments that are proposed since the bonus threshold is no longer met. We should make them aware of these adjustments as soon as possible. b

IMPACT

FOCUS → EBITDA

Since management has the potential to earn additional compensation based on EBITDA, the members may have been biased to make decisions that increase EBITDA. In particular, they may have had a bias to recognize revenue sooner, buy versus rent equipment, capitalize expense items, and classify expenses into categories that get added back to the calculation, such as interest, taxes, or amortization. c A number of the errors I have identified for adjustment have this impact.

ways of "manipulating" EBITDA.

ID:	determine the existence of possible bias on the part of management
ANAL:	examine the accounting adjustments overall (manipulation)
CONC:	reach a conclusion on management's conduct (impact)

a In this case, Anne is DFT's Chief Executive Officer. She is the link between DFT and the external auditors. She is also the one supervising the accounting for transactions, such as the $300,000 bonus (A6). It would be erroneous to think that she is part of management and, as a result, that she will participate in the bonus program. The Chief Financial Officer, or the comptroller, does not usually receive a bonus based on financial results! In addition, it would be inappropriate to speak of the possibility of fraud, simply because there is no indicator of existence to that effect in the case. The mere fact that there are errors in the accounting for certain transactions is insufficient.

b Of course, the analysis must be performed in light of the total arrived at by the candidate. It is, indeed, unlikely that a candidate would arrive at the exact figure of $13,766,000 (A20). In this discussion, it is not the accuracy of the figure that matters, but its interpretation.

c This is a "LIST OF" ways to manipulate results, which can be set out more concisely in the form of an enumeration. Note, as well, that each of the ideas put forth starts with a verb in the infinitive.

ways of manipulating + concrete examples from the case = INTEGRATION

Examples include the following: a

A12 **Recognizing revenue sooner** — Recognizing the Indo shipment even though Indo has not taken out the inventory yet, recognizing NRE margin that is partially connected to future product sales, and recognizing government grants when received although related to products still in development. A10 A13

It would be a good idea to indicate that the reference is to the Ares product to avoid any confusion.

Capitalizing expenses — Continuing to defer development costs related to a specific product no longer under development, and recording the GST reassessment as a prepaid expense. A14 A15

Classifying expenses into categories added back for EBITDA — Including impairment related to production equipment in capital assets amortization expense. A16

TAKE A POSITION WHERE THE CONCLUSION IS CLEAR.

Be a professional accountant → Be honest

All of the above accounting decisions worked in management's favour, and it seems that management has done whatever it can to manipulate the financial statements (in other words, it has used its bias in the selection of accounting policies when there were choices amongst alternatives or when decisions had to be made). b This has been done in order to meet the EBITDA threshold and therefore obtain the bonus. We should question management's integrity and bring this to the attention of the board of directors. c

Since DFT is a public company, the presence of a Board of Directors is a given.

IMPACT

Integrity of management? → notify the Board of Directors

"Competent with distinction" level

Ironically, it may not be the decisions of management that result in a bonus being paid or not. It may well be the decision of Indo to take out inventory prior to September 30 that determines if management gets a bonus. If Indo takes the entire inventory shipment worth $1.85 million prior to year-end, DFT will be able to record $1.85 million of sales and $1.11 million of cost of sales (based on 40% gross margin), resulting in an increase of $740,000 to EBITDA, which will put it over the $14 million threshold. This type of item affecting the bonus may not have been anticipated when the plan was set up. A20

In light of the restricted time frame of 70 minutes for the DFT case, I understand that it is not obvious to flesh out this particular fact. However, in the analysis of the proposed solution, one must note that an adjustment, the outcome of which, for the time being, is uncertain, may make a difference as to the payment (or non-payment) of bonuses to management. (A20)

---

a The examples taken from the case and that justify one of the ways of "manipulating" the EBITDA are succinctly set out per category: Increase in revenues, Decrease of expenses or Inappropriate classification. There is no need to summarize the previous analysis of the accounting issue identified. Incidentally, it is not the importance of the topic that matters, but what it teaches us about the conduct of management.

b Upon reading the case, one must identify the "potential bias" of management to want to maximize its bonuses. From experience, I can tell you that it is relatively easy to pick up on the existence of this bias in the DFT case . However, one must be sure to keep this information in mind all throughout the drafting process and to refer to it as needed.

Reading notes A8

IDENTIFYING THE BIAS FROM THE OUTSET AND NEVER AGAIN REFERRING TO IT IS NOT VERY USEFUL.

It is unfortunately easy to resolve each of the accounting issues, one after the other, without asking oneself any questions. In this case, the accumulation of accounting choices made by management, all heading in the same direction, must draw your attention. At some point during the analysis, you must take a step back and flesh out the similarity with which each of the various aspects analyzed behaves.

c Questioning the integrity of management may influence the planning of the audit engagement. (e.g.: CAS 300.A5 *Planning An Audit of Financial Statements*)

For Assessment Opportunity/Primary Indicator #3 (Enabling Competencies — Professional Skills), the candidate must be ranked in one of the following five categories:	Percent Awarded
Not addressed — The candidate does not address this primary indicator.	10.1%
Nominal competence — The candidate does not attain the standard of reaching competence.	20.9%
Reaching competence — The candidate recognizes the potential for management bias towards a higher EBITDA due to the bonus.	16.0%
Competent — The candidate discusses the potential for management bias towards a higher EBITDA due to the bonus.	52.9%
Competent with distinction — The candidate discusses the potential for management bias towards a higher EBITDA due to the bonus, and comments on the elements that are driving the bonus (Indo-Tech transaction).	0.1%

not taking a step back in the analysis of the DFT case

One must recognize that it is easy to "SEE" management's potential bias.

← professional skill to be demonstrated

comment on what determines the bonuses ↓ transaction with Indo-Tech

(Candidates were asked to discuss the impact of the adjustments and errors in EBITDA on the management bonus. To achieve competence, candidates were expected to discuss the potential for management bias towards a higher EBITDA due to the bonus. Candidates were not clearly directed to this indicator, although the partner did indicate his particular concern with issues that affect earnings because of the expectation of a more profitable year and the new management bonus program based on EBITDA.)

A candidate who takes the time to identify the "particulars of the context" during the reading process increases his or her chances to see this type of situation.

"*The existence* of a bias *means that* its impact must be assessed."

(Candidates performed as expected on this indicator. Many recognized that the bonus caused a bias on the part of management, and that the way transactions had been recorded was favourable to management. They were able to identify some of the inappropriate issues, such as revenue being recognized too early, and most were able to sufficiently explain the impact on the bonus calculation (early revenue recognition skews earnings in management's favour; therefore, earnings meet the bonus threshold and management receives a larger bonus). However, some candidates focused their discussions purely on the impact of management's bias on the extent of the audit work rather than linking that bias to the bonus.)

One must go beyond just "seeing" the bias; one must justify it, and then assess its impact.

individual accounting topics → OVERALL IMPACT

(Strong candidates were able to explain why management's accounting decisions were a concern (often after their discussion of the individual accounting issue) and then recognized the potential impact on DFT as a whole. These responses were clear, concise, and often summarized in one succinct section of the responses. Weak candidate responses merely repeated case facts without additional comments or recognition of the bias or the impact of the accounting choices on EBITDA or the bonus. Most did not recognize the potential for management manipulation at all.)

One must go beyond the basic issues.

integration ↓ consequences for DFT

COMMENTS:

- The previous assessment opportunities (#1 and #2) are mainly intended to assess the candidates' knowledge in accounting and audit. This assessment opportunity is instead focused on the enabling competencies of a professional accountant. To achieve the passing standard, one must TAKE A STEP BACK, and GET AN OVERALL PICTURE.

  The presence of a conclusion assessing the entire situation is incidentally generally required at the "Competent" level.

- The analysis of the impact of the bonus program is set out in a separate section at the very end of the proposed solution. It is undeniable that grouping together ideas in the same place makes the submission of arguments and the development of the conclusion easier. It is then easier to assess whether the discussion put forth is complete.

  However, it sometimes happens that a candidate will touch on such and such an issue here and there in his or her answer. This candidate may have stated, during the analysis of the accounting issues, that such and such an adjustment leads to a decrease of EBITDA, without any further explanation. Such a candidate must, once the Accounting issue is completed, refer to his or her prior observations, supplement them, and ultimately reach a conclusion that spans the entire situation. Such a manner of presenting the analysis is, of course, acceptable, since the crux of the ideas is still put forth.

Enabling Competencies — Professional Skills

Reaching competence	**Competent**	**Competent with distinction**
RECOGNIZE management bias	DISCUSS management bias	DISCUSS management bias + COMMENT elements driving the bonus

- Personally, I believe that, by "seeing" the bias generally, by way of a mere reference thereto at the outset of the answer, for example, one can achieve the "Nominal competence" level. At the next level, namely "Reaching competence", I think it is necessary to tackle the issue of bias by integrating one's statements to DFT's specific circumstances.

- The report is directed to the partner and not to the client. This allows the candidate to express a firmer and more direct conclusion (A34) as to management's conduct.

traditional simulation ↙ ↘ ACCT AUDIT

IMPACT ACCT ↓ EFFECT BONUS

(This was a fairly traditional audit and accounting simulation, and candidates seemed to be comfortable responding to this type of scenario. Candidates performed well on Primary Indicators #1 and #3. Most candidates appeared to be familiar with IFRS and were able to discuss the appropriate accounting treatments for the relevant issues in that context. They were also generally able to recognize the impact the management bonus program had on the recording of certain transactions (in other words, that the most favourable result to management had been reported) and explained the effect on the bonus calculation. Where candidates seemed to have more difficulty was on Primary Indicator #2. The main struggle for them was in recognizing the need to revisit various aspects of the initial audit plan, given the additional information that had been gathered subsequent to its preparation in July 2012.)

It is important to properly situate oneself in time in order to be able to flesh out the most important aspects.

SECONDARY ISSUE

ASSESSMENT OPPORTUNITY/SECONDARY INDICATOR/MINOR [a]

Strategy and Governance

medium term → less imp

It is normal to question the effectiveness of a NEW bonus program implemented at the beginning of the current fiscal year.

Assessment opportunity/Secondary Indicator #1	*(IV-2.4, IV-4.1)*
The candidate discusses the structure of DFT's new bonus plan.	
The candidate demonstrates competence in Strategy and Governance.	

MANAGEMENT ASPECT

Management is now part of a new bonus program that is based on earnings before interest, income taxes, depreciation, and amortization (EBITDA). The bonus begins to accumulate once EBITDA exceeds $14 million. It was instituted at the beginning of fiscal 2012 with the objective of "motivating management to contribute to profitability by being innovative and developing new product ideas." A4

The means of compensation chosen must promote the achievement of the stated objective.

A short title can replace this introductory paragraph.

CONCEPT: motivation

The board and management may want to consider whether a bonus plan, based on EBITDA, will motivate DFT's management the way it intended. Currently, management is being rewarded in a manner that is highly dependent on the decisions of a customer (Indo) rather than as a result of management's direct efforts developing a new product. An additional consideration is that the bonus calculation is affected by non-controllable factors such as the impairment of equipment and prior-period adjustments. b (Using EBIT or a return on capital employed would eliminate the impact of some of the uncontrollable factors — PPE would be a cost no matter what.)

CONCEPT: non-controllable factors

investment centre → ROC

EBIT: The amortization expense is an integral part of the targeted result.

It appears that management was attempting to inflate earnings to achieve a higher bonus payout. Basing your bonus on EBITDA may be causing unintended results.

One must try to find a compensation method that aligns the goals of the incumbent staff with those of the entity.

practical sense

Bonus plans, structured properly, can be motivating. They can align management's efforts with the company's objectives. DFT needs to determine what it should reward that is linked most directly to its objective — in this case, "being innovative and developing new product ideas that contribute to profit." Using EBITDA may not tie the bonus closely enough to the objective for it to accomplish what you had hoped. c

---

a It is not necessary to tackle this secondary issue to successfully complete the case. However, for learning purposes, it is useful to analyze the proposed solution. The bonus issue is certainly important from DFT's point of view. However, it is not within the strict consideration of the required/requirements, which basically focus on the accounting and the audit. From this perspective, one can understand that the merits or the determination of management's compensation method is a secondary issue. Incidentally, the principal role of an auditor is usually not to run the business.

b The events referred to in the DFT case serve as examples to buttress the ideas put forth: the impairment loss of $100,000 on production equipment (A16) and the reassessment of $125,000 related to GST/HST (A15).

c Since management attempted to manipulate the financial statements in order to receive bonuses, one could say that the current compensation scheme is not suitable. In other words, the members of management tried to secure bonuses by manipulating the results rather than reaping the rewards of their efforts by developing new products, for example.
The Board of Directors could, incidentally, ask itself whether management is capable of achieving the objectives that have been set by acting with integrity.

"*Where there is* a discussion of the performance indicators, *one must think of* the balanced scorecard."

Board of directors ↓ OBJECTIVES

You may wish to consider a process that is more closely linked to specific measurement objectives, using the following general approach: a

2 aspects: – entity – individual

1. Corporate scorecard b — You will want management to share the success (or failure) of the company. This is a good incentive to remain loyal and work towards the company's success. The scorecard should be a mix of long-term success planning metrics, short-term success planning metrics, and employees' satisfaction surveys. Assign weights to the components (adding up to 100%) and measure them against the expectations for the year. For example, you may wish to reward new product ideas that were developed that contributed a higher-than-set-minimum contribution margin.

   Then, if the company reaches expectations (scores exactly 100%), 10% of net income would be put aside for the bonus pool. If it exceeds expectations (scores 150%, for example), 15% of net income would be put aside, and so on.

expectations ↓ metrics

ST + LT

link to the particulars of the case

simple examples illustrating the ideas put forth

2. Individual scorecard — You will want your top performers to receive a higher bonus than others. Consider tagging performance (for example, with Excellent, Good, Satisfactory, and Below Expectations) and associate a percent of the bonus pool to each tag (such as 150%, 110%, 90%, and 60%). By doing this, you make sure that two people in the same position will get different bonuses if their performance differs. Again, performance can be tied to the aspects that best contribute to the success of the company — for example, creativity, innovation, customer relations, identify trends in the industry, share price, et cetera.

CONCEPT: compensation based on performance

Also, test the bonus structure before fully implementing it. Consider how can it be twisted and altered so people gain the bonus with minimum effort. You will likely understand the importance of this step already, as it appears that management may have attempted to manipulate the accounting to inflate earnings this year, knowing that a higher EBITDA would increase the bonus.

take into account past experience

You may want to consider a broader compensation plan, not just a bonus. Since DFT is a public company, you could use stock options or shares and tie their issuance or vesting to reaching set targets, if you believe it could help achieve the set objective. Since innovation can translate into long-term financial results, this might be a suitable incentive.

other suggestions to reward efforts

public company ↓ shares

In a case, most of the compensation programs are based on short-term criteria although one must also consider the long-term horizon. This is especially important for a business that must "constantly reinvest in research and development..." (A4)

---

a One must seek a solution for any deficiency or problem identified.

b It would also be appropriate to make direct reference to the four hallmarks of a balanced scorecard: Financial situation, Customer, Internal process, Learning and growth.

For Assessment Opportunity/Secondary Indicator #1 (Strategy and Governance), the candidate must be ranked in one of the following three categories:
Not addressed — The candidate does not address this indicator. **Nominal competence** — The candidate does not attain the standard of competence. **Competent** — The candidate discusses the structure of DFT's new bonus plan.

1- justify the issue
2- propose solutions

(Candidates were asked to discuss the structure of DFT's new bonus plan. To achieve competence, candidates were expected to discuss the structure and recognize that a bonus based on EBITDA may not motivate management to be innovative and develop new product ideas. Candidates were also expected to suggest an alternative basis for determination of a bonus for management. Candidates were not directed to this indicator, although previous analysis of accounting issues and a recognition that the bonus caused a bias on the part of management may have led them to comment on the structure of the bonus plan.) a

link with specific objective of DFT

One must justify one's opinions
↓
WHY?

(Most candidates did not address this secondary indicator. They either did not address the bonus structure at all or merely stated that EBITDA was not an appropriate basis for calculating the bonus, without further explanation as to why it was not appropriate for a company like DFT.)

secondary aspect in light of the requirement

(Strong candidates were able to explain why the current structure of the management bonus was not beneficial to the company as a whole (for example, potentially sacrificing product development for inflation of revenue), and then suggest another basis for determination of the bonus, a management compensation plan, or both.) b

When one reads this part of the proposed solution, one realizes that the particulars of the context of the case are constantly considered: (A8)

- public company;
- constant reinvestment in research and development to ensure that its product remain relevant and can integrate with the latest technology;
- contribution to profitability by being innovative and developing new products.

---

a This assessment opportunity relates to the MANAGEMENT aspect of the bonus program. Is it an appropriate method of compensation? If not, what are the other possibilities? The concepts touched on include motivation, the need for assessment based on controllable factors, the alignment of the method of assessment and the objectives sought to be achieved, the assessment of the performance of the entity AND of the individual, the consideration of the short-term horizon AND the long-term horizon.

b To achieve the "Competent" level, it does not appear necessary to issue a conclusion or recommendation as to the improvements to be made to the bonus program. One must remember that the questioning of the new program has just been raised and it would be premature to determine a new manner of proceeding. Besides, such a decision is within the purview of the Board of Directors.
THE IMPACT of the bonus program on the analysis of the accounting issues is part of assessment opportunities #1 and #3 and the IMPACT of the bonus program on the year-end audit is part of assessment opportunity #2. One must know how to distinguish each of these aspects when assessing the value of the ideas put forth.
The context in which an idea is put forth is important.

I wish you all great Success,
and Thank you for appreciating my work.

CPSIA information can be obtained
at www.ICGtesting.com
Printed in the USA
LVOW02s2323281015
460113LV00002B/5/P

9 781928 067054